managed to get tickets for the matinee show. I had read in the music papers that the band never did encores at the matinee shows. The long-awaited day came and we went to the show at Green's Playhouse in Glasgow. The band didn't disappoint, they were incredible. I was very privileged to see that tour. The show ended and the band left the stage. John and I knew they wouldn't be back on so we left the crowd cheering for an encore. Renfield Street was almost empty as we headed away for our bus home. We walked for about three blocks when we heard screaming from back at the gig. A limo was approaching and the lights beside us were red. We looked at the limo and saw David looking straight on and suddenly Ronno stuck his head out at the window and waved at us. In later years I reminded Ronno that he was the first Rock Star to acknowledge me.'

Derek Forbes, *Simple Minds*

'Even now 50 years on Ronson's guitar solo at the end of 'Moonage Daydream' still sends me to heaven.'

Daniel Ash, *guitarist of Bauhaus*

A proper biography of Mick Ronson, with a focus on the city that moulded him, was long overdue. Thankfully Rupert Creed and Garry Burnett have not just provided it, they've done so with style and panache. Mick Ronson was a genius who would never answer to such a description. His self-effacement in an industry bloated by hyperbole was one of the things that made him special – the other was his soaring musicality.
It's very good and worth the wait for all those millions of fans of Ziggy Stardust and the Spider's from Hull!'

Alan Johnson, *award-winning author, and former MP*

'I feel the stage show *Turn and Face the Strange* celebrating Hull's very own Mick Ronson deserves a world-wide audience, and I feel the same about this book.'

David 'Burnsy' Burns, *BBC Radio Humberside*

'A fascinating and brilliantly-researched guide to the life of a great and much missed musician.'

David Quantick, *music writer*

'Released in 1970 "The Man who Sold the World" was Bowie's first record with Mick Ronson and was Bowie's attempt to shrug off his failed 'one-hit-wonder folkie' tag (achieved through the albeit limited success of "Space Oddity"). And strike a light did it do the job! Step in Bowie's very own Jeff Beck, the Spider with the Platinum hair, my fellow northerner, Mick 'Ronno' Ronson. This is a lovingly crafted tribute to his life and his music.'

Marc Riley, *BBC Radio 6 Music*

'Mick came from good stock. A no-nonsense Yorkshire lad who would rather get things done than talk about them. Need the public gardens in Hull sorted out? Done. Need some strings arranged on a Mott song? Done. Need a stunning guitar solo on Mott's last single? Done (that one took 3 meticulous days). Need to beef up Dylan's Rolling Thunder Tour with some proper rock guitar? Done. Want me to dress up and make up like a platinum-haired rock god? Done (with a touch of persuasion from Bowie). And a hundred other brilliant musical deeds. He didn't live nearly long enough - but by gum, this book shows he LIVED!'

Morgan Fisher, *Mott the Hoople*

'The wonder you felt if you were lucky enough to meet or encounter a musical genius like Mick Ronson, and the curiosity you couldn't help but contemplate at that intangible gift which enabled, someone like him, to create such beautiful music and melodies, was truly fascinating to experience. His humble gift and legacy has been appreciated by many millions of people around the world and looks likely to remain just as impactful for many, many more to come. What a legacy it is. Hull and Yorkshire – be proud. Be *very* proud.'

Kevin Cann, designer, *writer, and music promoter*

'Ronson's innovative use of the wah-wah pedal is still being appraised and appreciated by contemporary discerning guitarists. His track record as a player and composer is second to none. He was a massive influence on a whole generation of musicians. I first saw him play when I was 15. He blew my mind. A genuine guitar god!'

Martin Bramah, *singer-songwriter and guitarist, and founding member of the Fall*

'I worked with Ronno at Trident Studios where he was responsible for producing the song that Bowie had written for me, "Andy Warhol", which came out on my *Weren't Born A Man* album when I was also signed to MainMan (as well as some other tracks) and not forgetting that his "Slaughter on 10th Avenue" came out as a single with me on the flip side. The first ever string arrangements that Ronno ever did was on my album. It was a sort of try out for him so he could then do what he wanted to do, which was to write arrangements. If you listen to the 'found' demo tracks that were discovered by Tris Penna and came out on my MainMan double album 2 years ago on Cherry Red Records, then you'd hear two rare tracks of "Andy Warhol", with Ronno and Bowie playing, which had never been heard before until this release.
To work with Ronno was such an honour as his talent was extraordinary, especially his unique guitar sound. I will always consider it an honour to have worked with him, and he will always be missed by me. Love Dana'

Dana Gillespie, *actress, singer-songwriter*

'My first recollection of hearing David Bowie was on a Saturday morning in 1969 whilst ice skating at Crossmyloof in Glasgow, Scotland. The radio was blaring out 'Space Oddity' and I was hooked. My interest took me on an adventure of exploration, seeking out everything I could from this weird alien God. My best friend, Ian Reekie, bought *Ziggy Stardust and the Spiders from Mars* and this lit the touch paper for my meteoric rise to lead guitar playing. Mick Ronson had a style of his very own, even the clothes he wore had me imitating him in my days at College. I would wear white Oxford bags, a striped red and white v-neck T-shirt, with platform shoes borrowed from my brother John. Ziggy was coming to Glasgow, and my brother and I

TURN & FACE THE STRANGE

THE MICK RONSON STORY

RUPERT CREED AND GARRY BURNETT

Published by McNidder & Grace
21 Bridge Street
Carmarthen SA31 3JS
Wales, United Kingdom

www.mcnidderandgrace.com

Original paperback first published 2022, reprinted 2024
© Rupert Creed and Garry Burnett

All rights reserved. No part of this work may be reproduced or transmitted in any form or by any means, electronic or mechanical, including photocopy, recording, or any information storage and retrieval system, without permission in writing from the publisher.

Rupert Creed and Garry Burnett have asserted their right to be identified as the authors of this work in accordance with the Copyright, Designs and Patents Act 1988.

Every effort has been made to obtain necessary permission with reference to copyright material. The publisher apologises if, inadvertently, any sources remain unacknowledged and will be glad to make the necessary arrangements at the earliest opportunity.

A catalogue record for this work is available from the British Library.

Image credits: cover illustration and chapter heading illustrations, Cecile Piverotto.
Author photo credits: Rupert Creed, Quentin Budworth; Garry Burnett, Tracey Taylor.
Turn & Face the Strange Show photo credit: Tracey Taylor

ISBN: 9780857162267
Ebook: 9780857162274

Designed by Sooky Choi
Cover design: Tabitha Palmer

Printed and bound in the United Kingdom by Short Run Press, Exeter

For Tracey
and for Louise

and everyone involved in making the magic that is the legendary
Turn and Face the Strange show:
the TAFTS family!

Foreword

by Midge Ure

It's 1977 and the band I had recently moved from Glasgow to London to join, Rich Kids, were sitting in a pub discussing who we might want to produce our, what transpired to be, only album. We had various names suggested to us by the label but we suspected the names given were for their sales prowess rather than what they might bring to the music. I then suggested someone who I hugely respected and admired as a producer, guitarist, pianist and arranger. Mick Ronson.

It's 1973 and I'm sitting in the Glasgow Greens Playhouse eagerly awaiting the matinee show from Ziggy Stardust and The Spiders from Mars. I was playing in my own bands that evening hence the matinee but I wasn't about to miss this moment. It was love at first note! The band. The look. Bowie seducing the audience and to top it all, Mick. Mick with his beat up Gibson Les Paul, his Marshall half stack and his wah wah pedal pulled halfway back giving the guitar its unique, slightly strangled voice playing like there was no tomorrow and at the same time giving Bowie a run for his money when it came to stagecraft and showmanship. Eyes darting from one to the other like watching and supporting both tennis players in a match and never quite knowing who to root for more. It takes quite a powerful force to outshine David Bowie but more than once the spark from the side of the stage outdazzled the spark in the centre!

Mick producing Rich Kids gave me the opportunity to spend time with this unassuming, sometimes shy, understated man. Always happy to pop down the pub or smoke his roll ups. He seemed to be the antithesis of the guitar hero I had witnessed a few years before but his skills and abilities remained. I even found myself the keeper of the 'holy grail' of guitars when Mick asked me to look after his Gibson for a few months. Musician friends would come and gaze in wonder at the instrument responsible for the classic 'Moonage Daydream' solo. I'm not convinced in hindsight that the ensuing album was the 'musical marriage made in heaven' we all anticipated but it brought this genius into our lives and we were all better for it.

Mick agreed to play guitar for me on my 1986 Gift tour. Maybe because I was wanting to hear 'that sound' I always associated with Mick or maybe I was living some sort of unattainable schoolboy dream it didn't work out. I came to the conclusion I was restricting him by having him play parts rather than be himself, rather than be the brilliant musician I loved hearing. A few weeks into rehearsals I had to make the most difficult phone call in my life and explain to Mick I didn't think this was working. Being who he was he took it with enormous grace and said he understood but I'll never really know because we never had the opportunity to meet up again.

His melodies. His unique guitar and piano playing. His absolute northern down to earthiness. I miss it all.

He never wanted to be the centre of attention.
He never sought the limelight.
He was happy being a musician.
Not just a sidekick. THE sidekick.

Midge Ure, 2022

Preface

by Garry Burnett

When I was twelve, *Top of the Pops* was one of the most popular programmes on the telly. We never missed it! I remember the momentous night when David Bowie put his arm around Mick Ronson in the middle of 'Starman' and feeling waves of silent disapproval emanating from my father's fireside chair. I glanced over uncomfortably to see his newspaper lower six inches below his eyes and his brows rise almost to his hairline. 'Bloody hell!' he scoffed. 'Is that a lad or a lass?' Then he recognised Mick. 'That's him off Greatfield! He cuts the grass in East Park!' I just kept my mouth shut because I thought it was brilliant. And the way he played guitar! Like thousands of others, from that moment on I wanted to be just like him.

I bought the *Aladdin Sane* LP the week it came out, from Cleveland Records on Craven Street Corner. I couldn't wait to get home and play it. In those days we had a radiogram record player in our front room which was as big as a sideboard, and if you put a record on, everybody had to listen, you had no choice. So you can imagine how relieved I was that I was on my own the first time I played *Aladdin Sane*. The lyrics! Track 1 on side 2 was 'Time'. 'Time he flexes like a *whore*. Falls *wanking* to the floor...' I blushed. I didn't even really know what *wanking* meant at the time. All I knew was it was one of those words that you didn't ask Dad the meaning of. So I came up with a diversionary tactic: to cough loudly every time it came on.

It seemed to work fairly well until one day, disaster struck. There must have been a piece of dust or fluff on the needle because the record began to jump, exactly on *the* word. 'Time, he flexes like a whore, falls wanking... wanking... wanking...wanking...' It must have sounded like I was having a coughing fit. I didn't realise Dad was in the kitchen. He just strode over and booted the record player, all the way to 'Jean Genie'. He never said a word, just disappeared behind his newspaper, as if nothing had happened. But when I went to give him his goodnight kiss that night, he just held up his hand. 'Men don't kiss men,' he said. And from that time on I had to shake hands with him at bedtime. Every night, I'd kiss my mum and shake hands with dad. And though I laugh about it now, I remember going to bed that night feeling ashamed and embarrassed, as if I'd done something wrong, and also a bit scared, because I knew everything had changed.

Drifting through my open bedroom window were all the night noises from East Park where Mick had worked, the peacocks and owls, and I thought, 'Yes, Mick, you had something to do with all this'. And it was through you I that knew you could be from *round here, from East Hull*, there was nothing wrong with that, but you didn't have to be the *same* as all the rest, that it was okay to dream, to be *different*.

And so most of my life Mick Ronson has been with me, as firstly a neighbour, then a role model and always an inspiration. Our families grew up and worked in many of the same places. And now he is buried in Hull's Eastern Cemetery, close to home in the same grave as his parents, just round the corner from my own grandparents and uncles. It is a peaceful place, an oasis of calm sandwiched between two tough estates and opposite what was my old school. Turn your head and you can see cranes turning on the edge of the Humber, or smoke chuffing from the funnels on the North Sea Ferries, and catch the smell of the river and the woodyards in the air.

Listen carefully and you might also hear beautiful music, birdsong, sometimes woodpeckers, in the trees near the chapel, or tinkling wind chimes from the baby cemetery at the far end. One day as I put some flowers down I even thought I caught the four notes of 'This is for You', one of Mick's haunting solos playing on the jingling chimes as a light breeze blew through.

Heaven, and Hull.

Preface

by Rupert Creed

In contrast to Garry, my teenage years were spent in Brighton. In the late '60s and early '70s, 'London by the seaside' was a cool place to be. I hung out with hippies on the beach, saw Pink Floyd, King Crimson, Free and Dr John play at the Dome, and sprawled on bean bags, listening to the latest albums on headphones in the smoke-filled booths of Virgin Records on North Street. In 1974 I swapped this vibrant southern scene for what felt at the time, the grey parochial grimness of Hull, moving north to study Drama and German at Hull University. Unlike Mick, who'd had to head to London to make his name as a musician, I was travelling in the opposite direction to train in theatre. By the time I arrived in Hull, Mick had relocated to America. I never got to see him play, let alone meet him in person, despite living in his home city for the next two decades. In fact, until his death in 1993, I didn't even know that he came from Hull – such was the city's lack of interest at that time in promoting or celebrating its stars. Close to half a century after first coming to the city, I am still here. I have made a career as a writer and theatre director, documenting and portraying the stories of this unique place and its remarkable people.

In 2016 Garry approached me with the idea of collaborating on a project recording the untold stories of Mick Ronson and celebrating his life and music in a stage show. With a commission from Hull City of Culture we embarked on *Turn and Face the Strange*. Over six months in 2017, we recorded the memories and stories of Mick's family, friends, fans and fellow musicians. What emerged was the story of a young man whose personality and attitude were firmly rooted in the culture of the city, but whose ambition and sheer musical talent drove him from the safe and familiar into a new uncharted world of creativity. As sideman to David Bowie onstage, and a key collaborator in the making of his music, Mick played a crucial role in the history of popular music. Although he didn't maintain the same success achieved with Bowie and the Spiders from Mars, his story doesn't stop there. He sustained a prolific music career as a guitarist, song arranger and album producer right up to his death.

Most rock histories portray Ronson primarily through the prism of Bowie in his Ziggy period, or alongside stars such as Lou Reed or Ian Hunter. We wanted to flip the traditional narrative back to Mick and offer a more Hull-centric focus. Our story sheds a more nuanced light on how the city and its culture shaped his personality, offered him a safe haven, and gave him a thorough grounding as a musician. It also gave him a culture he would ultimately kick against. Leaving Hull to join Bowie released the creative genie from the bottle and he never looked back. With his Spiders from Hull, Mick played a crucial role in the development of glam rock, journeying from a geographical backwater to the cosmopolitan mainstream. Alongside David Bowie they redefined and reset the boundaries of popular culture. It's a story of the unlikely juxtaposition of northern attitude and London cool, and how the two at times clashed and combusted, but more often than not coalesced to produce the creative spark for songs that have inspired and been enjoyed by generations of listeners.

Being 'on the ground' in Hull, Garry and I had access to a rich resource of local people's memories and stories of Mick. Some featured in the stage show *Turn and Face the Strange*, but many more appear for the first time in this book. The stage show sold out its initial run in 2017 and this success continued with further performances at Hull Truck Theatre from 2018 to 2021, and at Hull New Theatre in 2023. The show attracted visitors from as far afield as America, Scandinavia and Europe – a testimony to Mick's enduring popularity at home and abroad. We have gathered more stories in the interim, all of which offer first-hand accounts of Mick's life, character and skill as a musician. From estate kid to superstar, Mick Ronson was a man who stepped beyond his predetermined path, who turned and not only faced the strange, but chose to embrace it.

Contents

	Foreword by Midge Ure	ix
	Prefaces	xi
	Introduction	I
1	Childhood and Early Years: 1946–1963	7
2	First Bands: The Mariners and The Crestas: 1963–1966	15
3	The Rats, Part One: 1966–1968	31
4	The Rats, Part Two: 1968–1970	51
5	Bowie, Hype and The Man Who Sold The World: 1970	69
6	From Ronno to Ziggy: 1970–1971	86
7	Ziggy Played Guitar: 1972	99
8	Ziggy's Rise and Fall: 1973	114
9	From Sideman to Frontman: 1973–1974	126
10	Musician and Producer for Hire: 1974–1977	135
11	The Long Road Home: 1977–1993	146
12	The Legacy	160
	Afterword by Kevin Cann	171
	Appendices	
	Who's Who	176
	Mick Ronson Timeline	178
	Bands and Artists that Worked with Mick Ronson as Musician and/or Producer	192
	Mick Ronson's Hull	194
	Acknowledgements	198
	Select Bibliography	200
	Image Section Photo Credits	202
	Index	203
	About the Authors	215

Introduction

```
Once upon a time, not so long ago
People used to stand and stare at the spider
    with the platinum hair
They thought you were immortal
```

('Michael Picasso' by Ian Hunter)

It's 4 July 1973. Guests are arriving at the Café Royal on Regent Street in London. It's the post-Ziggy 'Last Supper' party and the social event of the year. The previous night David Bowie and the Spiders from Mars played the final show of a world tour that had taken them the length of Britain, crossed America from east to west coasts, and on to Japan — finally to return to London. In just a year and a half, Bowie and his band have gone from half-empty pubs in North London to sell-out gigs in the States. They've made iconic albums that have sold worldwide, generated a frenzy for glam rock and achieved international stardom. It's been a wild ride, and tonight there's that post-show buzz in the air of sweat mingling with sweet success. Bowie's main man, Mick Ronson, with his tanned physique and long flowing hair, looks like a Greek god as he steps into the gilded, art deco lift and ascends – if not to the heavens, then at least to the upper floor. The night before, he'd played the gig of a lifetime. To a packed Hammersmith Odeon crammed with adoring fans and rock glitterati such as Mick Jagger and Rod Stewart, Mick Ronson played his blond Les Paul with phenomenal power and passion, blasting a raw energy of sound throughout the auditorium. Jeff Beck had played alongside him, guesting on a couple of numbers. A guitarist emulated and idolised by Mick for years, was now publicly acknowledging Mick's status, a new guitar great. Then at the end of the concert, before the final number, Bowie declares to a stunned audience that this is not just the last night of the tour, it's the last night ever of Ziggy Stardust and the Spiders from Mars. Bowie is killing them off, he's breaking up the band. Mick knew it was coming and had a solo career lined up thanks to Bowie's manager Tony Defries, but for drummer Woody Woodmansey and bassist Trevor Bolder it came as a complete surprise, a knock-out blow delivered in public, leaving them shocked, angry and deeply hurt. They'd been on this rollercoaster ride together, they'd helped make it happen, but now it looks like they are out of the picture. As they leave the stage they can't help but notice that Mick, their fellow musician and long-time mate from Hull, is avoiding eye contact. It feels like betrayal. The following evening in the crowded throng of the Café Royal, Woody is making the best of it, trying to work out if he still has a job, but Trevor has stayed away. Mick is surrounded by fans, family and friends and the champagne is flowing. There's Mick and Bianca Jagger, Paul and Linda McCartney, Ringo Starr, Keith Moon, Cat Stevens, Lou Reed, Barbara Streisand, Britt Ekland, Tony Curtis, Elliot Gould, Ryan O'Neal, Spike Milligan, Peter Cook and Dudley Moore. Anyone who is someone, and in London, is here. And at the centre of it all is David Bowie and the man who helped make him a star. Though the lyrics said, 'Ziggy played guitar', everyone knew it was in fact Mick Ronson. How did this kid from a council estate in east Hull get to be here? From the edge of nowhere to the pulsing heart of popular contemporary music? How did this happen? And where did it start?

Michael Ronson was born in 1946 in the city of Hull in the north-east of England. As a baby boomer he was the product of his time and place, born into a working-class family in an industrial northern city where manual work was the norm and jobs were plentiful up to the 1970s. His destiny should have been to tread the path mapped out by his parents and previous generations: leave school at 14; find work on the docks, or in a factory or ancillary trade; earn enough to marry and start a family; holiday on the East Coast at Bridlington or Scarborough; and, more likely than not, live a life pretty much within the city. Mick chose a different path. By his mid-twenties he was a rock superstar touring the globe, an icon of glam rock renowned for his good looks and mastery of the guitar. His career drew countless accolades, not only for his guitar-playing but for his arrangements on piano and strings, his skill as a producer in the studio, and his enthusiasm for working his magic with unknown bands as well as established musicians. Having left Hull in the '70s, he never returned to his home city, apart from visits to family. He lived in London, then mainly in the States, and wherever the work

Introduction

took him – a guitar-playing, album-producing nomad, jet-setting across continents.

His journey, however, is no simple stellar trajectory, but a series of failed early attempts to make his mark as a musician. His burning ambition was tempered by self-doubt, the need to earn a regular working wage, and the lure of staying firmly in the comfort zone of known musical parameters and familiar home territory. Mick's formative years tell the story of a boy born into a community battered and bruised after the Second World War, where the pressure to get a 'proper job' was suffocating to someone blessed with artistic talent. He grew up in a largely working-class community, where negative attitudes to the arts and culture created enormous peer pressure to do the opposite of what he was restless to achieve. The male head of the household was expected to hold down a dependable job sufficient to pay the rent and put food on the table. This had been true for generations. Mick, however, was to lead a fairly maverick, hand-to-mouth lifestyle, and despite having huge earning potential was always focused more on the music than the money. He died poor with little to show of the financial rewards usually associated with being a rock superstar.

Hull's location would also play a part in shaping Mick's character and early music ambitions. The city lies 40km (25 miles) inland from the north-east coast, on the broad sweep of the Humber Estuary, isolated from the main north-south transport routes of the UK. It's a one road in, one road out, 'end of the line' town. It has a rich maritime history of fishermen and merchant seamen pioneering the distant horizons, but in equal measure it has a paralysing culture of looking inward, being insular and resistant to change. In the 1960s when Mick was first looking to make a career in music, the only real option available was to take the one road out of Hull and head for London. Dread of getting into debt and the lure of familiar home territory would invariably pull him back. Hull had a cultural drag anchor as strong as the Humber tide, that could easily snag and sink a young man's ambition and dreams. Having failed to make it as a musician in London in 1966, Mick was highly reluctant to ever leave Hull to try it again. It took the persistence of drummer John Cambridge to convince him that it was worth one more go – and it was only then that the Bowie-Ronson partnership opened the door to mutual success.

Mick had advanced practical knowledge of classical music and musical theory well before he even picked up an electric guitar, which set him apart both from his mates growing up on a Hull estate and from many of the musicians working the circuit at that time. He had the talent and credentials to hold his own with any of the top musicians he later played or collaborated with, be that Bowie, Dylan, Ian Hunter, Lou Reed or Morrisey. Through years of studious listening, practice and performance, he had developed an innate sense of melody, and how a hook or riff could enhance an embryonic tune. This, combined with the driving rock guitar he perfected in the Rats, offered Bowie the 'magic music bullet' he needed to enhance his own singer-songwriter skills and give his career a decisive and stratospheric breakthrough.

The years before, playing in the Mariners, Crestas and the Rats, were the musical equivalent of his day job marking out sports pitches, methodically exercising his craft, moving comfortably, predictably and proficiently within predetermined lines. Partnership with Bowie broke beyond those boundaries, rejected the orthodox rules and encouraged creative risk-taking. Bowie once said of Mick's ability to interpret: 'I would literally draw out on paper with crayon or felt-tip pen the *shape* of a solo. The one in 'Moonage Daydream', for instance, started as a flat line that became a fat megaphone-type shape and ended as sprays of disassociated and broken lines. Mick could take something like that and actually bloody play it, bring it to life. Very impressive.'

With Bowie and the emergence of glam rock, Mick also played a part in legitimising more liberal attitudes to homosexuality and gender. The community he grew up in held firmly to the orthodox distinction between male and female identity. Any transgression of the norm would often result in overt homophobia and violence. Given their background, it's not surprising that Mick and his fellow Spiders from Hull were initially resistant to Bowie's glam rock ideas. Long hair was acceptable, not lipstick or mascara. However, a growing cult following meant that it didn't take long for them to embrace both, and by doing so, they helped generate momentum toward a more tolerant, inclusive society.

There's no doubt that Mick's striking good looks and fit physique also contributed to the huge popularity of the bands he played in. It gained him a loyal female following, some of whom were quite happy to be counted as not just a fan but one of his amorous conquests. Mick had significant relationships with at least three women, one of whom he married, and all of whom bore his children. His rock lifestyle and constant touring, however, meant he was never consistently at home for either partner or child, and none of these relationships endured. Nicholas, his first son, was born in 1971 and grew up without ever knowing his father. His third son, Joakim, was born in 1990 and still a toddler when his father died, his mother having separated from Mick a short time before. Only his middle child Lisa, born in 1977, enjoyed a childhood with her father, and Mick's relationship with her mother, Suzi, did not sustain beyond his daughter's teenage years.

On one level Mick Ronson shows a consistent personality. Unlike Bowie he has no chameleon qualities. Fame doesn't change him, neither his broad flat-vowel Hull accent, nor his qualities of friendliness, generosity, modesty and his dry Yorkshire humour. At the height of rock stardom, he was still the person he'd always been – down-to-earth and grounded. But his story also shows contradictions and complexities. Like many performers he was shy by nature and not a natural extrovert, but once on stage, particularly on the Ziggy tours, he would become larger than life, interacting physically and theatrically with Bowie, personifying and inhabiting, shaman-like, the raw power of sound that he could summon from his guitar. There are further contradictions to his personality. He was admired, revered and held in almost universal affection by those who came into contact with him. He showed generosity, friendliness and a readiness to connect with people on equal terms regardless of their status. He was modest and rooted in values handed down from his parents. His father George taught him the need for discipline, hard work and living within one's means. From his mother Minnie he learnt to be generous and kind, values not always associated with rock stars. Yet when it came down to decisions regarding fellow musicians, the drive of his ambition could lead him to be ruthless. As a committed artist, he prioritised the music above loyalty to friends. His friendliness and desire to be liked made this a particular challenge for him and he tended to avoid confronting, or addressing difficult situations with band members.

When Mick died from cancer in 1993 at the far too young age of 46, the universal response was a massive outpouring of sadness and loss – from people in the music industry internationally, to friends and fans in Hull. Mick's story was not only a soundtrack to their lives, it was a guiding light, a compass, giving direction and meaning to their own sense of identity and aspiration. He helped them make sense of the person they were, and who they could become. Whatever contradictions or inconsistencies he might have shown as a person, the overriding emotions he evoked were admiration and affection. The epitaph on his gravestone in East Hull cemetery rings as true as his music: 'To know him was to love him'.

1 Childhood and Early Years: 1946–1963

The Mick Ronson Story

Its official title is Kingston-upon-Hull, named after the river that flows south through the city into the much larger Humber estuary, which in turn flows east to the coast and the North Sea. Few people call the city by its full name, as the shortened version 'Hull', sits far more satisfyingly on the tongue. Michael was the first child of George and Minnie Ronson, a working-class couple, who lived at 1 Grosvenor Terrace, a small two-up two-down terrace house just north of the city centre. He was born in a nursing home on the nearby Beverley Road.

Mick's mother was born Minnie Morgan in 1924 in Hull, the second daughter of Harold Morgan and Hilda Shortland. The Morgan family came originally from Wales and the Shortlands from Lincolnshire, both families drawn to Hull by the jobs on offer in the expanding industrial city. Mick's father, George Ronson, was born in Hull in 1920, the son of a deep-sea trawlerman also called George, who worked the tough and dangerous trade on the storm-tossed seas off Norway and Iceland. The Ronson family came originally from Lancashire and by 1911 George Ronson Sr, Mick's grandfather, had settled in the city, marrying Maria Dunn from Ireland. Maria died in 1933 when Mick's father George was only 13, and the evidence suggests George was now brought up by a guardian relative. With a father at sea and mostly absent in his life, he came to value the stability and security that family life could offer, the importance of taking responsibility for oneself and being financially self-sufficient. George Ronson was a strict father to Michael and exerted a big influence on his son's attempts to forge a career as a musician, constantly stressing the need for his son to get a 'proper job' and keep music as a hobby. The Morgan, Shortland and Ronson families all lived in the Hessle Road area of Hull, a close-knit community of densely packed terraced houses adjacent to the fish dock in west Hull, with its constant flow of trawlers landing their catch or setting sail on the tide.

Minnie Morgan and George Ronson had met prior to the outbreak of war, but it wasn't until January 1944 that they were able to marry. In 1945 victory brought peace, and for the citizens of Hull, an end to the aerial bombardments they had endured for five long years. The city had suffered a grim tally of both physical and human costs: over 5,000 houses destroyed, almost 1,200 civilians killed and 3,000 injured. The people of Hull had been battered by the war and that shaped the attitude of their generation and what they passed on to their children. Young lads such as Michael were told to get a trade or join the army, become a skilled hand at something that would 'sort them out'. It was an important part of what it meant to be a man. Work was not only essential to pay the bills, it was something to take pride in: it helped define your sense of identity and place in the community. Music, as with any other form of entertainment, was there to be enjoyed, but unless it could pay the bills and put food on the table, was no substitute for a proper job. The 1960s were to usher in a different set of social attitudes, but born only a year after the end of the Second World War, Mick grew up in a city and time that carried physical and emotional scars of war, along with the prevailing attitudes of his parent's generation.

For George and Minnie Ronson, the birth of Michael, their first child, marked a significant new chapter in their lives. Peace and a return to civilian life provided the stability and relative security to invest in a family and a future. Despite living in an age of austerity, with food rationing not ending till 1954, a new era was beginning. It offered a new contract with the people: a National Health Service for all, improved work and welfare benefits, and a massive programme of home rebuilding. For baby boomers like Mick, it offered the life for which the older generation had fought and sometimes died – the chance to inherit a new age with the sound of music, not bombs.

One of Mick's first childhood friends was Rod Block, who lived down the same terrace and remembers that early time: 'When I first met Michael we both lived down Grosvenor Terrace, down Grosvenor Street, which is off Beverley Road between Leonard Street and Wellington Lane. We both went to the same school, Park Road School, which is near Pearson Park. Michael used to sit next to me in class and I do recall writing and looking at him and saying, "What you doing, Michael?" He said: "I'm copying off you", and I said: "I'm writing my name!"' The Ronson family had acquired a second-hand accordion and Rod recalls Mick as a child displaying an extraordinary ability to play a tune from memory: 'I remember one evening I was sat on the table listening to the wireless when Mrs Ronson and Michael came into the house and Michael had an accordion strapped to his back and Mrs Ronson said: "I've just taken Michael to the Strand Cinema to watch a movie, now just listen to this." And he played the theme tune to the movie by ear, which was "The Man from Laramie".'

The bombing of Hull required a substantial post-war programme of house building on new greenfield council estates in East Hull, named Bilton Grange, Longhill and Greatfield. The houses came with indoor toilets and plumbed-in bathrooms, until then a dream for many working-class families, previously having to make do with an outside privy in the backyard, and a tin bath once a week in front of a coal fire. The estates were built on the 'garden city' concept, where curved avenues and closes with plenty of outdoor spaces were replacing the older housing of dense, cramped terraced streets and poor sanitation. George, Minnie and Michael Ronson moved into a new-build council house on Hopewell Rd, on Bilton Grange estate, where Mick attended the local Wyvern Primary School. Minnie Ronson found work at the Imperial Typewriter factory on Hedon Rd, and George Ronson got a job at British Industrial Solvents, later to become BP, at the petrochemical works at Saltend on the eastern edge of the city's commercial docks.

Recognising her son's innate musical talent, Minnie bought him a piano for £73, which in the 1950s was a serious amount of money. She arranged lessons with Mrs Bolder, a piano tutor who just happened to be the grandmother of Trevor Bolder, one of the future Spiders from Mars. According to Minnie Ronson, 'Mrs Bolder sent me a note saying: "This boy needs to drink more milk"' – no doubt a response to Mick's slim build. Estate friend David Harvey remembers his mother responding in a similar way: 'Mick sometimes would walk past my house and I'd go out and see him. My mum always used to say, "Ask him to come in because he looks like he needs something to eat! Tell him to come in, I'll make him a sandwich, I'll give him some soup or something." Mick always looked very slim, even in his later years when he was playing with David Bowie and Mott the Hoople. He always was very slim on stage, but he'd always been a slim lad from when I first knew him.'

Susan Baird grew up on Bilton Grange Estate and remembers Mick's early music talent: 'We used to go in his house and he would be playing the mouth organ and playing the piano. He seemed to be able to play anything really. I remember him being quiet and he seemed shy, he didn't go boasting that he could play. He used to play spoons and the mouth organ – yes, he used to play the spoons! When he came down to our house it was because we had the [tape] recorder. I don't think he had one. He would come down and we would just have a laugh outside. At the side of our house was our bathroom and the window. We used to put the tape recorder on the floor and put the wire through the window and we used to put it in the light socket, and then we used to be sat at the side of the house with the tape recorder. He used to sing and we used to sing as well. He would play the recorder or the mouth organ and then we would play it back to listen to it.'

For the first eleven years of his life, until the birth of his sister Margaret in January 1957, Mick was an only child – and doted on by his mother. Minnie not only encouraged her son's musical talent, she

Childhood and Early Years: 1946–1963

taught him the values of kindness, politeness and generosity, of treating people as equal, which were values he followed throughout his life. Growing up meant inevitably getting into scrapes, and when in trouble, punishment was traditionally meted out by the father. George was strict and like many fathers of his generation didn't show much overt affection to his son. According to Minnie: 'Michael had a sometimes strained relationship with his dad and had a few "clouts around his head" when he was growing up.' Susan Baird remembers Mick throwing stones one day and breaking a window in their house. 'His mother come round and said, "Don't tell his dad, his dad will go mad." So my dad said, "It's alright." My dad had some picture frames and he cut the glass out of a picture frame. His own dad was quite strict. But his mother, she was real good with him.'

In September 1957 Mick started at Maybury School, where he became friends with Ian 'Taffy' Evans, who would later be a roadie with Mick in the local band The Rats: 'When we first went to Maybury it was a big school. There was rugby teams, there was football, there was sports. Mr Coverdale used to come out on a morning in middle of winter and say: "Are you cold boys?" and we said: "Yes, sir". And he said: "Last one back from the end of that football pitch gets the cane" and we was off like stink! But Mick was never the last, he was always quite athletic, he was good at PE.' Taffy recalls: 'Smoking in the bike sheds, Woodbine tipped. We just had a good time, we were a really good class together.' The school encouraged Mick to develop his interest in music: 'The music teacher at the time was Mr Harris and he realised Mick had some musical talent and put him in the recorder group for the school which appeared every morning at assembly on the stage to accompany us singing hymns.'

In 1958 the Ronson family moved from Hopewell Rd on Bilton Grange, to 8 Milford Grove on the adjoining Greatfield Estate. Their council house was modern, closer to the bus stop into town, and like the Hopewell Rd house had a small back garden. Mick took on a paper round, and two brothers, Dennis and David Wright, helped him with deliveries: 'We used to do both sides of Hopewell Road and one side of Lingdale. Most times I would meet Mike where they dropped the papers off at the telephone kiosk near Hopewell Road School. I used to meet him there and I'd do one side of Hopewell Road for him. I would have my own little bag and he would give me the papers and he would do the other side. We used to race each other and I often used to win, but I think that was Mike letting me win so he didn't do so much work!'

The Mick Ronson Story

At Maybury School Mick's musical range was expanding, as Taffy Evans recalls: 'They arranged for extra violin lessons for half an hour after school, where he would receive violin lessons. When Mr Harris left we had a man called Geoff Slaughter, a great bloke, and he clicked on to Mick as well and kept him going and started him with the piano. I don't know what his mother was doing with him with the piano, but he certainly was targeted for extra lessons.'

For some of the kids on the estate the sight of one of their own playing violin, or walking home carrying a violin case, was so out of the ordinary it invariably provoked a response. Childhood friend Ray Jordan lived in the house backing on to the Ronson family: 'He used to play the violin and I remember vividly 'cause it was unusual. We was all from working-class families. It wasn't usual to see a kid playing a violin. So we used to creep up to his window, knock on his window and pull funny faces, and he was there playing his violin. And he took it all in good fun and we used to laugh and we used to run off, but I always remember him playing the violin.' Another friend Tony Ward recalls: 'We used to play football outside and we used to tease Mick when he was going across to his music lessons with his music case. We used to tease him like mad.' Mick used to pay some of the older estate kids to carry his violin case for him, in effect his first roadies. In a 1976 interview from *Guitar Player*, Mick reminisced about that time: 'Violin was quite fun but after about three years I got fed up with it because people used to make fun of you if you carried a violin case. I used to pay people to carry my violin because I was afraid to myself. There were some tough lads there!'

The taunts and jibes of his peers didn't deter him, however. What stopped him from playing the violin was the more tempting proposition of another stringed instrument – the guitar. In an interview in *Rock Scene* from March 1975, Mick recalled the transition: 'I first studied on the piano, then recorder and violin. The guitar came much later. I got thrown out a lot in my violin class because I kept holding it like a guitar and plucking the strings. I was playing those kind of things on the violin and the teacher threw me out. I mean I was playing good violin, but as soon as his back was turned I was plucking and I was thinking like the Shadows and the Beatles, and then after that I thought, I've got to get a guitar. I put my violin away and got a guitar and I stopped playing piano and I was just playing guitar. So guitar became a big part of my life for a long while.'

In 1960, at the age of 14, Mick left school and started full-time work.

Childhood and Early Years: 1946–1963

Fourteen might sound like a tender age to enter the adult world of employment, but in those days for working-class kids it was the norm. A professional or academic career required further education, which in turn placed a financial burden on families that was simply unaffordable. With the young baby Margaret now part of the family, Mick would be expected not only to look after her when he could, which he more than happily did, but also to contribute financially to the household by giving his mother a regular amount from his weekly wage. His first job was with the Co-op, working on the mobile van that toured the estates selling groceries. David Wright remembers it well: 'He was working on the Co-op van and he used to always pop in. He knew me mam real well. Me mam could play the piano and there was always a key out of tune, and Mike used to tell me mam: "Edie, that bloody piano key, it's out of tune!" and she'd play up hell with him and say: "No, it isn't. You don't know how to bloody play the piano. Get yourself back on that van!" and she would kick him out in a nice way.'

With his good looks and polite, friendly manner Mick became a well-known and popular figure to the local mums and their impressionable young daughters, as Lynn Mitchell recalls: "He was about 15, I think. He used to work on the Co-op van. It was a maroon one with Co-op written on the side, and the back opened up and they stood inside, him and this chap. Every day it stopped right outside my mum's house, and me and my mum used to go and buy our little bits of shopping, 'cause there was no shops around there at all then, and that's how we met him. I mean I was only 9 or 10 I think, but he always had five minutes for me. He always used to have a little chat. He was blonde and I thought he was real nice looking. I was in love with him! I never missed going to the van with my mum. And then I remember him telling her that he'd been bought a guitar. Whether it was a Christmas present, birthday present, I don't know, but he said, "I'm practising like mad."'

The guitar was a cool instrument exemplified by skiffle bands, performers like Duane Eddy, and emerging guitar groups such as the Shadows and the Beatles. These were the early years of rock 'n roll, and for Mick the guitar was not only more acceptable within the working-class culture of a council estate, but it also allowed him to pursue his passion for music more intuitively. It offered a route out of the formal and tightly prescriptive music lessons, as he described in a 1988 article in *Music Maker Holland*': 'I used to play classical piano and violin and I learned to hate practising the scales. When I took up the guitar I decided not to practice anymore, just play.' Mick did practise, endlessly, but on

The Mick Ronson Story

his own terms. His mother remembers him playing incessantly at home: 'His fingers were constantly moving, practising guitar on his knee at the table in the kitchen.' The guitar was becoming his total passion, but at this point still a hobby, slotted between work and family obligations, and with no audience other than friends. His younger brother David was born in November 1962 and as with his sister Maggi, Mick would come home in his lunch break to take David out in the pram. His mother recalled, 'He always made sure everybody else was alright. At Christmas he would be the pot washer and he just wanted everybody else to relax and enjoy themselves.'

At this stage in his life Michael was simply the good-looking lad on the estate who worked on the Co-op van. His obsession with the guitar would soon set him on a new path, taking him out of the estate he grew up in, out of the city of Hull, into a future he could barely imagine.

2 First Bands: The Mariners and The Crestas:
1963—1966

The Mick Ronson Story

It's December 1965. Mick Ronson is onstage playing guitar with the Rolling Stones. He's one of them, one of the band. Jagger's out front, strutting his stuff, and nobody seems worried that Keith is missing. There are two Micks in the band now and the fans love them both. It's a big venue, a sell-out gig with the audience going wild. Girls scream, drowning out the amplified sound. Some are in distress, hands on temples, imploring the gods onstage to acknowledge their longing, their desire, their adoration. Mick's hand slides up and down the guitar neck, fingers shifting fluidly and effortlessly into the shapes of each chord. He feels the waves of sound wrapping around him and the band, the energy flowing back from the audience. They're playing so tight tonight, and he feels the perfect pleasure of being onstage doing what he loves most. He's fuelled by euphoria.

That feeling stays for a short while on waking, but before he's even left the house it's dissolving into the winter grey of another dull day in flat town. Reality has checked in. A dream is just a dream, and that level of success and adoration is not going to happen with his band: the Crestas are going nowhere. They've reached the end of the line. Four of them have left in the last six months, faced with the responsibility of married life, or the draw of a regular job putting more pound notes into their pocket. They're all older than he is, and they've run out of steam. By the time he's reached the bus stop he knows what he's got to do. Leave Hull. Go to London. It's the only way. That evening he tells his mother. She's worried by the idea of him being so far away, but she knows how much he wants this, and gives him her support and love. His father, George, is not impressed. He's told Mick before, 'Music should be your hobby. It's not going to pay your way in life.' He adds, 'If you're not careful, you're going to end up on the street, selling matches.'

At the start of 1963 Mick wasn't even playing in a band. He was still working at his day job on the Co-op van, and the closest he got to mixing with other musicians was in Gough and Davy's music shop in town, or on the top floor of Hammonds department store where they had a small music section. Both had impromptu gatherings of musicians, as Peter Alton-Green describes: 'Gough & Davy's had a shop down Saville Street. Every Saturday morning a gang of local guitar players, including

First Bands: The Mariners and The Crestas: 1963–1966

myself, would go down and try the gear and sometimes buy, and meet other people. It was like a little Saturday morning club where all the local guitar players used to go. Mick got to know this, he came in and he would start talking to us, and we'd start showing him things, which was the reason he was there. At that time I was doing national tours and I was pinching the licks off the professional people, and then I was passing them on to the local people. So that's how I first met Mick. He was a teenager. He was polite, he was nice, he was interested. He liked what we did and if he wanted to know something, he would ask, and I was happy to tell him.' Mick would mix socially, pick up tips on guitar-playing, and showcase his own developing skills. Just five minutes down the road was a similar Saturday scene at Hammonds Department store, where Rick Kemp was the manager of the music department: 'It was on the top floor in the area next to the radio and TV space, where the staff walked through to the canteen. There was a small display of electric and bass guitars, just one drum kit. It was a cool place to hang out on Saturdays. Musicians would come in, try out guitars and we'd jam together. That's where I got to know Mick and realise just how good a player he was.'

The Kemp family had moved up to Hull from London after Rick's father was promoted by his insurance company. Rick's first job was selling encyclopaedias door to door, then for a while he was the Man from the Pru, working in insurance like his father. Being a keen guitarist, he soon teamed up with other local musicians, as his then wife Christine, now Christine Park, describes: 'He was bored working for the Prudential, plus he had to go back out on a night as well, which wasn't very nice when you've got two babies, so he got a job working on the music department in Hammonds. Life changed for both of us then. He got to know more and more musicians coming in on a Saturday, and Mick Ronson was one of them. One day Michael Chapman came in, and Rick and him hit it off immediately. He was a tutor in Leeds in the college there, and he'd given up his job, and him and his lady Andru, they came to Hull to live down Louis Street. They had a flat down there. So Michael Chapman was coming to our house in Hessle and they were making music together, and we were going to their place and having meals, and really having a nice time.'

Rick Kemp would go on to play bass with Steeleye Span, and his early music collaborations in Hull, particularly with Michael Chapman, would help Mick Ronson on the path to a professional music career. It was Rick who got Mick his first job in an actual band in November

The Mick Ronson Story

1963: 'I was in a band called the Mariners, and the person that ran it was called John Griffiths, and he said to me one day, "Wouldn't it be good if we had somebody that could play guitar better than you?" So I said, 'Yeh, I do know such a person – his name's Mick Ronson and he's about 17. I managed the music department in Hammonds, so I knew that Mick was a great player. And he came along to play with the Mariners and the first gig was at the Beverley Arms Hotel in Beverley. Just before you get to the gig, there was at that time a garage on the right. So when I pulled in to get petrol before this gig, the petrol attendant said: "Sorry about JFK" and I said: "What about JFK?" and he said: "Kennedy was shot and killed today in Dallas." So a very memorable day to be doing this first gig with Mick. Also somebody shouted out after the second song: "He's better than you!" and I said: "I know, that's why he's here!"'

In May 1964 the Rolling Stones headlined at Bridlington Spa and Mick with the Mariners played support, albeit at the bottom of a very long bill of bands. A young Janet Padwick, who lived close to Mick on the same council estate, remembers a story from that time which gives a hint of his ambitions: 'He told me and Jennifer Curtis, who lived a few doors away, that he was playing at the Brid Spa and the Stones were top of the bill, and he would try and get their autographs. When he brought the books back he had signed it himself, and we said we didn't want *his* autograph, but he said he might be famous one day!' Sandra Nelson was at that Stones gig. Not long after, Mick auditioned for John Tomlinson's band the Buccaneers, and for a while played with them as well as the Mariners. Sandra swapped her attention from the Buccaneers' lead singer to Mick and they soon began dating. Rick Kemp's wife Christine remembers Sandra and Mick babysitting for them at their house in Hessle, a suburb of Hull: 'Mick used to bring Sandra down sometimes during rehearsals and I'd said how tough it was to get babysitters and afford them, so Sandra offered to babysit for us with Mick.' Christine remembers him as, 'Quite shy, quite a shy young man. He was just really very ordinary, talked about everyday things.'

In 1964 drummer Dave Bradfield joined Mick in the Mariners, the first of three bands in which they played together. 'They asked me if I wanted to join, so as you did in those days, if you thought it was a better band you just dumped the band you were in and joined, 'cause it was pretty merciless, you know. More status, more money.' The two became good friends and Dave remembers some of the venues they used to gig at: 'We played all over the place. We had a residency at the Marquis de Granby in Hessle. We used to play there every week. There

First Bands: The Mariners and The Crestas: 1963–1966

was the Ferry Boat Inn in Hessle, which was one of what we called "the fishermen pubs". When the fishermen came home they'd go to the Ferry Boat to fight. And Halfway House on Spring Bank, that was the other main fishermen's pub. It's where they went when they came in for a couple of days before they went back out to sea. There was Maybury pub, there was the Anchor down Southcoates Lane, and then of course there were a lot of working men's clubs in Hull, the Ambassador, Rayne Street Club. Music was very big in them days, very big. We also used to go out of town to the West Riding. And there was a pub, I think it was somewhere near Thorne, called Moor End, and that was a big fighting pub, tables and bottles all night, and you just stay on the stage and try and keep out of it. If you needed to go to toilet, it terrified you, 'cause you didn't know whether you were gonna come out. Ferry Boat was like that. I mean the people I saw get laid out at Ferry Boat was unbelievable.'

Live music in and around Hull was a vibrant scene. It ranged from smaller coffee-club gigs at places such as the Gondola and Kontiki Clubs, to a wide spread of pubs, and the larger venues such as the Locarno Ballroom, run by the Mecca organisation, the Skyline Ballroom, Hull City Hall and Beverley Regal. There was also an older tradition of musicians playing in resident cabaret bands in working men's clubs, where they would provide backing for guesting singers. Bands also played regularly in church halls, village halls, youth clubs and schools.

The Mariners played covers, as Dave Bradfield recalls: 'Everybody in those days used to play whatever was in the pop charts at the time. So you played the Hollies, the Beatles, Chuck Berry. You did everything that was popular 'cause that's what you had to do, that's what people wanted.' Years later, in a 1992 interview filmed at Hammersmith Odeon, Mick fondly recalled the guitar players who had influenced him in his early career: 'I started off in bands where we'd play Everly Brothers songs and Beatles songs, and later on that progressed to more of a blues band, you know, soul band. I used to like listening to Eddie Cochran, George Harrison, Hank Marvin – the Shadows was one of the earliest ones. I was always a big melody lover. I used to play classical music, classical piano, violin and I was always fond of a good melody. The Shadows were always great at that, a great instrumental band. And from there, Eddie Cochrane, George Harrison was quite a big influence, not right away, I think I was more of a Rolling Stones type of fan early on, and then I got into this Beatles guitar, very good, great, and Jeff Beck, I used to like Jeff Beck, still do.'

By the age of 18 Mick was starting to establish himself in the local music scene. In 1964 he left the Mariners to join the Crestas, a band that was higher up on the local pecking order, as Peter Alton-Green explains: 'There were the First Division of bands, like the Aces, the Tycoons, and the Mods, and there was a Second Division like the Mariners that were coming up. They got loads of work 'cause they'd do it cheaper than we could do it.' The Crestas were definitely First Division and were a hybrid of another Hull band, the Aces. The Crestas were unusual in that they had two lead vocalists in Johnny Hawk (real name Ray Ward) and Eric Lee, with the pair variously fronting on alternate songs, taking alternate verses, or duetting with harmonies.

John Robinson, the Crestas manager, remembers how Mick was recruited: 'I used to see him play in Halfway with the Mariners and we realised he was pretty good, he was too good for the group he was in. When the lead guitarist out of the Crestas decided to chuck it, we says we'll go for Mick. But none of us knew where he lived, so we didn't want to ask one of the Mariners, because they would have known we were going to poach him, so I rung the Co-op shop and asked him to give us a ring. When I mentioned *Did he want to join the Crestas*, he jumped at the chance, he couldn't believe it, he was real chuffed.'

Mick knew he was stepping up a level by joining the Crestas. Alongside Johnny Hawk and Eric Lee on vocals, the line-up included Tim Myers on bass, Henry Temple on rhythm guitar and Mike Kitching on drums. They were all older and more experienced than Mick, so Johnny Hawk felt he needed to visit the Ronson family to assure Mick's parents that he and the older band members would take good care of their 18-year-old son. Eric Lee recalls Mick being 'like the young kid coming to school. If we was going to a gig and we were playing with a named group, in the van he'd be saying, "What are they like, what do you think?" We'd say, "Don't worry, Mick, just watch us, you'll be ok. Play, don't worry!" Mick was nervous – 'cause these bands were on a higher level and he needed to build his confidence. He was shy, that's how he was. But it all went away once he plugged in – it was just him and his guitar. He was a boy on the way there, but he was a man on the stage.'

The Crestas got a gig at Dewsbury Town Hall supporting a popular band at the time called Reverend Black and the Rocking Vicars. The Crestas went down a storm, resulting in promoter Derek Arnold booking them for regular Saturday night gigs around the Leeds and Bradford areas and across South Yorkshire. With constant local gigging as well, the band were playing or rehearsing most nights. Roadie Ted Park recalls: 'It was quite a hectic scene, really. I was working in the day

First Bands: The Mariners and The Crestas: 1963-1966

like Johnny Hawk at the same place, and dashing home on a night. My mother would have a bath run, I'd jump in the bath, she'd have me some food ready, I'd get changed, pick up the van and then go round and pick all the lads up. We played a lot of gigs round Hull. The Halfway House on Spring Bank was a big scene. Two nights a week at least we were playing there, and we played Beverley Regal on Friday night, and The Duke of Cumberland in Ferriby on Sunday was a regular booking. It was the in place to be on a Sunday night. People used to come from all over and absolutely packed the place. We also did the out-of-town gigs on a weekend.'

Mick brought a fresh energy to the Crestas, adding vocal harmonies alongside Eric Lee on Everly Brothers songs, and with Johnny Hawk on the Beatles' ballads. He also brought a new guitar style, according to Eric: 'Mick was a breath of fresh air, he was just brilliant for us. We'd never had a guitarist who played that sort of style. Styles of playing changed and fuzz pedals and distortion came into the game. Before Mick got a pedal, he used to turn and face the amplifier with his guitar to get the feedback, and it used to scream like hell. On a solo, if the solo was good, he used to turn back for us to come in on the vocal, and we'd say: "No, carry on" – and he'd do a double solo. He was bringing it up a notch. He's playing his own style, like Hendrix, that's the way it was going. Faster, more scales, more improvised, you could hear it, it was different. He was a massive asset.'

The Crestas would rehearse Thursday evenings in a room above the Green Gingerman pub on Lombard Street by the former central bus station. As well as their usual set list of Chuck Berry, classic R&B rockers, and Beatles tracks, they would practise new songs of bands appearing on *Top of the Pops*, which began broadcasting in 1964. Mick recalled the way he learnt guitar parts in an article in *Melody Maker* from 1973: 'When I was starting, I listened carefully to my favourite guitarists on stage and records, notably Jeff Beck, Jimi Hendrix, Keith Richard and George Harrison, and watched exactly how they played, where they put their fingers, and how they got the sounds. I put two and two together, went home and practised until I could do it myself.' Ted Park can vouch for Mick's dedication to his guitar playing: 'When I dropped Mick off on a night, he always took his guitar home. And because it was an electric guitar the sound was very small, so he didn't wake up his mum and dad and his sister. He would go home and have half an hour sat in his chair with his guitar on his own before he went to bed. Just practice, practice, the guy never stopped practising.'

The Mick Ronson Story

Although shy by nature, Mick had a slim physique and good looks that were making him increasingly popular with young women. Ted Park remembers a Crestas gig in a mining community near Sheffield, where they nearly came to grief: 'We were playing Mexborough Town Hall. The night had gone well no problems. It got towards the end of the night and one of the bouncers came across and said to me, "Look, there's a bit of trouble brewing with a lot of local miners. So what I suggest you tell the lads is, as soon as you come to the last number, get your gear out, get yourselves packed up and get away." A couple of weeks prior, I don't know whether this is a true fact or not, but the man did say that a band called Johnny Kidd and the Pirates had been involved in quite a fracas with these miners. So as the night ended we were unplugging the gear and we were getting it together as quick as we could, and getting it in the van. The van was parked on a slope near the dance hall, so we jumped in the van, drove down the slope and as we came out the other side there was all banging on the side of the van. Nothing serious just a few bangs and screams, but we're OK, we're on the road."

The problem was, they'd left the gig without Mick: 'All of a sudden they're shouting in the back, "Stop the damn van – Ronno's missing!" So we pulled the van up, put the lights on, no Ronno, missing completely. Me being the roadie, seven stone, couldn't fight me way out of a paper bag, was given the job to go back to this dance hall and find Ronno. So I shot back down the road as fast as I could, picked up a bouncer on the door and he said, "I'll come inside with you and we'll find him." We wandered through the dance hall, and there was Mick stood at the bar, a young girl on his arm, chatting her up as Mick did, because he was definitely a ladies' man and they loved him. So I went across with the bouncer. I grabbed Mick's arm and we carefully lead him out the dance hall with his lovely girl hanging onto his arm. We got to the door and as we got round the corner there was this load of miners. You could see they were looking for trouble. So I said to Mick, "Turn left and just walk. We're not going to run 'cause that'll attract attention, we'll just walk." So we set off walking I don't know about 150 yards, walking very steadily then all of a sudden Mick slapped me on the back and said, "Leg it, leg it, they're coming!" So we both legged it up the street, but they weren't. He was just winding me up. We got back to the van with the engine running, ready to go. So we all piled in to a big cheer from the lads and drove back to Hull."

The band had a strict rule that girlfriends weren't allowed to travel in the van home from out-of-town gigs. Pat Lee, fiancée of singer Eric

First Bands: The Mariners and The Crestas: 1963–1966

Lee, had become good friends with Mick's girlfriend Sandra, and one night the pair decided to test the rule: 'This one time when they were playing out of town in Dewsbury we had the brilliant idea of following them, 'cause we weren't supposed to go out of town with them, so we thought we would. We got the train, and we didn't get there while about half past ten, and it finished before midnight. We just turned up and they were quite surprised to see us. Then when it came to going home, they wouldn't let us in the van, 'cause we'd broke the rules. So we decided we'd go to the police station because Dewsbury closed down at 11 o'clock. We told them that we'd nowhere to go, no hotels were open, so they decided they would take us to the railway station. They opened the railway waiting room up for us, and the station master kept an eye on us all through the night, and they brought us hot drinks now and then. Then I went home on the first train home, we both did. Eric had been to see my mother on the Sunday morning to tell her that we weren't in, and she hadn't even missed me till then! And when I got home, that was it, I was grounded for two weeks, and I was engaged to him at the time! But that was it – we never did it again.'

Mick acquired the nickname 'Ronno' when he joined the Crestas. Benny Marshall was the singer in the popular Hull band the Rats, and remembers the first time he heard it being used: 'I came across Michael when he was playing with the Crestas at the Halfway House. He was the new guitarist who had joined. Eric Lee was the singer and he was a good friend of mine and I used to go in and watch him. Anyway, this day the new guy turned up, and I said to Eric: "Who's the guy then?" and he said: "Ah, that's Ronno." And that's where his name came from. It stuck with him the rest of his life. It was Eric Lee who actually gave him the name Ronno, that's where he got the nickname from. Of course, we picked it up straightaway.'

Gigs in the '60s would have several bands on the same night, and this meant local musicians would get to know each other, check out each other's skills, and see how each band was progressing. This networking led to many Hull musicians being part of Mick Ronson's musical journey in Hull and beyond, including among others: Rick Kemp, Michael Chapman, Benny Marshall, Geoff Appleby, John Cambridge, Keith 'Ched' Cheesman, John Bentley, Woody Woodmansey and Trevor Bolder. Some helped Mick up the ladder to success, while others were drawn in the slipstream of his achievements. In 1965, drummer John Cambridge, who was to later play such a pivotal role in introducing Mick to David Bowie, remembers first seeing Mick play at Beverley:

The Mick Ronson Story

'My first band was called the Gonx when I was 15, and we'd do Beverley Regal. We used to play with the Crestas, who I thought was probably the best band in Hull at the time. I liked them and I would go and see them play the Halfway House on Spring Bank, a really little pub with a back room. So that's how I got to meet Mick, through things like that.'

Shared gigs were also a route to poaching other band members and reconfiguring line-ups. The scene was constantly fluid, with musicians keeping an eye out for the main chance to improve their opportunities. Mick was no exception. Benny Marshall remembers Mick making it clear, even at their first meeting while he was still in the Crestas, that he considered the Rats to be a band he was keen to join: 'The Rats were doing quite well – we had a couple of singles out, two TV appearances, all was well with the world, and Mick knew this. He came over and said, "If you ever need a new guitarist, I'd be interested." "Ah, would you?" So jokingly like, 'cause we already had a guitarist, I said, "There'll have to be a transfer fee." So the transfer fees used to come up, and every time it changed. The first time it was two army badges and a Barmy Drain frog, and it would get so: "No, no, you'll have to have a pair of racing bike handles as well" and "I've got a used pair of football boots, are they any good?" He would do this every time we met up, and I used to see him around the town quite a lot.'

In 1965 Mick's music ambitions nearly came to a premature end one Sunday night at the Duke of Cumberland in North Ferriby, a small village to the west of Hull. The band were setting up as people were arriving. Accounts of what exactly happened vary, but roadie Ted Park remembers: 'Mick walked up to the mike stand, touched the mike stand, and he went down like a ton of bricks. We thought at first he was messing around. Mick often did. Of course, in another second we realised the guy was getting a severe electric shock. I remember the drum kit went all over. I jumped on the stage. It was either Timmy Myers or a roadie mate of mine called Stuey George, who flew over the drums to unplug the system completely from the wall. By that time Mick was on the floor and was in a bit of a state. He'd had a serious electric shock. I think Tim Myers or Eric put him in the recovery position and we rang for an ambulance.'

Singer Eric Lee recalls: 'We were rigging the gear up, and we had two amps plus a PA amp into the plugboard. Unbeknown, there's a loose wire in the board. Now several musicians have been killed this way, died onstage. What happens is, you've got one hand on your guitar, you go and grab a microphone stand, and you create the circuit, and you can't

First Bands: The Mariners and The Crestas: 1963–1966

let go, it's killing you. We heard a shout and scream, turns round, and Mick's dancing all over the stage, all over the place. He's writhing about, jumping and swirling about, trying to let go and he can't. Some people thought he was messing about. After the event some people said they thought he was doing an Elvis impersonation. I didn't and Ray (Johnny Hawk) didn't – we've known this happen before. We shouts, "Pull the plug out – quick!" Me and Ray went up to him, kicking his 335 off of him, his Gibson, kicking it off, trying to pull the microphone stand off him, and we got burnt, pulling it off him.'

John Robinson was also there that night: 'I tried to get the mike out of his hands and I got a shock as well. John (Hawk) just took a running kick at it and kicked it off the stage into the audience. Somebody had rung for an ambulance, and the ambulance was there within about five minutes, and they took Mick out on a stretcher, and oh, it was deathly quiet in there, you know, you wouldn't hear a pin drop. Everybody was panicking 'cause they thought he was dead when they took him out.' Mick was taken by ambulance to Hull Royal Infirmary and fortunately made a full and quick recovery, to the extent that he turned up and played the following night's gig at Halfway House.

In June 1965, Johnny Hawk told the band he intended to leave, as he was starting a job in Goole, west of Hull, so he played his final gig in July. Rhythm guitarist Henry Temple also left, followed by Mike Kitching, who was taking on a regular job in his father's butcher's business. Mick's former Mariners bandmate, Dave Bradfield, took over on drums: 'We'd meet in the pub and everybody would be drinking pints, but Mick would just go quietly to the bar and get a little orange, get his cig out 'cause of course in those days you could smoke in the pubs, and then just sit there with his cig. I never ever saw Mick get angry or aggressive. He'd just sit there with his cig and glass of orange and then go on and play. He was always laughing, was Mick. He was a joker, rubbish jokes, but he was always cracking jokes. If we were playing at Halfway, we'd finish up at Supa Bar and all have curry and chips.'

The Supa Bar was on Princes Avenue in Hull, one of the first Chinese takeaways in the city: 'After the gig we'd get into the group van and we used to go there straight from Halfway, it took five minutes to get there and we'd all get what we wanted. Mick always got about four or five cartons of curry and I used to say, "What you gonna do with them, Mick?" He said, "I have 'em for me breakfast cold." Yeah, curry sauce in a tub, he liked pots of curry.' Roadie Ted Park confirmed Mick's post-gig culinary choice: 'He wanted his curry and chips, did Mick, so we're sat in the van and he used to get the curry and just drink it. Sometimes he didn't even get the chips, just the cartons of curry sauce and just drink them. Amazing.'

Dave Bradfield remembers the long drives home after out-of-town gigs: 'In those days it used to take you about five hours to get from Huddersfield, and if you went down to Lincoln you had to go right round Goole, there was no Humber Bridge, and it would be an all-nighter getting home. I don't think we ever got home earlier than four or five in the morning 'cause there was no bridges, there were no motorways.'

Mick was increasingly steering the musical direction of the band, and Dave remembers his growing confidence in rehearsals: 'He wasn't your average rock guitarist. Mick was much cleverer than that. For a start, he understood classical music, which you can of course transfer onto a guitar or any instrument. Most people at that stage would play three or four chords to every number. Mick was clever, he would be playing 9ths and 13ths which only jazz players play, and of course he knew all the scales, so he could do runs that other people wouldn't know where to start or where to finish. He knew all the theory, so it made him a wonderful musician. I've seen him when we rehearsed at Londesborough Street Club with the Crestas. If we were learning a new number he'd say, "Right, they're the notes you should play – bass player Tim – and these are the harmonies I want you to sing." Straight out of his head on to a Park Drive packet. He knew harmonies and chord structures inside out, so he'd often say: "Right, you're singing the tonic, you're singing the third and you're singing the fifth. These are the notes. Have you got 'em? Right, we're doing it" – and that was it. He was very clever, he was a very clever lad.'

Soon after Johnny Hawk left, the band's other singer Eric Lee, his wedding imminent, also decided to finish: 'I was ordered by my mother. It's the truth. She said, "You can quit that game. That dun't work with a marriage!" I loved the Crestas, it was a great band, but to tell you the truth when Ray (Johnny Hawk) left, it wasn't the same. Ray was a major spark in the band, and he was good fun, and that was what the band was about, having a good laugh. But when he went something was missing. The spark had gone.'

Four of the six Crestas had left in the space of a few months. It was clear to Mick that despite the band's success and popularity, and his own growing confidence and status within it, the overall commitment just wasn't there to take it to a higher level. The strain of constant gigging, with late-night drives home from out-of-town gigs, did not sit easily

First Bands: The Mariners and The Crestas: 1963-1966

with trying to hold down a regular day job or a serious relationship. The Crestas carried on for a while with a new singer, Malcolm 'Mally' Hunt, but the band was coming to the end of the road.

In the space of two years Mick had gone from a hobby guitar player at home, to a touring musician with an ever-growing fanbase. Despite his father's warnings, his desire to make a career out of music was growing stronger – with each band and every gig his ambition was being vindicated. He knew he was popular and he knew he was good. A 1975 interview in *Hit Parader* magazine gives a vivid insight as to just how consuming his passion for music had become: 'I used to go to bed and dream. I remember one night I dreamed I was on stage with the Rolling Stones. There I was in Keith Richard's place and I was playing and the audience was going crazy and it felt so good and I never felt anything like it in my life before and I always remember that. I guess every kid who starts off playing guitar or drums, or piano, or whatever it is, must go through all that and dream about it and keep striving for it.'

By Christmas 1965 Mick had made his mind up. He was going to London. If Hull was the end of the line and the road to nowhere, then the one road in was also the one road out, the road to somewhere better. He tried to persuade Dave Bradfield to go with him: 'Mick got itchy fingers, he was wanting to pursue his dream, which was to become professional, and successful and famous. He said to me: "Come down with me, Dave" and I said: "No, I'm not coming Mick. I've been there, done it, you go down and get a band and I'll come down and audition," so that's exactly what we did.'

At the age of 19, soon after New Year 1966, Mick moved down to London. He stayed for a while with a friend of the family who lived with her husband in Harlow, Essex. With no income at this point, his savings were dwindling fast: it cost him a pound a day to travel back and forth to the capital. He would scan the classified ads of music papers such as *New Musical Express* and *Melody Maker*, seeking musicians to join or form bands. An endless routine of phone calls with the occasional audition finally paid off when he got a job with the Voice, replacing guitarist Miller Anderson. He moved into a shared house in Chalk Farm and when the band's drummer decided to leave, Mick was straight on the phone to Dave Bradfield. The Voice were supporting the Yardbirds at a gig in March at the Top Rank in Brighton. The Yardbirds at that time were fronted by Jeff Beck, a guitar hero of Mick's, and on the day he got to play on the same bill as the musician he idolised, his Hull mate Dave Bradfield successfully auditioned for the job as drummer with the

Voice. Dave moved in with Mick in London to work in what was their third band together and started a daily routine of rehearsals and gigs: 'We lived near the back of the Roundhouse. We used to get up about half nine. There was a little café round the corner. We'd go and get an English breakfast for half a crown, then we'd come back for Mick to pick his guitar up. My drums were always left with the band and we'd get on a Tube and go right across London to this pub where we used to rehearse. If we had a gig, we'd finish early and go to the gig. If we didn't, we'd practise or then come home and just chill. We never went to the pub because Mick didn't drink. I drank but I was never bothered. We just used to sit in the communal room with all these hippies and crazy people and just watch telly. There was no doors anywhere. Typical '60s London, Bohemian lifestyle. Then we'd go to bed and do the same thing the next day.'

The Voice offered the Hull lads potential for bigger things, as the band was managed by Micky Most. He had produced hit singles for the Animals, Herman's Hermits and Lulu and would go on to produce Jeff Beck's seminal album *Truth*. Bradfield remembers the music played by the Voice at that time: 'We did quite a lot of soul, some Motown, we did good stuff, and there were people in the band who wrote. The keyboard player was Eddie Hammill and he was a good writer, so we did some of what they'd written. It was different to being in Hull in a pop band. We did more refined music. And it was good music, it was enjoyable, very enjoyable.'

Dave Bradfield soon realised, however, that the Voice was not just a band, but part of a larger quasi-religious cult: 'There was a singer, a keyboard player, a bass player, Mick, and myself. The other members were all members of this religious cult called The Process, and that was a right odd situation. They used to give Bob and Mary Ann all the money, and every week they gave them a pound back to live on. They lived in a big mansion in Hyde Park – I mean *mansion*.' The Process was run by two former Scientologists: Robert (Bob) De Grimston Moore and Mary Ann McClean. In 1964 they started a therapy group called Compulsions Analysis, which soon morphed into a religious cult called The Process Church of the Final Judgement, or The Process for short. By 1965 The Process had moved to a mansion in Mayfair at Balfour Place. Dave Bradfield was not impressed: 'I kept away from it. I didn't get involved. I never went to the house. I'd seen pictures of it and I knew what was going on, and I knew about the control 'cause they took all our money. It just seemed even to an outsider, it seemed controlling and dark, and I

First Bands: The Mariners and The Crestas: 1963–1966

didn't want nowt to do with it. One of the guys used to talk about it – how Bob and Mary Ann took the money, how they told them what they could and couldn't do, and where they could and couldn't go. I mean I'm not intellectual but I'm pretty bloody savvy. I soon clocked on that these kids were being took for a ride.'

In late June, Dave and Mick went home for a weekend in Hull. 'When we got back to London and we got into our flat, all our gear was on our beds and there was a little note saying, "The deal with Micky Most has fallen through, so we've decided to go with Bob and Mary Ann. They've bought an island in the Bahamas. We've decided to go off with them and give up music." So then we were a bit stuck. I said to Mick, "I'm not going to stay down here in London, Mick." I'd been professional before and I hated London anyway. I hated it, I still do. So I came back. Mick stayed down there.'

Alone and with the Voice having folded, Mick was struggling to make ends meet. He got a day job at a garage, cleaning cars and working as a mechanic. He was determined not to give up on his dream and by July had joined a semi-pro band the Wanted, playing Motown covers. The band soon folded, however, leaving Mick even further in debt. In a letter to his girlfriend Sandra Nelson, written late in August, he said, "Things are bad. I'm most probably coming home in two weeks to settle myself down to an ordinary simple way of life for a while. I think that is the best thing to do, don't you?" He later described that time in a 1970 article for the *Hull Daily Mail* as a 'real battle even just to live and eat, and in the end I had to get a job in a garage because I wasn't earning enough from my music. I still could not afford to live, so I came back to Hull.' In another interview with the same paper from 1975, the full extent of that difficult and demoralising time was apparent: 'When I went to London the first time, I got £100 into debt – and that was without making the equipment payments. I owed rent, paid it off and then borrowed some more money, and had to cash an insurance policy. I was working during the day and earning £9 a week and had equipment and my room to pay from it. After forking out for that, I was left with nothing and used to eat dry bread.'

In September 1966, after nine months in London, he came home – with little to show for all his efforts. His father's warning that he could end up selling matches on the street now sounded too close to the truth. His dreams of playing in a top band, of getting a recording contract and making actual records had all proved illusory. He couldn't earn even a basic living from music. He was in debt and the pressure was on to get

The Mick Ronson Story

a proper job. He applied for a post with Hull City Council in the Parks Department. He was turned down the first time, but his mother Minnie insisted he go back, and he finally got a job as a council gardener. Mowing the grass and lining school and municipal sports fields in Hull was a long way from being a rock star, but it gained him the respect of his father, the comforts of family life, and the reassuring familiarity of being once more on home turf. It wouldn't be long, however, before rock 'n roll would start shaking it all over once again.

3 The Rats, Part One:
1966–1968

Back in Hull, tending the city's parks and playing fields, Mick started to pay off his debts. This was a period of consolidation. The demoralising experience of trying to find professional music work in the capital had in no way diminished his desire to be playing. What had been difficult and frustrating in London, now proved relatively simple back on home territory. Following up on those earlier exchanges with Rats singer Benny Marshall, Mick joined the band he'd had his eye on before moving to London. Drummer Jim Simpson recalls his recruitment: 'We arranged to meet him in the back of the Barham pub. So went there and he's expecting us of course. He knew we were coming and he knew what we were coming for. It wasn't so much a discussion about whether we wanted him to join the band. It was more a discussion about whether he wanted to join us.' No one remembers if the requisite 'transfer fee' was agreed, but since Mick at this stage wasn't in a band, perhaps it was no longer required. The search was then on for a fourth band member as Benny recalls: 'We needed a bass player and we went to a guy called Joe Wilkinson. He was a part-time agent, he used to give us a few gigs, and we said have you got any bass players? He says, "This kid called Geoff Appleby – he's not doing much at the minute." So he gave us his address, we phoned him up and he decided to join.'

Geoff Appleby was born in Hull in 1949. He joined his first band, the UFOs, in 1963, which then became the Yorkies. The Yorkies folded in 1966 around the same time as the Rats were in flux and Mick Ronson was coming home. With the line-up of Benny Marshall on vocals and harmonica, Jim Simpson on drums, Geoff Appleby on bass and Mick Ronson on guitar, the Rats were back in action.

The band had pedigree long before Mick joined. They had started life in Hull in 1962 as Rocky Stone and the Stereotones. Apparently singer Rocky Stone's adoption of a faux-American accent occasioned not only the dismay of his bandmates, but also his speedy replacement by Peter (Benny) Marshall, under the stage name of Peter King. Jim Simpson replaced David Barron on drums, and with Frank Ince on lead guitar and Brian Buttle on bass, the line-up went under the name of Peter King and the Majestics. In 1964 Grimsby booking agent Martin Yale joined Barry Paterson to manage the band and pushed for a trendier name. The success of the Liverpool-based, Merseybeat bands no doubt influenced the proposed name of the River Rats, shortened simply to the Rats. Robin Lecore joined on keyboards and that year they recorded various tracks at Pye and Olympic studios in London, releasing the classic Willie Dixon track 'Spoonful' in the US in December 1964 and in

The Rats, Part One: 1966–1968

the UK the following February, where it reached No. 67 in the Hit One Hundred record chart.

In Lancashire there was another band also called the Rats, and this led to them both appearing in March 1965 on *Thank Your Lucky Stars*, the TV music show hosted by Brian Matthew. On the same bill were the Dave Clark Five, Georgie Fame and the Blue Flames, Screaming Jay Hawkins and a very young unknown guitarist called Jim Page (in the days before Led Zeppelin). The appearance of the two Rats, though, was a televised Battle of the Bands, the audience voting to choose which band would keep the name – and the Hull-based Yorkshire Rats won. Drummer Jim Simpson was an apprentice fridge engineer at the time and was finding that the late-night drives after Rats gigs were in danger of losing him his job: 'I used to get home sometimes just in time to be late for work.' With the need to take time out for the TV appearance, he feigned a work injury: 'I'd had so much time off, I daren't ask again, so I pulled something off a workbench and it made a big thud and I pretended I'd dropped something on my foot. They took me to the hospital and the hospital said that I had to rest up for a couple of days. We got to the studio and the cameraman says: "I'm going to open the shot with a close-up of your bass-drum foot", which was a little bit upsetting 'cause that's the foot I said was poorly!' The TV appearance gave the Rats confidence that the band was really going places, but their second single 'New Orleans/I Gotta See My Baby' failed to make any impression on the UK charts. In 1966 Brian Buttle and Frank Ince left the band, followed by Robin Lecore. Singer Benny Marshall and drummer Jim Simpson were still keen to continue, and with Mick Ronson's return home from London that September 1966, and with Geoff Appleby on bass, the band had a new line-up and a fresh impetus.

Jim Simpson remembers how with Mick joining, they moved towards the heavier rock sound of the new emerging bands: 'We were a blues band. So we were playing Muddy Water's stuff and things like that. Then when Ronno joined it became Jimi Hendrix, Cream and that kind of music. We didn't change him, he changed us, surreptitiously, in his musical ability. He didn't show the intense talent that he had, but I suppose if you looked carefully you could see the beginning of it. We were all learning, everyone was learning. It was new to everybody, but he just progressed and progressed and progressed. I think that was the making of him to be honest. In the end it became his band. It didn't take very long actually.'

Mick had seen Cream play that September along with a friend and drummer Dave Harvey: 'Mick and I went in 1966 to see Eric Clapton, he was playing with Cream at the Skyline Ballroom in Hull. I wanted to see Ginger Baker and so we went to see them together. I was stood directly in front of Eric Clapton and the stage was only one foot [30 cm] high, so I could virtually play Eric Clapton's guitar. Mick Ronson was right next to me so the pair of us could have strummed along because we were that close to him, literally one foot away. Mick could watch all the techniques that Clapton used. He told me at the time, he liked to see the way he bent the notes, and got the sounds when he did the blues stuff.'

The mid to late '60s saw a growing shift in musical styles and an embrace of new genres. The American blues and old school R&B were morphing into psychedelia, prog rock, folk rock and all manner of crossover forms, often typified by a heavier sound, extended guitar impros and drum solos. The clean-cut guitar sound of bands like the Shadows was giving way to the use of distortion, fuzzboxes and wah-wah pedals. Bands were beginning to see the potential of writing their own material, and a number of independent record labels such as Island were challenging the dominance of the major record companies, who in response set up their own 'independent' sub-labels to cash in on this new wave. It was a time for innovation and change. Mick's interest in the guitar playing of Jeff Beck, Eric Clapton and Jimi Hendrix started to feature prominently in the music of the Rats. They remained a covers band, but the setlist was increasingly encompassing this new emerging sound, as Benny Marshall describes: 'When Mick started playing there was no custom gauge guitar strings. He used to put a banjo top string on 'cause it could bend more, but after a while when the custom gauge came out, he used to go through all the strings in a box and get the right gauges out for himself. Then we came on to playing Led Zeppelin, and there was no way I could reach the notes that Robert Plant reached, so everybody tuned down a semitone, the whole band tuned down a semitone so that I could hit the right notes, and Mick could get a better bend on his strings.'

The shift in music was mirrored by a change to what was worn on stage. Jim Simpson remembers the early Rats wearing suits: 'We bought the suits off Johnny Hawk and the Aces because they'd split up. I remember one was black and gold lamé and the other was red. Nobody fitted any of them, but we had to do it. It was fun in the dressing rooms getting dressed up. We'd no make-up or anything like that, but actually getting dressed up to go on stage made you feel as though you were doing it properly. Then after that it was sort of shirts and trousers with

The Rats, Part One: 1966–1968

creases in them. Then it got lazy and it was jeans and T-shirts."

With Ronson in their ranks, the band quickly built up a local and regional touring circuit. Jim Simpson recalls: 'There was a lot of gigs in those days and you could be working seven nights a week if you wanted, and we did sometimes. We used to go to Sheffield for £25. Five of us, with a driver and petrol. It certainly wasn't about money. We used to spend hundreds of hours in the back of the van getting to jobs, because we were getting popular. The biggest joke was supposed to be who would carry the drums because they were the heaviest things. As time went on, the drums were the lightest thing. Amps got bigger and bigger, and the PA system got bigger. But the joke before that, was who was going to carry the drums, because it's the bane of every drummer's life having to carry them. Mick always used to manage to get everything out except the drums. Not once did he have to carry them!'

The Rats auditioned that year for Mecca with the aim of securing a residency or touring on their circuit of venues. It didn't go well, as Dave Harvey recalls: 'In 1966 I was working for the Mecca company on Ferensway, and people from the head of the music department from London came up to Hull to audition bands, sometimes for holiday relief, but also sometimes for permanent jobs on the Mecca circuit. Mick's band, the Rats, came to audition. There was another band on before, playing the waltzes and the foxtrots and the quick steps and a little bit of what they called soft pop. Then the Rats came on and they set up and started to play. Mick was using distortion on his guitar, which not many people were using, and playing really well, and the band sounded really good. It wasn't what the Mecca establishment wanted at the time, so the head of department said to me, "Could you go up and ask them to stop playing?" I felt really embarrassed 'cause these were my friends and I had to go over and ask them, "Would you mind stopping. They don't want to listen to any more." They just said OK and stopped. But it was embarrassing for me to go and ask them to do it. That was an audition that they'd failed!"

In the spring of 1967, the Rats got the chance to tour abroad. Through an agency in London they were initially booked to play American airforce bases in Germany. Drummer Jim Simpson was not keen on going: 'I was getting towards the end of my apprenticeship, and I'd already had that much time off from work that it was really important I learned something quick or I wouldn't get another job.' On hearing what the tour deal actually involved, he was not impressed: 'There was no money till the end of it, and they had to find their own accommodation or sleep in the van and all that sort of stuff. It was just nonsense really. I can't understand how they all fell for it, to be honest.' As the tour van was Jim's, the hunt was now on not only for a replacement drummer, but a roadie and a van. Mick approached John Cambridge, but he declined, and they eventually recruited Clive 'Spud' Taylor, who had previously drummed with Geoff Appleby in the Yorkies. Mick then enlisted Ian 'Taffy' Evans, his former friend from Maybury School, for the crucial transport and roadie duties: 'One evening a knock came on the door and there was Ronno stood there. He said, "We want you to come and drive for us, we're going on tour to Germany." I said: "Right, what van have you got, then?" "Oh we haven't got a van yet." So the day before we went, we bought a van from Millhouse Garage on Southcoates Lane – a Ford Thames – and it had windows! No group in town had a van with windows and a side door, and we were just feeling absolutely spot on.'

With no advance for the upcoming tour, and mindful of his recent financial problems in London the previous year, Mick needed to find some source of funding. His 21st birthday at the end of May was only a few weeks away and he persuaded his mother Minnie to give him some birthday money upfront. Minnie recalled: 'I didn't know how I was going to get the money. I thought I'd have to work something out with his father. It was £50, which doesn't sound like a lot of money, but it was back then.' Given his father's attitude to his son trying to make a living from music, it is unlikely that George was made aware of what the birthday money was in fact for; he would not have approved. Cash for the tour was in fact so tight that Ian Evans had to borrow money from his aunt to pay for the recently purchased second-hand van.

Shortly before they were due to set off, another problem reared its head. Mick was playing a Fender Telecaster by this stage, and it developed a fault with one of the pickups. Ian Evans takes up the story: 'Before we went away Mick had a Fender Telecaster, his white one, and they only have two pickups and one of them had broken, it wasn't working. In them days you couldn't just pick up another Telecaster, it had to be sent for from America, so we had to go to find another guitar. We went to Gough and Davy's – and nowt there. So as always it was on to Pat Cornell's, and we spotted a Fender Stratocaster Sunburst and we went in and said, "How can we get this?" They said, "Well, we can do it on finance but you're too young, so take this form away and get your dad to sign it and then bring it back." So we took it out the door and Mick signed it in his dad's name. We went back 20 minutes later and Pat Cornell said, "Twenty minutes? From here to Greatfield and back?"

The Rats, Part One: 1966–1968

And he just looked at us and he obviously knew, but we got this Fender Stratocaster and that's what we went on tour with."

The forging of his father's signature would come back to bite Mick, but at this stage he had sorted out the various obstacles, and with a sense of excitement and adventure the band set off on their first trip abroad. With all their gear in the van and Ian Evans at the wheel they headed south down the A1 to Dover via London. Unfortunately the van got only as far as Grantham when a major fault in the engine forced them to get a tow to the 3Bs, a nearby garage. It took another three days to find and fit a replacement engine from a local scrapyard, with the band members sleeping in a caravan in the garage forecourt. They finally continued their journey down to London, where the booking agency informed them the tour was now rescheduled for France. They got the Dover ferry across the channel arriving on the continent on the morning of 1 May.

The schedule in France was organised by promoter Jean Besnard, who brought English bands over to play in venues in Rouen and Paris. The Rats spent their first week in the capital playing the Golfe Druot Club in Montmartre. The Club was situated above the Café d'Angleterre and started life as a tea room. In the 1950s the owners decided to install a nine-hole, mini golf course on the first floor, hence the club's name. Bartender Henri Leproux installed a jukebox, playing the records of Bill Haley, Jerry Lee Lewis and Elvis Presley. The club became more popular for dancing than golf, and from the end of the 1950s hosted regular singers including Johnny Hallyday on a Friday night, open mic slot. Between the early '60s and its closure in 1981, the club hosted over 6,000 bands and singers, including many English rock bands such as the Yardbirds, Free and the Who. It was also the stage for the first gig played outside the UK by David Bowie with the Lower Third, who appeared there on New Year's Eve 1965, with Arthur Brown on the bill. He would not have known it at the time, but Mick was doing his first European gig on the same stage as, and in the footsteps of, an artist with whom he would forever be associated.

After a week in Paris the Rats were booked to play a club in Rouen, which Benny Marshall remembers having some rather dodgy connections: 'We were playing in this club called L'Oubliettes in Rouen and it was run by a guy and he was one of the Mob. He once took us up to show us all his armaments in his wardrobe, which was full of rifles and pistols and God knows what else, it was quite an eye-opener.' Ian Evans also recalls the venue having some dubious criminal links: 'As you walked in there was a staircase and then you walked left into the bar area with a spiral staircase in the corner, which went down into a cavern, very similar to the Cavern in Liverpool. The stairs to the first floor led to a bedroom where we used to get changed, with just one single bed and a wardrobe, and we were told in no uncertain terms, *Do not even think about looking in the wardrobe*. It was full of guns and ammunition. One evening we'd finished playing and a knock came on the door or the bell rang, and the doorman said, "No we're closing". (They never used to let anybody in after twelve.) About ten minutes later they tried again to get in for a drink. "No, go away!" Five minutes later a brick came through the window and the doorman flew upstairs, picked up something that was in the wardrobe, came down and blasted this guy. It was mayhem, absolute mayhem. The doorman pumped the hell out of this car with this... it wasn't a rifle or a pistol, it was a sub-machine gun. It was terrifying.' Benny and Ian were in no doubt that the club was connected to criminal activities: 'The café opposite where we used to have our breakfast was owned by an English man, Eric, who'd married a French girl. He said, "What was all that noise last night? What's going on?" So we told him what had happened and Eric said, "You do realise who you're employed by – it's the Mafia."'

The Rats were proficient musically, and audiences in both Paris and Rouen were enthusiastic for British rock and roll bands. Mick was constantly experimenting with the sound of his guitar, and as Benny recalls, he hit on something that stayed with him for years to come: 'When we were in France, we had this battery-operated record player, a little tiny thing. It was Mick's. One record, that's all he had. It was Stéphane Grappelli and he used to try and get his sound like Stéphane Grappelli's fiddle. He played it over and over, this record. It was nearly worn through. He was trying to get this sound when he was playing. He used to have a wah-wah pedal, and he found out that if you clicked it on and then rocked it back and then left it, it used to give it that edge he needed. He would play and not touch the pedal, just leave it clicked on and rocked back, and that was how he got his sound.'

Whilst abroad, Mick was paying the day-to-day expenses of the whole band out of his own pocket, and by necessity they were living as frugally as possible. Ian remembers how they cleaned the van: 'In Rouen we used to put the van halfway down the "horse wash" and wash it. It was just a slope into the river. Just used to put the van halfway down, then just give it a wash and pull it out. We were quite practical when we wanted to be!'

Mick's relationship with Sandra Nelson had ended the autumn

The Rats, Part One: 1966–1968

before, but as Ian remembers: 'Mick always had good female company.' Bassist Geoff Appleby nearly came home with a French bride: 'Geoff fell in love with Nelly in Rouen and she actually tried to drag him to the registry office. She wanted to marry him. We had to go and get him out. Nelly was a French girl, she was absolutely gorgeous. She just fell in love with Geoff like you would not believe, it was amazing. Them two just hit it off, and with Nelly being able to get through a little bit of English they were just fantastic, lovely couple. He should have married her.'

The five Hull lads, barely out of their teens, and with little French between them, were pretty much Brits abroad for the first time. Mick had a passion for gambling, whether on fruit machines or the horses, and he didn't let language barriers stop him from placing bets as Ian recalls: 'He liked a gamble, did Mick. Horses. He'd study form. He could find a racing paper anywhere, lots of racing in France. On two or three occasions we would have to pick him up physically, two of us, and drag him out of a betting office. We used to drag him out 'cause he had the money. He had the money that we were eating with!' Mick rarely drank alcohol and if he did, it was only ever in small quantities, as he knew it would affect his playing: 'It only took one pint and he was like, he was "happy". We used to drink this thing called a Black Velvet – it was half a Guinness and half a cider. One pint of that and we used to sit back and be entertained. Mick was so funny, never nasty, just funny, laughing and good humour. But that was it – one pint – that was all it took!"

Ian also remembers a time on that tour where alcohol definitely came into play: 'They asked us to go back to Paris for one night to play at a millionaire's daughter's 21st, which we did. When we got there, it was on floating pontoons in the park in Paris. We put all the equipment on the pontoons, parked the van up, and then we were pushed off into the middle of the lake. On this big pontoon was three tables with drinks and, of course, we just got nicely used to drinking whisky. There was three waiters on each table and it was, "Just help yourself, boys." We daren't let Mick have a drink. When we finished and managed to get the gear off, I'd ended up in the water, my trousers shrunk to my knees and we had to drive back to Rouen. Everybody had had a drink and things just got a little bit out of hand!' Benny offers further details: 'We were playing in Paris, and there was like a small island in the Seine, and it had a very upmarket venue on it, and there were two bands playing, us and another band. And the only thing they were serving, and it was all free, was champagne and whisky. So we got on and played. Taffy disappeared, and the next time we saw him, he was sick in the van. He'd

The Mick Ronson Story

drunk so much whisky, he couldn't drive the van. The kitchen staff had washed it out with disinfectant to try and take the smell away, and I had to drive the van back to where we were staying. I didn't have a licence or anything, I just knew how to drive, but I was on the wrong side of the road!"

By the time the tour came to an end, the Rats had still not been paid. On the journey home at Dieppe they confronted the tour booker, as Ian recalls: 'We ended up on the dockside in Dieppe. Our agent in France, Jean Besnard, didn't really like English bands, but they were the thing of the moment and he was told to put them on. He came to us at Dieppe and we said, "We need money, we need paying, we're going back to England." "I have no money for you," he said. "You are Rats by name and Rats by nature." There was an argument, and it wasn't me that did it and I can't say who did, but they removed the wallet, took the money out of it, lobbed the wallet, and he ended up in the water. We jumped on the ferry 'cause it was about to leave and we disappeared."

There was only enough money to get them as far as London: 'We got back to the agent's office in London and he said, "Because of what's happened in Dieppe, we can't do anything for you now." His office was in a block that used to have these filling stations underneath, a BP filling station, and on his desk was his account number of the filling station and I read it upside down. We then filled up the van on his account, signed for it and we managed to get back to Grantham." Running out of fuel and stranded halfway home, the band stopped at the 3Bs garage that had helped fix the van when it broke down on the journey out. The mechanics suggested the Rats play at a new club in Grantham called the Cat Balou, which was opening that very night. The band played and the gig not only gave them enough petrol money to get home to Hull, it also secured many more bookings in the future, including one where they supported Mick's hero, Jeff Beck.

Mick knew that trouble was looming back home. A phone call to his mother had alerted him to the fact that the paperwork for the HP agreement on the Stratocaster had arrived in the post, addressed to his father at their home on Greatfield Estate. Seeing his own signature on a document he had no knowledge of reading, let alone signing, George put two and two together and knew that Mick was responsible. Or in his view, highly irresponsible. Minnie made it clear on the phone to Mick that his father was really very angry with him. Mick had hoped the tour would leave him and the band with money spare, but they were all penniless. His birthday money had all gone on subsidising the trip, and

The Rats, Part One: 1966–1968

after several weeks they had nothing to show for it. Having the cachet of a foreign tour under his belt, along with some good memories, wasn't going to cut the mustard as far as his father was concerned. He was back in the same dire financial straits as when he came home from London nine months earlier: once more in debt. Ian Evans was in a similar situation: he still owed his aunt the £35 she had lent to purchase the van, and he also owed his father money for a car he'd bought.

Driving back into Hull, neither Mick nor Ian dared go home to face the parental music. For Mick, it turned out that going home wasn't even an option. As Benny remembers: 'When Mick came back his father read him the riot act and he said: "Leave immediately!" and kicked him out.' It wasn't any easier for Ian Evans: 'We came back from France absolutely penniless and we daren't go home at the time because we just felt we had failed. We literally daren't go home. We'd borrowed money to go out with, and we came back and we didn't have any money. George [Ronson] was quite a disciplinarian and I think we was a bit afraid. We used to go home during the day for a bath while our fathers weren't there, and our mothers paved the way for us to go back home.' They spent the next three to four weeks sleeping at friends' houses, and Mick stayed for a while with Benny Marshall until peace could be made with their respective parents. The pressure was back on to earn money and the priority was to get paid work. Gigging at night with the Rats brought in some cash, but they all needed a day job. Ian found work with a building company, but the late nights home from gigs, coupled with early morning work starts, weren't sustainable and cost him three jobs in one week. It took him a year and a half to pay off his debts.

Mick went back to his day job with the City Council Parks Department. He was once again happy to hold down a regular 'proper' job and forego any musical ambition other than performing evenings and at weekends with the Rats. The 'road to somewhere' had turned out once again to be the road back to where he'd started. He wasn't prepared to risk the wrath of his father, or the pain of being poor again in the pursuit of his music. If security was the enemy of ambition, then so be it. For the next two years his reputation would continue to grow in his home city, but he was focused solely on being the best guitarist in the best covers band in this north-east town.

Although Mick had lowered his musical horizons, the Rats still had a very busy gigging schedule both in the city and out of town, as Ian Evans describes: 'It was very difficult to have a proper relationship at that time because we were busy, we were here, there and everywhere.

You're playing nearly every night, you're driving to different places. There would always be a following. People used to get there on the train and expect to come back in the van. Sometimes there was two people stood on the back step or clinging on to the guttering all the way back from Scarborough.'

In a *Hull Daily Mail* interview from the '70s Mick reminisced about those early days with the Rats: 'Sometimes we travelled 80 miles [130 km] to play and never made any money. When we did make anything, we'd treat ourselves to a slap-up feed. It wasn't the money we were after because we had jobs during the day at that time anyway. It was getting the opportunity to play.' Taffy Evans remembers a particular quirk of Mick's: 'One of the things Ronno loved was having his feet massaged. It didn't matter who did it. It used to send him into a different world. He'd take his socks and shoes off, sit on the back seat of the van with his feet on the engine cowling. "Oh Geoff, just rub that there oh, oh", and he used to be miles away absolutely miles away.'

When not on the road, rehearsals were just as busy. Ian remembers lengthy late-night rehearsals in Benny's ground floor flat on St George's Road: 'That's where we used to rehearse until God knows when in a morning. Mick would listen to an album, and he'd done his work before he came to rehearsal, and he was obviously the master of ceremonies, he knew exactly what was what and we just put it together. Mick would play and play and play, we never used to come out of there until 4 or 5 in the morning, until we got it absolutely right.'

At some point during the summer of 1967, a young Keith 'Ched' Cheesman saw the Rats play – and it made a lasting impression. Ched knew of the band through family connections and his own interest as a budding guitarist: 'In a way I kind of had a relationship with the Rats from their early days, because Brian Buttle who was the bass player in the original line up, his brother was married to my sister. So I had a connection and knowledge of the Rats and what they were doing, right from the early days. My brother became a friend of the Rats and he used to see them quite a lot. He was a couple of years older than me, so he was out on the scene at that time.'

His brother suggested he should see the band as they were playing nearby, and their setlist included tracks that Ched was trying to master on his own at home: 'They were playing a weekday residency, I think at a pub in Anlaby that had a backroom called the Birdcage Club. I walked in and, sure enough, Mick with the Rats was playing all these things that I'd been learning. As I approached the club, I heard this Jimi Hendrix

The Rats, Part One: 1966–1968

song being played, which I thought was a record. And I walked in and it was Mick actually playing it live. It was that good. He was playing a Telecaster guitar, which I could only dream about at that time. At the end of the night when they'd finished playing, as he was packing it away into his case, I went over to have a look at it. He saw me looking and he just took it back out of the case and said, "Here you are, have a go on it." He didn't know who I was. I thought, it was quite nice of him just to say: "Have a go" to someone he'd never met." Ched wasn't to know at the time, but in just over a year he would be on that same stage playing alongside Mick in the Rats.

In the autumn of 1967, John Cambridge replaced Clive Taylor on drums. 'Cambo' was born in Hull in 1949 on Albany Street, off Spring Bank. His father was a plasterer by trade and had moved to the city from Salford, as the damage to Hull's housing from wartime bombing offered plenty of work. In 1954 the Cambridge family moved into a council flat on Brisbane Street near the city centre – the home where David and Angie Bowie would stay when visiting in 1970. John spent a lot of his youth listening to local bands and by 1964 had acquired his own drumkit. In 1966 John joined the Hullaballoos, starting a friendship with guitarist Mick Wayne which two years later would take them both on a new journey with Juniors Eyes and David Bowie. Although John had declined to join the Rats earlier that April for their French tour, by October '67, when Mick asked him again, he agreed. He played his first gig with the Rats on 20 October at the Purple Onion Club in Cleethorpes. Ian Evans remembers John bringing something new to the already proficient mix: 'Cambo came to work with us and brought a different feel to the band, he brought rock music with harmonies, and we played a few different numbers that made it just sound that little bit different, "Rock and Roll Star", the odd Tamla thing. He made a great difference, did John, really did.'

John was aware of Mick's anxieties around the risks of going fully professional, but could also recognise his innate drive to achieve success as a musician. John's ambitions were similar, so they were well matched initially. Their future had yet to play out the way it did, but at the start there was a strong sense of shared friendship and fun. John Cambridge had, and still has, a cheeky sense of humour that slotted easily into the band's internal dynamic of laddish wind-ups and jokes, and he could match Mick's dry Yorkshire wit: 'I remember Mick saying to me: "I've always been in a band with good drummers", which I thought was a nice compliment. I said: "I have always been in a band with good guitarists, but I'll make an exception when I join you" and he saw the humour."

During this time, Ian Evans was not only doing the usual roadie duties, but was increasingly organising gig bookings. The band were now using heavier sound gear such as Marshall stacks and they decided to enlist the help of Stuey George, to help carry the gear and protect it. Stuey was a familiar figure on the Hull music scene as a doorman and security at various venues. There are a number of stories about Stuey, most of them apocryphal, one being that he managed to sell a house in Hull that he didn't actually own – at the time he was just the tenant paying rent. Stuey was tough, and his height and ethnicity made him very distinctive, being one of the relatively few people of colour in a predominantly white city. On 22 October, the band played the Broken Wheel Club at Retford, where Stuey came in very useful, as Ian Evans describes: 'We had Stuey on board then, because he was muscle. We used to take him with us to the Broken Wheel at Retford, which was a club on the third floor of a disused warehouse alongside a canal and we played there several times. The only problem with the Marshall stuff, it was back-breaking, like at Beverley Regal trying to get them up the back staircase was incredibly hard, and that was the same at Retford. It was an area where it was still mods and rockers, greasers, and if you looked a bit modish, they would just try and get on stage and wreck your gear. It was all on finance, so we were very protective of the gear. If we didn't have it, we couldn't play. I used to be stood at one end of the stage with a mike stand to repel boarders, and Stuey used to be at the other end. It just kicked off. A fight started, and they come surging at the stage. Stuey hit this lad and he hit the doors, what used to be the loading doors off the canal, and the doors opened and he ended up in the water three storeys down. By the time they had fished him out, we had all the gear packed up, and we was in the van and we'd got the money and gone. That's how Stuey started to come with us.' Stuey George would go on to be a bodyguard for David Bowie and toured with him worldwide throughout the Ziggy period and beyond.

Other roadies for the Rats included Chris Adamson and Pete Murfin. Pete emigrated to Australia in 1971 and still has fond memories of Mick and those times: 'Mick was a great bloke – always cared after the group. It didn't matter where we were, he made sure everybody was OK – all the time. He was a gentleman at heart, and he always had nice things to say about everyone. He never had a bad word, or never had a go at anybody. If he couldn't say anything nice, he just wouldn't bother talking. He really was a nice guy.'

The Rats, Part One: 1966–1968

Neal Owers worked as a photographer in Hull in the late '60s: 'I told them I took photographs of the band at their gigs and they suggested I give them the photographs and they'd pay me a small amount. I remember one time going to the Gondola Club with some photographs and Stuey telling me the band couldn't pay me this time, and then generous as ever, Mick gave me the cash out of his own pocket.'

Pete Murfin recalls the wide variety of venues the Rats played in. 'We did a lot of universities, did a few RAF bases, a lot of schools, school dances and stuff like that, and a lot of pubs, and quite often at Skyline, backing up the real, big name players. Sometimes I never went to bed for days. We used to get stopped all the time by the police, especially driving back home after a night and you were coming back in at 3 or 4 o'clock in the morning. They used to pull me up all the time and want to have a look in the van. That used to get to me, so I had some really nasty remarks for them! It was a good time, though, 'cause the music was right and I was right into rock n roll.'

The Rats were increasingly playing with bands that were either big or breaking on the national music scene. In September 1967, they supported Pink Floyd at the Skyline in Hull. In November it was the Move at the Railway Institute in York, and again the following year in May 1968 at the Skyline. The next night it was Geno Washington and the Ram Jam Band in Huddersfield. In December they played support to the Crazy World of Arthur Brown at Hull City Hall. The Rats were gaining ever bigger audiences in their home city and region, but as they were all holding down day jobs, there was a limit to what they could achieve.

One option was to move from only doing covers to writing some original material. John Cambridge was keen to do this: 'Mick wasn't really a song writer, and I've always been interested in writing songs, and I said to Mick, *Basically all we are doing is covers of Hendrix*, you know, *why don't we do some original stuff?* I said *I've got some ideas for a song*, and it was called "The Rise and Fall of Bernie Gripplestone".' John wrote the lyrics and Mick came up with the music: 'I am sure Mick said he'd nicked the chord sequence off "Eleanor Rigby". We just put bits together.' They recorded the track in December at Keith Herd's new Fairview Studios at Willerby, just west of Hull. *Recording studio* is perhaps a grand term for what was at the time his front room, the walls covered in egg boxes for sound proofing. It was the precursor of his purpose built-Fairview Studios in which many local bands recorded over the next few decades, including the Red Guitars, the Housemartins, the Beautiful South, and the Paddingtons. The song had a middle section that needed some technical recording trickery to get the effect John and Mick wanted: 'We ended up doing it playing it backwards like the Beatles on *Revolver*, which meant we could never play it live on stage.'

Although they would record again at Fairview Studios, the Rats never repeated this attempt at writing an original song. They would spend hours rehearsing existing songs and perform them powerfully onstage, but when it came to writing new material, the skill, the group chemistry or the will to do it, just wasn't there. As Mick's guitar work was very much the star turn, there was more than enough material out there to replicate, from the output of Beck, Clapton, Hendrix and Page. This lack of songwriting ability would increasingly frustrate some band members in the future – particularly Ched Cheesman, in 1969 – and it was also a factor in why the band Ronno failed to make any impact in 1970–71. It wasn't until Mick began working with David Bowie that his own particular skill would marry with a gifted songwriter, releasing both artists' full potential and generating a catalogue of classic songs.

The Rats rounded off 1967 with a busy calendar of local gigs that continued the momentum into 1968. In March they were back at the Cat Balou Club in Grantham playing support to Mick's guitar idol Jeff Beck. In a 1976 interview for *Nineteen* magazine Mick said of him: 'I love what Becky does. There are lots of good guitarists around, but none can get it on like him. I used to spend days listening to his records, copying his ideas, when I was younger.' According to John Cambridge, Mick's interest was closer to an obsession: 'He not only idolised Jeff Beck, he wanted to be Jeff Beck!' There were several Beck songs in the Rats set list, and Mick wanted to learn more. He was keen to master the various sections of the Beck guitar instrumental 'Jeff's Boogie', which had appeared on the Yardbirds 1966 album *Roger the Engineer*. While backstage that night at the Cat Balou, Mick took the opportunity to ask Jeff Beck to show him how to play key sections of the song, as Benny Marshall recalls: "He taught Mick how to play the fast run, the pull-off run, nobody else was doing it then. I was there when he taught him to do it. And Mick was saying to Beck, "Can you play it a bit slower?" And Beck would play it again more slowly. And Mick said, "Can you play it a bit slower than that?" In the end Jeff Beck said, 'If I play it any slower, I'll bloody stop!'" The Rats had a reel-to-reel tape recorder with them that night and they recorded Jeff Beck's entire set. They would play back the tape in rehearsals until they'd mastered the tracks they wanted to play. This meant they were playing songs live off the Beck album *Truth* before

The Rats, Part One: 1966–1968

its release in the UK in November that year.

In 1968 the Rats replaced their tour van, as John Cambridge describes: 'All the local bands had a van and a roadie, but the vans weren't very big until Needlers Chocolate Factory, they had these great big vans and they were selling them off cheap. A couple of bands in Hull got them, so we thought we'll get one. It was basically a big van with just one door at the back, you opened it and you went straight down and there were shelves on either side. So what we did, we cut it in half for all the gear in the back, and we altered the shelves to make sort of bunks. So now we could stand up in the van, we could even go to sleep in the van, and lie down rather than just sit down going to gigs.' According to Taffy Evans, the seven-and-half ton Bedford van was expensive to run, doing only 10km (6 miles) to the gallon. For the band, however, it offered the opportunity for a basic 'camper-van' conversion and a summer holiday that August. John and Mick, with two of their roadies, Chris and Eric, drove down to Great Yarmouth on the Norfolk coast and parked up on the seafront, where they could take advantage of a nearby public toilet and use the facilities at the local swimming baths. Their daily routine would involve time in the amusement arcades, where Mick could indulge his passion for gambling. John Cambridge remembers it well: 'Mick used to love the "bandits" and he'd put all his money in, all the tanners and shillings, and he'd be waiting to win the jackpot. And every other day, "I've won the Jackpot!" and what would he do? He'd put it all back in again. And we'd go to the next amusements down the line, and we'd come back and Mick was still on the same bandit. Or he'd be sat playing bingo. Honestly, he loved bingo and the one-armed bandits!'

One day they decided to forego the amusement arcades and take a walk into town. They were approached by a couple of elderly ladies, as John Cambridge describes: 'They was Romany gypsies, with the bandanas on and big long cardigans and the dresses right to the floor. And they was carrying great big baskets, massive big baskets under their arm. As they got close one of them started going, "Lucky white heather, lucky white heather!" Well, Mick just made a beeline – he went straight for this elderly lady and said, "Do you read palms, tell fortunes?" And she went, *Yes, cross my palm with silver sort of thing.* So she's starting to read his palm, and I'm thinking what a waste of bloody money. Then she says to me, "Do you want your palm reading?" "No, I'm alright, no." And Mick went, big dig in the ribs, "Go on, go on!" So she's reading my palm and holding my hand and looking down at it, and I'm not really paying much attention, until the very last thing she said, which was, "Are you anything to do with music?" Well, I thought I'm not going to give her any clues, so I just sort of said, "Why do you ask?" She said, "You're going to be very successful in music." I said, "Oh, thank you very much"' And I went to walk away, and with that, Mick gets his palm and shoves it right under her nose, and he says to her, "Did you see anything with music with me?" And she just looked at his palm, looked back at him, and said, "No." But looking back, I think she must have been cross-eyed and mixed us both up!'

On the local music scene Mick had become a well-known and popular figure. He still had a natural shyness, but his ability onstage as a performer gave him greater confidence with people. Being friendly by nature, he could also offset any shyness by taking the initiative and offering a handshake. A number of friends like Ched Cheesman have commented on this: 'Mick always had this thing of shaking people's hands. Not necessarily every day and all the time, but if I hadn't seen him for a couple of days, there'd be a handshake. He always looked good, had a great image, plus he was playing the guitar better than most people around, so he was an attractive personality to everybody really. He ticked all the boxes – he looked good, he looked the part, he played the part, and he had the knowledge to back it up. And to top it all off, he was a down-to-earth guy who you could sit and have a normal conversation with, who'd always talk to fans, and never be the big "I Am".' Jim Simpson remembers Mick as, 'A lovely guy. He had everything. He had the talent, he had the style, he had the looks, but he didn't have the ego and that was his biggest trait, that he was so normal.'

Another Hull friend, John Close, points to Mick's distinctive appearance: 'He had quite chiselled, sharp features and his hair was blonde, natural blonde and always long. He always had that same style even back in the day. He was quite striking looking.' Or as Ian Evans describes: 'He was tall, slim, he had blond hair and he looked like a pop star basically.'

Musician John Bentley grew up in Hull and has a strong memory of the first time he saw Mick: 'I was just sitting in the back of the car. My parents were driving me somewhere, I think heading out towards Hessle, and there was a dual carriageway with a verge in the middle. As I glanced out of the window, I noticed this council worker stripped to the waist mowing the central reservation as we drove past. He looked like nothing I'd ever seen before, and beyond anything I could ever have imagined. To me back then he looked like a fantasy superhero, Greek god, only with a better haircut! My impressionable jaw hit the floor, and that image has lived in my memory ever since. I can still remember it vividly because he looked so stunning with his platinum blonde hair. It was Mick Ronson. Even if you didn't know who he was and you saw him, you'd think, "Who's that man?" When I found out who he was, I thought, why is such a brilliant musician cutting the grass for a living? Of course, this was way before he was famous, but he was already. Mick was famous before he was really famous. He was famous in Hull – everybody knew Mick Ronson.'

Another Hull musician, Jeff Parsons, who would later play in the band Dead Fingers Talk, remembers Mick's good looks marking him out for female attention: 'Mick was well known on the local scene when I first started going to gigs, round about 1968, '69 as a young teenager. He was one of the standout players on the local scene. I just remember him being offstage at the end of gigs, being surrounded by girls. He was just one of those guys who was magnetic to women. He had an aura – there's no doubt about it – and it was magnetic. So people wanted to speak to him, the girls wanted to be seen with him, the girls wanted to walk out of the dance floor with him, on his arm.'

Mick's work for the Council Parks Department meant he could often be seen lining sports fields adjacent to schools. In summer the vision of a fit and sometimes bare-chested Mick Ronson proved irresistible to many teenage girls, as Tony Ward recalls: 'I went to Newton Hall School on Greatfield Estate. I can remember when he was the parks department gardener cutting the grass, there was all our girls from school just swooning and watching him with his long blond hair, going up and down cutting the grass. They were 15-, 16-year old girls and there was this 19-year-old bloke, slim, brown, long blond hair cutting the grass and they all used to just look out the window. They were always getting into trouble off the teachers – "Pay attention, you girls!"' Ian Evans reckons it got to the stage where Mick was asked not to work at certain times at certain locations: 'Barham Girls School and Estcourt Girls School was on Hopewell Road and Mick was banned from both places 'cause he distracted the girls from lessons as he was lining or cutting the grass. So he couldn't go there. He just distracted all the lasses staring out the window.'

If this all sounds unlikely, Susan Webb, née Fewless, was a teenage schoolgirl at Estcourt High School on Greatfield Estate, and remembers the riveting vision of a fit and tanned Mick Ronson: 'My first sight of Mick was him cutting the grass outside our school while he was working as a gardener for Hull City Council. As an all-girls school, he raised quite a lot of interest. We had a second-floor science lab and I'm sure he must have looked up at some point to see a row of excited little noses pressed up against the glass watching him. It was the highlight really of our science lesson, much to our science teacher's disgust!'

Lynne Mitchell had a crush on Mick from the days when she and her mum would buy their groceries off the Co-op van that Mick first worked on. Fast forward a few years, and that infatuation hadn't lessened, as she wryly recalls: 'Me and my friend used to go in park quite a lot and I saw him a couple of times shovelling up leaves, and he always used to shout, "Hiya." Obviously I was too young to be his girlfriend, more's the pity ... but I will tell you one thing ... I was a bugger... I'd gone to top of street to meet my friend and she hadn't turned up, and I saw him and I said, "Hiya, Mike." He said, "Oh, hiya, how's your mum?" I said, "Oh, she's fine." I said, "Are you busy?" He said, "No, I'm just going to go get my dad his cigs." I said, "Well, if you like, why don't you pop in and say hello?" He went, "Aye, alright then." So he took his dad his cigs and walked down the street. I knew full well my mam was at bingo! So anyway we were sat chatting on my mam's settee and he said, "Will she be long?" I said, "Oh she must have just slipped out, never mind." I made him a cup of tea and then I said, "Oh, she might have gone to bingo, she won't be in while four." He said, "Oh, I better get off then." So that was awful, that was really bad of me, but that was my claim to fame at the time!'

Mick started a relationship with Denise Irvin, who lived on Bexhill Avenue not far from Mick's house. Denise was younger than Mick, and a schoolgirl fan of the Rats. Their relationship would lead to the birth in 1971 of Mick's first child Nicholas, but at this stage the notion of being a father was a long way from Mick's mind. The music came first.

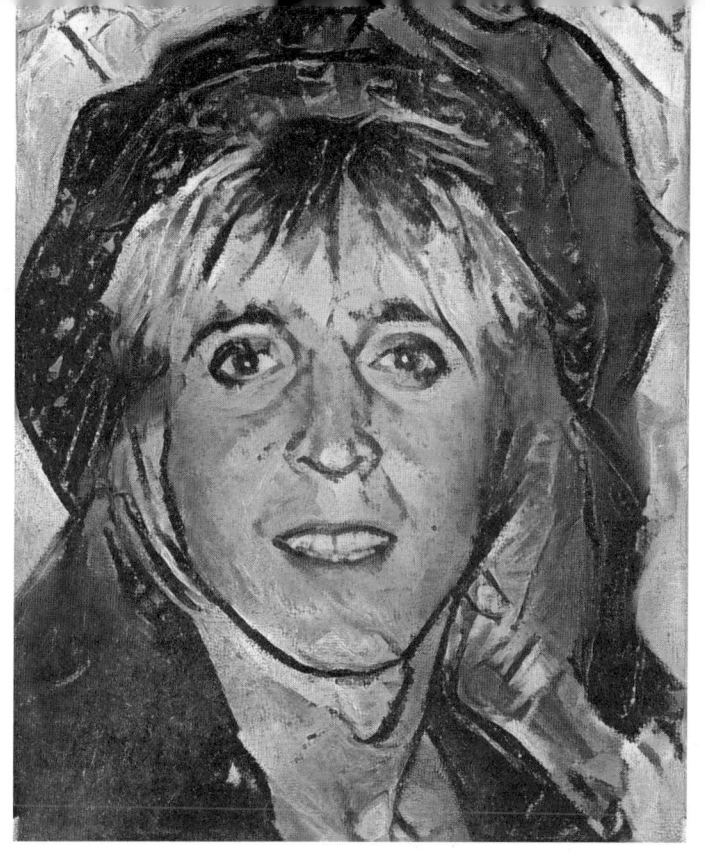

4 The Rats, Part Two: 1968–1970

The Mick Ronson Story

In November 1968 Rats bassist Geoff Appleby was going to get married. He gave the band notice of his intention to leave and offered to continue playing until they found a suitable replacement. At the end of September, Mick asked Keith 'Ched' Cheesman if he was interested in taking his place: 'I was sat in the Gondola Club in town, on a Saturday afternoon, which was the meeting place for anybody who thought they was anybody. That was the place to be. I was sat in there, drinking my hot coke and lemon, as you did. Mick Ronson walked in and sat right opposite me and he said, "Do you want to join the Rats?" I daren't answer because the band were known for their mickey-taking – they were all good at winding people up and having a bit of a laugh. So when Mick said that, I thought *There's a wind-up coming here*, so I daren't say yes or no. Their thing was to put a hand over the mouth and point, like pretend laughing, as if you'd said something stupid. I kind of expected that. He said, "No, I'm serious. We want you to join the Rats as a bass player." I said, "I've never played bass, I don't own a bass. I'm a lead guitar player." Mick said, "That's OK, we'll borrow one, we'll get it sorted out." I said, "Well, if that's the case I'd love to." It was my favourite band, I was quite shocked to be asked. I went home and took two strings off my acoustic guitar and started practising to play bass!'

Underlying Ched's delight was a lurking anxiety that the whole thing was still a wind-up: 'To me, they were like the top band around, playing the music that I liked, and it was an aspiration for me to be in that kind of band. I was only just starting out, a beginner. So it was quite a shock. They were all older than me as well. Plus the fact that they were piss-takers basically. You could never believe whatever they were saying, they were all like that, and John was probably the worst of all of them. I think we'd been to Benny Marshall's house and we were on the way back in the van. I said to John, "I've made this acoustic guitar into a bass, so I can practice and learn the songs." And he said, "Why? Are you joining a band?" That was the kind of humour and you never quite knew.'

Ched started learning the set list and recorded the band on reel-to-reel tape when they played in early October at the Duke of Cumberland. A week later he joined them onstage for a couple of songs at the Birdcage in Anlaby, where he had first seen Mick play a year earlier. He played his first full set in November at Willerby Youth Centre. Ched's four string acoustic guitar was fine for practising, but it still left him needing a bass guitar for gigs. With little or no money to buy one, Ched would borrow a bass from either Robert Palmer of the Mandrakes, who would go on to achieve success with hits including 'Addicted to Love', or from his former

The Rats, Part Two: 1968–1970

bandmate in the Jelly Roll Blues Band, Trevor Bolder. When Ched left the Blues Band to join the Rats, his place was taken by John Bentley, who persuaded them to change their name to Flesh. Flesh would rehearse in the scout hut adjacent to the village hall at Woodmansey, just north of Hull, where the Rats rehearsed. John Bentley later moved to London and found fame playing with Squeeze.

Some rock histories assert that Hull-born bassist Trevor Bolder played with the Rats, but the truth is he only ever did one, stand-in gig in July 1968, a few months before Geoff Appleby left. The band were playing Elizabethan Hall, Greatfield High School, and Geoff kept getting an unexplained electric shock from his guitar. In a 2003 interview from the *Hull Daily Mail*, Trevor recalled that evening: 'Though I'd seen Mick lots of times I never really got to know him, until I hooked up with him in Ronno. Before that, he was in the Rats. I went along to see them playing at a school youth club. Their bass player at the time was a friend of mine, who wouldn't play bass at the gig because he was afraid of getting electrocuted, so they asked me if I'd step in for it. I said: "OK, I'll play", so I got up and played.' Mick must have been impressed by Trevor's playing that night, or at subsequent gigs when he was playing in Flesh. Mick recruited him for Ronno in 1970, and to play with Bowie from 1971. As one of the Spiders from Mars, Trevor played on the classic albums *Hunky Dory*, *The Rise and Fall of Ziggy Stardust and the Spiders from Mars*, *Aladdin Sane*, as well as the covers album *Pin Ups*.

At the point when Ched joined, the Rats were called Treacle. They'd changed the name earlier in June that year at the suggestion of their then new manager Don Lill. Ched recalls: 'They were taking a slightly different line musically to where they'd been in the past. There were bands at the time like the Move, who were a rock band, but a pop rock band if you like, doing commercial singles with vocal harmonies. The Rats or Treacle at this time were trying to be that kind of pop rock sort of band, which they did very well. They were good at it.' Don Lill was a drummer with a Hull band called the Majority and for a time they had a residency at the Playboy Club in London, where Don had picked up contacts in the music business. Ched recalls: 'When I met him, he was name-dropping all the time. He reckoned he had these connections but they never came to anything. There was a promotion at the time. I remember this little orange fold-up thing and each page had a different band member, and John Cambridge *likes Coco Pops for breakfast*, that kind of thing. Very corny, pop band publicity. So that's what Don Lill was trying to do with the band. He was trying to mould them into a more commercial pop thing. I remember him telling the band off for something they'd done onstage, *not being professional* or something. I mean personally it all just smelt of bullshit to me. I had no evidence either way but somehow it just didn't feel right. I didn't know him that well. I only met him, maybe once, twice, because he didn't last long after I'd joined.'

Ched wanted to shift the Rats' focus back to their blues rock roots: 'The band that I'd joined was becoming a pop rock band, that was dependent a lot on the vocal harmonies. They all could sing – Benny, Mick, Geoff Appleby – he was a good singer, and John Cambridge could sing harmonies, so they had four-part harmonies. When I joined I had no experience of singing harmonies and never really classed myself as a singer anyway. So I couldn't really do that. My background was more bluesy rock kind of stuff, which Mick and Benny's was prior to this. Also at this time, in late '68, '69, the bands of the time were becoming more rock and bluesy – bands like Free, Zeppelin, the Jeff Beck group. So the two factors: one, I couldn't offer much to this pop rock band, but I could to a rock blues band. And two, that's the way things were going anyway. So the name Treacle didn't suit. I never liked the name from the off. I was sort of insistent and trying to persuade the others. I remember Mick at one point saying, "Why don't we call us the Yardbirds?" I said, "You can't do that!" He said, "Well, they've split up. They don't exist anymore." So much was his appreciation of Jeff Beck – he would have liked to call us the Yardbirds! I said, "You can't do that Mick."' The band did drop the name Treacle and reverted to the Rats from January 1969.

Although Ched drew the line at renaming the band the Yardbirds, he fully shared Mick's enthusiasm and admiration for Jeff Beck's guitar-playing. The reel-to-reel recording the band had made at the Jeff Beck gig back in April at the Cat Balou Club was invaluable for Ched when he first joined: 'The Rats had learned all those songs and they were playing the Jeff Beck *Truth* album live, before the album was released. So they gave me this tape recorder to learn the songs from.' Rehearsing Jeff Beck tracks also led Mick to refine the sound he had developed on tour in France while listening to the Stéphane Grappelli record. Ched recalls: 'On a lot of the songs on the *Truth* album Jeff Beck was using a wah-wah pedal. There are quite specific sequences where the wah-wah's making a quite throaty kind of sound, and Mick liked that and tried to recreate it. I remember at a gig at a pub in Withernsea, he brought this Vox wah-wah pedal and he used a Solar Sound fuzzbox. While experimenting he discovered he liked the sound if he just left it in a fixed position. Jeff Beck

The Rats, Part Two: 1968-1970

never actually did that. On a wah-wah pedal there is a kind of sweet spot. If you move it up and down there is a point where it goes quite throaty, a honky kind of sound and Mick found that. So from then on he used it quite a lot, even on rhythm guitar not just solo. That became the sound that most people remember him from in the Bowie days. It was a "half-cocked wah-wah" as we called it."

Mick had two Fender guitars – the blond Telecaster and the sunburst Stratocaster, the Strat purchased back in April 1967 prior to the French tour. Both guitars were still being paid for on the monthly hire purchase repayments. Jeff Beck, however, played a Les Paul guitar, and if Mick was to fully emulate his hero, that was the guitar he had to have. Taking on a third Hire Purchase agreement was a debt too far, so Mick offloaded the Fender Stratocaster to John Bentley: 'Mick wanted to buy a Les Paul but he couldn't afford the HP as well, so he sold it to me. I gave him £60, which was a hell of a lot of money, and I took over the HP payments. I think there was about £40 left on it. Strats were expensive guitars, even back then.'

Jeff Beck played a Les Paul Standard and Mick was only able to order a Les Paul Custom, but decided that was close enough. After a long wait it finally arrived for collection at the end of October, the day of Geoff Appleby's last gig with the Rats, as Ched recalls: 'They picked me and Mick up, and we went to Cornell's music shop on Spring Bank. I remember sitting in the van outside and Mick came out of the shop with his new Les Paul in a black case. The South Hunsley gig was the first time he used it.' John Cambridge also remembers Mick picking up the Les Paul: 'Mick opened it, looked at it, didn't even get it out and try it, "Come on, we've got to get going, got to do a gig." He gave his Telecaster in part exchange and just played the Les Paul on the night.' There was a problem, however, as Ched explains: 'As it turned out, it was very difficult to play. It had very low frets mainly designed for jazz playing, to be fast up and down the neck, but that didn't suit string-bending blues players. I remember Mick and I passing the guitar between us saying: "Can you do this?" and neither of us could. We tried to bend a string up, but you couldn't hold it under your finger because it was just like holding it directly on wood. The frets weren't lifting the string and you couldn't hold a string. It would just ping out from under your finger, so it was really quite difficult to play. He eventually got it re-fretted at a music shop in Leeds and got what we call Jumbo frets. They are quite big, fat, meaty frets so that made it playable from that point.'

Ched also recalls Mick making a number of other alterations to his

Les Paul: 'I remember him arriving at this gig with this little circle of white plastic in his hand that he'd made from something. I said, "What's that for?" Mick said, "I'm going to put it on the toggle switch at the top of the guitar, 'cause the original one that comes on the guitar is black, but Jeff Beck has a white one. So I'm going to put this on, to replace the toggle switch surround."' Throughout his time with the Rats, Mick's Les Paul was its original black, but he later stripped the paintwork down. Ched reckons the change was again to make it look more like the guitar Jeff Beck played: 'Later on in the Bowie period he sanded off the front, took the black paint off to make it just a plain wood colour. He also painted the pickup surrounds, which were black plastic, he painted them white. The whole purpose was to make it look like a Les Paul Standard. Jeff Beck played Les Paul Standards, as did the likes of Eric Clapton, and Jimmy Page, so he was trying to make it look like that.'

Jeff Parsons remembers seeing the Rats not long after Mick was playing the new guitar: 'He had the black Les Paul which he'd just bought, and that in those days was a talking point: *Whoa – he's got a Les Paul!* Even that added a desire to go and see the guy play. And it wasn't long before he sanded it down to that iconic wooden finish.' That particular Les Paul was the one Mick played throughout the Ziggy years and has gained almost iconic status.

Another change of music gear that was to reverberate down the Ziggy years came in December, when Ched went down to Grantham to pick up a Marshall Major 200-watt amplifier. He was unhappy with the sound quality through the amp he had acquired from Geoff Appleby, which was distorting his bass: 'Mick told me that they had loaned an amp to a band in Grantham which would probably be much better for me, so we went there to get it and it turned out to be a superb amp, and I used it for the rest of my time with the band. Later Mick used this amp on the live Bowie tours and it became famously nicknamed "The Pig".'

By the end of 1968, after two years of Mick playing with the Rats, the band had built an impressive following in Hull and the Yorkshire region. The bookings were probably at the limit the bandmates could sustain whilst holding down day jobs. The line-up had changed over the period with Jim Simpson, Clive Taylor and Geoff Appleby departing – all for different reasons, but each of their own volition. In 1969 that was to change when Mick's own musical agenda came into conflict with a colleague and friend.

The band began the new year with their usual frenetic touring schedule, ditching the name Treacle and reverting to the Rats. They sacked Don Lill as manager because he had failed to deliver on his promise of securing a record deal. They returned to Fairview studios, this time with Ched on bass, and recorded 'Stop and Get A Hold Of Myself', 'Morning Dew', and 'Mick's Boogie'. The latter was the party piece, instrumental track that Mick had now perfected, having badgered Jeff Beck to play it for him backstage at the Cat Balou Club the previous year.

The Rats were an extremely popular live band, tight and accomplished, and there was no reason for them to change the cohesive line-up of Mick, Benny Marshall, John Cambridge and Ched Cheesman. On top of the constant gigging was Mick's enthusiasm for extended rehearsals, which bordered on the obsessive. Music was the sole passion of most of the Rats members, but anyone having other outside interests could inadvertently sow the seeds of discontent and division, as Ched describes: 'John (Cambridge) unlike the rest of the band had other things in his life. He was probably what you would call a man's man, who does things like going to the pub with his mates, playing in a football team, maybe a darts team. He did all those sort of things. None of the rest of us did. He'd got other interests apart from music, where the rest of us was music and that was it.'

Things came to a head over the Easter weekend of 1969, while rehearsing at their usual place in the village hall in Woodmansey, just north of Hull. They had played a Wednesday night gig on Mick's home turf at Elizabethan Hall in Greatfield High School, and then rehearsed Thursday, all Good Friday and Easter Saturday. Mick then announced that the village hall was available for the Sunday, so he wanted to continue through the Easter weekend. John Cambridge put his foot down: 'I said, "I'm playing football" 'cause I mean I had other things. Benny, Ched and Mick were music barmy, so was I, but I had other things. I'd been in a darts team, I'd played football. I think Mick and Benny wouldn't have known a rugby ball from a football, you know what I mean. I said, "I've already done three days, I'm not playing."' For Mick, however, this was evidence that John was not sufficiently committed, and unknown to John, he quickly set in motion the search for a replacement drummer. As the youngest and most recent member of the band, Ched was out of the loop of any decisions made by Mick and Benny. 'I hadn't been in the band long. I still saw myself as a junior member, and I had no control over what was going on. All I really remember is that Mick said that John couldn't rehearse 'cause he was doing something else, and they thought that he didn't have enough interest in the band and so he was going to get the sack. I didn't have any involvement in it other than that.'

On Easter Sunday, Mick and Benny along with Ched, drove up to Driffield to recruit a new drummer – Mick 'Woody' Woodmansey. Ched recalls: 'Mick said he knew of a drummer, who he'd seen, which turned out to be Woody. They'd done gigs together when Woody was with the Roadrunners, and Mick was always impressed by his drumming. We went off in the van to Driffield to see him, and then we set up an audition at the place where we rehearsed at Woodmansey Village Hall, because everybody had got wind of this, and several other drummers had applied for the job. But it was all a sham because it was decided that Woody was going to be the drummer anyway.'

John Cambridge was swiftly and summarily dismissed. The following Tuesday Jim Simpson, who had been put on stand-by as temporary drummer, was despatched to John's house to deliver an envelope containing some owed gig money, along with the news that he was sacked. Mick's shyness, and desire to be liked, meant he would often avoid challenging or confronting people directly, and this pattern of avoidance would recur in the years to come.

With Mick Woodmansey now in the drummer's seat, the Rats carried on much as before. Ched felt there was something else that had to be resolved: 'I said, "We've got two Micks in the band now. We'll have to call you something different. We'll call you 'Woody'." So it was me who gave Woody the name, 'cause previous to that his nickname in Driffield had been "Pecker"– Woody Woodpecker.'

It's worth taking a brief detour from Mick Ronson, to focus on John Cambridge and Mick Wayne's backstory, in order to chart the route that eventually led Ronson to Bowie. After being sacked from the Rats that April, John Cambridge spent the next month or so working on plastering jobs with his father. He kept his drumming hand in with a residency at the Brickmakers Arms in Hull, along with former Aces and Crestas singer Eric Lee and former Rat's bassist Geoff Appleby, whose in-laws ran the pub. John had little or no contact with Mick or the Rats until later in the autumn. By then he was working professionally as a drummer in London, and mixing in the kinds of music circles of which Ronson and the others back in Hull could only dream. Sacked from

The Rats, Part Two: 1968–1970

the Rats for not having a sufficiently committed attitude, John had an ambition and talent that put him within a few months on the path to working with David Bowie. It's an oft-repeated myth that he left the Rats to join Mick Wayne's band Junior's Eyes, suggesting he left of his own volition. The truth is, he was sacked from the Rats, but soon after was offered the job by Mick Wayne.

Mick Wayne was born in Hull in 1945 and his friendship with John Cambridge began in February 1966, at the time that Mick Ronson was trying to make it as a musician down in London. John applied to a local anonymous advert 'professional group seeking a drummer'. The group was the Hullabaloos, which Mick Wayne joined, replacing their singer Ricky Knight. The band had started life back in the early '60s in Hull as Ricky Knight and the Crusaders. Barely known in England, they achieved considerable success in America as part of the British Invasion from 1964. They combined pop melodies with close-part harmonies, which along with their boyish good lucks and long blond hairstyles put them firmly in the Swinging Sixties mould of bands that were breaking in the States. They released two albums in 1965 on the New York-based Roulette label, both with a strong Buddy Holly vibe. They also appeared on two episodes of the weekly US prime time TV show of the same name – *Hullaballoo*, along with big names such as the Rolling Stones, the Yardbirds and the Kinks.

By 1966 the band was back in Hull and managed by John Chichester Constable, a local aristocrat who owned and lived at Burton Constable Hall a few miles east of the city. John Cambridge successfully auditioned to join as drummer and rehearsed there with the new line up of the band. The Hullaballoos in this line-up with John Cambridge and Mick Wayne played some local gigs from February to April 1966, but at the end of that month Wayne decided to pursue his music career in London, and the Hullabaloos folded for good. John Cambridge went on to play with local band ABC before joining the Rats and Mick Ronson in 1967.

During that period in 1966 Mick Wayne had been living such a hand-to-mouth existence at his flat on Albert Avenue in Hull, that John and his parents provided him first with meals and then with rent-free lodging at their own home. John's friendship and generosity was something Mick Wayne never forgot. Fast forward three years to 1969, and just a few weeks after getting the push from the Rats, John got a phone call from Mick Wayne, inviting him to see his new band Junior's Eyes play at Scarborough. John went along and agreed to drum on one of their songs, not realising he was effectively being auditioned in

The Mick Ronson Story

front of a live audience, with the rest of the band checking him out. A few days later Mick Wayne rang John to ask him to join Junior's Eyes. John immediately accepted and started rehearsing with the band, first in Norfolk and then in London. The band's one and only album *Battersea Power Station*, recorded with the line-up before John joined, was produced by Tony Visconti and released that June. The same month Mick Wayne recorded his distinctive guitar part on Bowie's 'Space Oddity' single and the record was released in the UK in early July.

Bowie decided to use Junior's Eyes for recording his second album *David Bowie* (aka *Space Oddity*), rather than bring in separate session musicians as he had done for the single produced by Gus Dudgeon. He also opted for Tony Visconti as producer. On 16 July the band with John Cambridge on drums started recording with Bowie at Trident Studios, as well as maintaining their own schedule of gigs as an autonomous band throughout July and August. This included a week-long stint at the famous Star Club in Hamburg, where the Beatles had played seven years earlier.

On 11 September they were recording the track 'Unwashed and Somewhat Slightly Dazed', and John Cambridge gave an opening to the Rats singer Benny Marshall, who had travelled down from Hull to visit him. Bowie clearly didn't need a singer, but his harmonica skills could be utilised, as Benny describes: 'I walked in with John, and Visconti's there, and John says, "You want a harmonica player on this, don't you? Well, there he is, there's your man." I hadn't got any harmonicas with me, so he sent someone out, they bought an F harmonica back. Bowie's sat there alongside of me, and he says, "You're not going to mess this up, are you?" So no pressure! I had no fear in them days! So I played it, and he thought it was wonderful. I saw Bowie live a few times after that, and he always had that harmonica with him and always asked me to play."

John Cambridge was back on his feet just months after getting the sack from the Rats. He was working with an up-and-coming professional band with bookings nationally and abroad. He was recording with a singer who was making an impact in the charts and he was living in London, mixing with musicians who were famous. He was at the heart of the new music scene.

The Rats, Part Two: 1968–1970

Back in Hull, Mick Ronson and the Rats were gigging locally while holding down day jobs. In August, Mick had his own chance to make an impact beyond the local music scene, courtesy of his former Mariners bandmate Rick Kemp, whose friendship with Michael Chapman had grown over the intervening years. Rick played on Chapman's first album *Rainmaker*, produced by Gus Dudgeon and released in July 1969. Chapman was now working on his second album, *Fully Qualified Survivor*, again with Rick Kemp on bass, and they were looking for a lead guitarist. Gus Dudgeon's instinct, being a London-based producer, was to use a session musician from the capital, and his first choice was Mick Wayne, who had impressed him with his playing on Bowie's single 'Space Oddity'. Chapman and Kemp, however, wanted to keep it really local and knew exactly who they needed – Mick Ronson from Hull.

Rick Kemp recalls: 'Gus Dudgeon called and said: "We're doing another album with Michael Chapman", who I was working with – that was my main gig at the time. He said, 'Do you know anybody who can play seriously good electric guitar, because while I love Michael's acoustic playing, I'd really like a separate electric player." So I said: "Yeh, I do know this man called Mick Ronson" and once again rode him in. I remember pulling up in the Morris Thousand with the wings flapping off, while Mick was mowing the grass on the verge at Hessle for the Corporation, and I pulled up and said, "Do you want to play on an album?" And his line was, and I still love it to this day, "What – you mean one that's going to be sold in the shops?" So I said: "Yeh", and he said: "That'll be good, where are we doing it?", and I said: "In London", and he said: "How are we getting there?" I said: "In this car if that's OK." And he looked a bit doubtful, switched his machine on again, and I drove away. Three or four days later off we were, down the old A1, and I remember he had this warm overcoat on and some sandwiches that his mum had packed for him. About Hatfield he was so cold, I don't think it had a heater, he was shivering really badly, and he wanted to call home because he had promised to, and it was very bleak, I remember that. Anyway, cut a long story short, we ended up in what I think was Trident to do Michael's album *Fully Qualified Survivor*, and he made an instant impression and asked of Gus Dudgeon if there was any more work like this, and immediately he was on his way. And he did very, very well. *Wherever you are, Mick, fantastic, you did very well. And I still think that the playing on that album is probably among the best I ever heard you do.*'

Fully Qualified Survivor was actually recorded at Regent Sound Studios in London in August 1969, and Rick Kemp admits he may have confused his reminiscence of the cold drive down with a separate occasion when he drove Mick to London the following year, possibly for a radio recording in early 1970. Either way, Rick is on the ball with his description of Mick's superb playing on what became Chapman's breakthrough album when it was released in March 1970. Mick's rock blues riffs complement Chapman's acoustic folk and slide guitar, being distinctive but never dominating, and are integrated well into each of the tracks. It was one of John Peel's favourite albums of 1970 and for Mick it was his first outing on vinyl, on a record that was 'sold in the shops'. Although interested in doing more recording work in London, he was still content with living in Hull and playing with the Rats, being adamant not to repeat the previous mistake of trying to make it by moving to the capital.

That August the Rats played the first of a series of festival gigs in Hull and the East Riding, including an all-nighter at Burton Constable Hall and free concerts in Hull's West and East Parks. The events were organised by Rick Welton, who had been appointed as Administrative Director of the embryonic Hull Arts Centre in April 1969. The Arts Centre wasn't to open until the following year, and Rick used the interim period to organise music events as profile raisers, and in the case of the Burton Constable Hall gig, to raise money for the new Arts Centre. The all-nighter took place on 22 August, a Friday evening that led into the early hours of Saturday morning. It was ticketed, with the grounds and facilities being provided free of charge by its owner John Chichester-Constable, who had managed the Hullabaloos a few years earlier. The event was billed as the first ever pop festival in the Humberside area. With its all-night bus shuttle to and from Hull, its market stalls, avant-garde and cartoon film showings, and its three-stage set-up allowing for a rapid changeover of bands, the event was clearly influenced by the many counter-culture festivals springing up in London and throughout the country. Nearly 2000 people attended the gig with a line-up of performers including the Pretty Things, Chicken Shack, the Third Ear Band and the Nice, as well as local bands including Alan (Robert) Palmer's the Mandrakes. The Rats played two slots, the Riding Stables at 9.45 p.m. and the Courtyard at 12.15 a.m. Thunderclap Newman, the billed headliners, didn't perform, having split up shortly before the gig. Benny Marshall recalls the event: 'They were all-nighters, used to be seven or eight bands on, maybe more. The main venue had two stages, and then they had places outside where they used to put bands on as well, mainly acoustic stuff. They were good. They used to get packed.

The Rats, Part Two: 1968–1970

And there were buses to and from Hull, so there was never any hardship getting there. It was a good gig to play.' Ched Cheesman also remembers the gig: 'You had a main stage and a smaller stage at the end that kind of jutted out into the audience, and we played on that smaller stage. This was so they could have quicker changeovers. Sam Cutler who had just done the Rolling Stones Hyde Park concert, he was the stage manager and I remember him buzzing around. It was an amazing event, they had a lot of the big names at the time all in one night. It was something very different, had never happened before as far as I know, an all-night concert, it was really quite amazing.'

A photograph of Mick playing that night at Burton Constable Hall shows him wearing a suede jacket with tassels on the shoulders. Ched remembers how this came about. 'There's two reasons why he's wearing that particular jacket. One is that we'd been to see Jeff Beck play at the Skyline Ballroom in Hull, and he had on these calf-length moccasin boots with tassels hanging down. That seemed to kind of influence us a lot. I had a guitar that I stuck a bit of suede on the front and put these tassels on. My girlfriend at the time, who is now my wife Cathy, she had this bright green suede mini-coat that she'd just recently bought, it was brand new. We were stood at a bus stop getting a bus somewhere, and I was eating a bag of crisps, when I spilt this bag of crisps and one went on her coat and I tried to brush it off and it made like an oily mark on this brand new green suede coat. At the same time we were thinking it's time we dressed Mick up a bit, because he was quite a conservative dresser at that point, despite what he became in later life. He always wore plain black trousers with a crease down the front, white socks, and usually just a plain ordinary shirt. He was a very conservative dresser and we thought it's time we rocked him up a bit. So Cathy decided to make him a jacket out of this coat that she now couldn't wear 'cause I'd put a grease stain on it and it wouldn't come out. So she cut it all up with our favourite tassels at the time, and he wore that and there's quite a few photographs of Mick wearing that jacket.'

Following on from the ticketed Friday night gig at Burton Constable, Rick Welton had also organised free concerts in Hull's East Park for the Saturday and Sunday afternoons. The Saturday gig with headliner Barclay James Harvest was washed out by heavy rain, but the Sunday gig went ahead with main act the Edgar Broughton Band. The Rats played that afternoon and the event is remembered vividly by a teenage Sheila Thornton: 'I was just completely overwhelmed by the whole thing, 'cause it was like going to a festival. It was when things like

The Mick Ronson Story

Woodstock and the Isle of Wight festival were on, and I was 14 going on 15, so there's no way I could have gone to any of the festivals, although I would have loved to have done. So for me being able to go to East Park in my flowing clothes, and I used to have leather plaits in my hair and all my bells on my feet, and me and my sister were weekend hippies! It was just a fantastic atmosphere to be able to go to this concert in the park, an open-air concert, and it was just like being at a festival – it was brilliant!' Teenager Lynne Mitchell still had her crush on Mick Ronson and also remembers that day: 'Me and my friend went and everybody sat on the grass, and the stage was there and we were sat down at this side of it. Mick was stood on the stage and I waved, and he waved and said, "Hiya, are you alright?" And all these girls at the back was going: "Oh he waved to me!" and I was thinking, *No, he didn't, he's mine, haha!*'

Also in the crowd was Rob Eunson, who would later play with Jeff Parsons in Dead Fingers Talk: 'When I saw him at East Park, you saw the band, but really you were just seeing him. Your eyes were on him, you was listening to him. I mean the others were good, but he was so outstandingly brilliant. And he looked great and he had this fantastic charisma. He was so entertaining, it was fantastic entertainment to watch someone who is that charismatic. He had everything and he was a great technical guitarist, he was creative. I didn't remember any of the others to be honest, I didn't remember the songs, I just remembered Mick Ronson. That's how much he stood out.' Rick Welton organised a similar free concert that year in Hull's West Park, at which the Rats also played. The stage had a covered area which provided more protection from the elements.

Down in London, drummer John Cambridge was now sharing a flat with Junior's Eyes guitarist Tim Renwick. It was the basement flat of an upmarket mews house in Gloucester Place, owned by the manager of the American band Blue Cheer. Rock celebrity neighbours included Alvin Lee, guitarist with Ten Years After, whose regular visitors included the Small Faces and Rod Stewart. Benny Marshall would often travel down from Hull to visit John, no doubt with one eye on the music opportunities, but also for other reasons: 'They used to send me down and say: "Bring some dope back" and I used to have to score the dope. Tim Renwick was like a master technician at rolling stuff. We used to call him the Rollie King and he used to roll them and just pass them on, roll them and pass them on, round and round and round. So it was, "Tim can you get us some of it?" "Oh yeh, OK", and he used to get it from wherever, and they used to say to me: "Don't forget – bring some stuff

The Rats, Part Two: 1968–1970

back" and they'd give me the money and off I'd go. I was going to see John, but that was like part of the deal.'

It wasn't long before all the Rats came down to stay for a few days at John's posh crash pad. Ched Cheesman remembers that trip to London: 'We all went down in the band van and stayed there. Some stayed in the flat, I actually slept in the van. We socialised quite a lot. I remember one occasion we were all sat on this mattress in a circle and Tim Renwick was playing records on a little Dansette record player, and rolling joints like a machine! He would roll a joint, pass it along, and before it had got round the circle he had another one rolled, and they were going round like that. And I don't smoke, I've never been a cigarette smoker, but obviously I didn't want to be left out of it, so I was just taking tiny little puffs and trying not to inhale. And Woody was the same. So this went on for some time then we decided to go into London to the music shops and by this time we were so stoned – I'd never been that stoned ever in my life. I remember me and Woody stood outside the music shop just staring at the traffic. We just couldn't do anything but stare! Mick mentions about being stoned at the Roundhouse in March 1970, and Woody mentions in his book about the first time he was stoned at Hornsea Floral Hall when they did some gigs as Ronno, but they're both wrong, 'cause they were both stoned with me at Tim Renwick's joint-rolling session!'

Rick Welton organised a second free concert in Hull's East Park, which took place on 28 September 1969. For the first time since his dismissal from the band six months earlier, John Cambridge playing with Junior's Eyes shared a stage with Mick Ronson and the Rats. Michael Chapman also played and an image of him performing that day, by Hull photographer Barry Nettleton, became the centrefold for his album *Fully Qualified Survivor*. David Bowie was billed to perform but his growing success on the back of the 'Space Oddity' single brought other commitments, so he didn't venture north for the gig. Trevor Bolder also played that day in Flesh, alongside his brother Ian, Keith Stutt on drums, and John Bentley, who was playing the Fender Strat he had acquired from Ronson the year before. John recalls: 'As we were playing our set, Mick who was standing on the sidelines must have heard that his ex-Stratocaster was out of tune. So he walked out onto the stage and proceeded to tune up my guitar for me while I was in the middle of playing it! He wasn't trying to upstage me in any way. It was a case of the older more experienced musician helping the younger novice – it was just a very kind gesture.' Mick's habit of retuning his fellow musicians' guitars onstage wasn't always taken so kindly, as Ched recalls: 'John's recollection of Mick tuning him doesn't surprise me. He used to do that to me also. Trevor Bolder told me that he used to get annoyed with Mick doing that to him. Trevor said that during some of Mick's wilder string-bending solos such as "Moonage", his guitar would go out of tune and Mick would come across and start tuning Trevor's bass as if it were him out of tune!'

In hindsight, that second East Park concert is quite significant. On the same day on the same stage are all the future Spiders from Mars, playing in different bands: Mick Wayne, who played on the classic single 'Space Oddity' and was instrumental in introducing John Cambridge to Bowie; John Cambridge, who in turn would soon be crucial in introducing Mick Ronson to Bowie; and the two drummers, John and Woody, who played in both the Rats and with Bowie. Also onstage are: Michael Chapman, who gave Mick Ronson his first recording credit on a professionally produced record album; John Bentley and Ched Cheesman, who would play at the 1994 Mick Ronson Memorial Concert at Hammersmith Odeon (along with Cambridge); finally, it has David Bowie billed to appear and even though he doesn't play, this is the gig that features all the Hull musicians who were to be crucial to his subsequent career.

By the autumn of '69, Ched Cheeseman was becoming frustrated by Mick's unwillingness to try writing or rehearsing any original material: 'The band had been kind of like my heroes in a way, but after having joined I became increasingly disillusioned and disappointed. It was mainly the lack of originality, and not making any effort to be anything other than a Jeff Beck cover band. It was a time when bands were really getting to write their own material – even bands like Free, they were playing music like us, but it was their own. They did some blues standards, but they were writing their own songs, and that's the way things were going. I thought we should really be attempting to do that. But it got to be quite annoying because of this mickey-taking. You daren't say anything, or contribute anything because you're either going to get laughed at or dismissed, so you couldn't really contribute anything. You'd just get: "Go on – write a song, then!" and you can't do it under those circumstances.' Two years after the one attempt to write a new song ('Bernie Gripplestone'), and the band still hadn't produced any original material: 'Mick wouldn't even attempt it – he wouldn't even try. I remember a specific time rehearsing at Woodmansey Village Hall and I don't remember what song we were doing, but I was trying to get

The Rats, Part Two: 1968–1970

them to do it our way, rather than a direct copy. Mick didn't quite know what to do, and I remember Benny saying: "Play an Indian solo" and that kind of annoyed me, 'cause I thought that's what everybody else is doing. An Indian solo, that's like a sitar type thing. It started with Jeff Beck doing the rundown where he mimicked an Indian sitar type thing, and a lot of people were trying to do solos like that, so it was a common thing. So when Benny said that, I thought, *That's just going nowhere*. It was sticking with the copying idea, and I remember getting a bit annoyed and throwing me guitar down and walking away. So I probably didn't handle it very well, but I was really disappointed that we just couldn't get anywhere on that front. There was what I can only describe as a laziness to move on and become an exciting band. It was basically rooted in *How good could we cover Jeff Beck?* So I became more and more disillusioned and disappointed.'

This narrowness of vision, restricting the band to copying the creativity of others, eventually became too much: "In the end I said: *I want to leave, I'm leaving the band but I'll stay for as long as you find somebody to replace me*. So this carried on for a while. They couldn't find anybody and I think I eventually said, "Oh well, I'll stay then and put up with it." We did a gig at Hornsea Floral Hall. The next day the roadie came round to see me and said, "The band don't need you anymore." I wasn't too disappointed because I'd become disillusioned anyway and I'd put in me resignation, although I kind of rescinded it a little bit, so it wasn't too much of a disaster to me.' Ched was replaced on bass by Geoff Appleby who returned to the Rats in November '69 after a gap of a year. The band did a third and final session at Fairview Studios recording 'Telephone Blues' and 'Early In Spring'.

Throughout the year Mick's relationship with Denise Irvin had developed and she would often be at local gigs. Benny Marshall recalls her somewhat surprising influence on Mick's musical taste: 'She used to take him to see things like the film *Mary Poppins* and all we got in the van, all the way to gigs and back, was the songs from *Mary Poppins* – "Chim Chim Cher-ee" and "Supercalifragilisticexpialidocious"! This was a rock guitarist singing all these songs. I think he'd been to see *The Sound of Music* as well because we got a lot of them songs. There was no stopping him once he got going!"

On 14 November, the album Bowie had recorded that summer with Junior's Eyes, featuring John Cambridge on drums, was released in the UK. Titled *David Bowie* (like his previous album), it was produced by Tony Visconti, apart from the single track 'Space Oddity' produced by

The Mick Ronson Story

Gus Dudgeon. Given that John Cambridge and Benny Marshall both play on the album, it's unlikely that its release in November 1969 went unnoticed by Mick Ronson. Whatever Mick felt about John Cambridge now achieving a level of success to which he himself aspired, it didn't alter his conviction to remain in his home city and limit his ambition to the Rats. All that was to change with the coming of the new year and a new decade.

5. Bowie, Hype and The Man Who Sold the World: 1970

The Mick Ronson Story

At the start of the 1970s, Mick Ronson's life continued much as before. He was still living at his parent's house on Greatfield Estate, working by day as a council gardener and rehearsing and gigging in the evening with the Rats. Hull at this time was still a working-class industrial city with a huge manual labour workforce. Jobs were plentiful, the worker was king, and the counter-cultural offerings of the alternative arts scene were small compared to the pre-eminence of sport, pubs, cinema, working men's clubs and the traditional annual Hull Fair. Drinking and fighting were arguably the most popular pastimes amongst the adult population, as John Bentley can testify. The seamen used to go out in the trawlers for weeks on end. They used to come back and they had these blue serge suits with huge baggy trousers, so you always knew to steer away from these guys that were getting incredibly drunk and spending their money. I remember getting beaten up at Hull Fair by a couple of seamen. I got nutted and they broke my teeth. It was quite rough in Hull.' Music was the most popular art form and could respond to a younger generation's tastes, even in a city that tended to lag several years behind whatever trend was happening nationally, or was big in London. The pole position of this thriving local music scene was still held, indisputably, by Mick Ronson and the Rats.

With the imminent release of Michael Chapman's *Fully Qualified Survivor*, the artwork for the album was being completed in Hull. Tony Ward, Ronson's former school friend, worked with photographer Jim Marshall on the photo shoots at his studio on Holderness Road: 'Mike Chapman came down and Mick just came down with him for a little nosey. I was just a kid 15, 16, and he was on the cusp of this massive thing with Bowie, but we were just chatting at the back, just ordinary. He said, "I can remember you when you was a hairy-arsed kid." Mick was a lovely chap. He was never big-headed, he was never ever above his station, even though he could have been. He accepted everybody as they were whether you were the richest person, the poorest person, the thickest person, the cleverest person. He was always warm to everybody. He always had time for people.'

Down in London change was on the cards for Bowie and Junior's Eyes. Tim Renwick was considering joining Terry Reid's band Fantasia, who were gaining recognition in America. Mick Wayne was missing scheduled gigs, partly due to his partner being ill, but also down to his enthusiastic drug habit. Bowie decided he needed a new band and in early January asked John Cambridge to stay on as his drummer. John and roadie Roger Fry moved in with Bowie and his girlfriend Angie

Bowie, Hype and The Man Who Sold the World: 1970

at Haddon Hall in Beckenham, sleeping first on mattresses in the communal living room area and then a separate room.

Tony Visconti, and his girlfriend Liz Hartley, were also living at Haddon Hall. Visconti was Bowie's most trusted creative partner at this time, responsible not just for playing bass, but also song arrangements, strings and overall studio production. Bowie and Visconti started the search for a new lead guitarist, given that Tim Renwick was unlikely to be available. John Cambridge was present but was very much the junior partner in these deliberations: 'I remember being at Haddon Hall in the room with Visconti and Bowie and they are talking about guitar players and we could get so and so, and so and so, and I am chipping in with "I know a kid and he's a real good guitarist in Hull – he's called Mick Ronson." And they thought, *Who the hell is he going to get from Hull? You Know.* So I said, "Look I am going back home, do you want me to bring him down?" "Go on, then, bring him, bring him", just to shut me up.' Junior's Eyes' final gig was scheduled for the Marquee Club on 3 February and the plan was to launch the new band, Hype, the same night. At the end of January, John Cambridge drove up to Hull to see his family and his girlfriend Angie, and to seek out Mick Ronson.

'I came back to Hull and the next morning I knew where Mick worked, being a gardener on the Greatfield Estate. I parked my car and I just walked onto the fields and I could see Mick in the distance, in his wellies and his donkey jacket, marking up this line. You couldn't miss him with his blond hair. He was marking out a rugby or football pitch with creosote. I shouted, "Mick, Mick!" I ran over to him. I hadn't seen him for a while. He knew I was playing in London. Usually anybody would stop and say, "Now then, John, how are you getting on?" Mick just carried on walking. I think it was like, "I've got to get this pitch done by so and so time, there's a match on later." So I'm following him walking. I said, "Have you heard of this guy called David Bowie?" He had just had "Space Oddity" as a minor hit, so he said, "Yes." I said, "He wants a guitarist." Mick then starts laying on about how he got ripped off when he was in London and all this sort of thing and "I'm not doing that again, I got ripped off there and I'm not going, no, no, I'm not going." I said it was Junior's Eyes last gig at the Marquee and we were supporting the first gig of David Bowie's new band, the Hype. I said, "Why don't you come?" Anyway I finally persuaded Mick to come down, so we drives back down to London in my Hillman Minx.'

It says much about John's character and his loyalty to a friend that despite being kicked out of the Rats by Mick less than a year before, he was prepared not only to argue the case with Bowie and Visconti in London, but then to persevere against Mick's own lack of enthusiasm back in Hull. John drove Mick down to London on the Tuesday of the gig and they went straight to the Marquee Club. John drummed on both sets, playing the final gig of Junior's Eyes and the first gig of Hype, with Tim Renwick on guitar for both. They then went back to Haddon Hall as John recalls: 'That's really when Mick met David. We went back after the gig and started picking up a couple of acoustic guitars. This is one o'clock, two o'clock in the morning and they started messing about. Next morning the same thing – I think David and Mick just hit it off.'

The gardener-guitarist from Hull made an instant impression on Bowie and Visconti. He had been playing in bands for over six years by this stage. Three years with the Rats had honed his guitar skills to the point where he could improvise, and add fillers or riffs to almost any tune or chord sequence on first hearing it played. He was also bringing a rock sensibility that the ever-evolving Bowie was keen to integrate into his songwriting approach. Bowie had a recording session lined up for John Peel's radio show on Thursday, 5 February. The play-safe option would have been to use Tim Renwick, who had stood in at the first Hype gig at the Marquee Club, but Bowie, always the creative risk-taker, opted instead for Mick Ronson. John Cambridge recalls: 'Bowie said to him, "We have a John Peel show in about two days." It was live at the Paris studios in London and David said, "Do you want to come and play with us? You can be the guitarist rather than Tim."' The fact that Mick Ronson was happy to play for the first time on national radio with a group of musicians who were unfamiliar, apart from John Cambridge, and perform a set list of entirely new songs with just two days' rehearsal, demonstrates a high level of confidence in his own ability. It also shows that Mick at this crucial moment was prepared to match Bowie's willingness to take creative risks. They were effectively taking a leap of faith together, which would sow the seeds for a strong collaborative partnership. And for Mick, with a long-held ambition of making it as a professional musician, this was the opportunity he simply had to seize.

The quality of Mick's musicianship became even clearer to Bowie and Visconti when they heard him play electric guitar through an amplifier during the afternoon soundcheck at the BBC Studios. Bowie's latest songs were moving into new territory, but he had still been performing primarily as an acoustic folk-orientated artist, and according to John Cambridge this new alignment with Mick Ronson was powerful and immediate: 'It's like Bowie was getting Jimi Hendrix

Bowie, Hype and The Man Who Sold the World: 1970

or Jimmy Page out of Led Zeppelin to back him. Mick Ronson's powerful guitar just made Bowie go "wow". With Bowie's songwriting and his nice chords, he thought, "This is good." That is how I think the two gelled.' During the recording John Peel asked Bowie, 'Are you going to be doing gigs with this band?' Bowie replied: 'Yes. We're going to do some gigs, are we, Michael? Michael doesn't really know, he's just come down from Hull and I met him for the first time about two days ago through John the drummer.' When pressed by Peel – 'So you're planning to go on the road with them?' – Bowie replied, 'Yes, very surely.'

Bowie was indeed committed to working with Mick and asked him to join his new band Hype with Tony Visconti and John Cambridge, who no doubt felt vindicated for his persistent advocacy of his former Rats bandmate. Mick returned to Hull to put in place all the necessary arrangements that a move to London would require. That Sunday, 8 February, the John Peel show was broadcast on Radio 1 and the Ronson family enthusiastically tuned in. Mick's younger Hull friend Kevin Hutchinson also listened avidly: 'Mike told us about it about three days before. He said, "I'm gonna be on radio, on the John Peel show, have a listen, tell me what you think." It came on and we just sat there in total silence listening to it. It was incredible, it absolutely blew us away. Two or three days later, Michael's back in Hull and said, "What did you think to the show, lads?" "It was incredible, Mike, absolutely fantastic. It wasn't just good, it was absolutely amazing." "Do you think so?" He just couldn't believe that we thought it was that good. He was totally knocked out by the fact that we said to him, "Mike, it isn't just good, it's incredible." And that was the time when we all said, "This is gonna be massive, you're gonna make it, Mike." Even then he was thinking, *naaah, I'm not*, but I think that was the point when us as kids knew. "You're gonna be a star."'

Once back in Hull, however, the old doubts and fears returned. Mick had serious misgivings about giving up a steady income with his job as a council gardener and taking the risk once again of trying to make a living from music. The Rats played at the Duke of Cumberland in Ferriby in what turned out to be their last gig. Ched Cheesman played a couple of songs with them. Ched recalls Mick still being conflicted about the decision to go to London: 'I remember having a conversation with Mick after the show where he was saying he was unsure whether to go or not. I remember him saying, "We're going to be paid £8 a week, £7 or £8 a week [or whatever it was] and I'm really unsure, I don't know what to do, whether to go." So at that point, although he did eventually go, he was very uncertain.' In a 1975 article in the *Hull Daily Mail* Mick recalled how agonising the decision was: 'I considered it for two weeks. I had got out of a few debts and had a steady job. I wasn't making any money but I wasn't in debt either. I thought, "Should I go? Am I going to have this happen to me all over again?" After two weeks I reached the decision I *had* to go because if something good happened with David I would kick myself for the rest of my life. I think the reason I made it, possibly better than anyone else from Hull, is that I took a lot of chances when I was younger. I don't see anybody getting on if they don't take gambles. I was very determined and also quite lucky. The two go hand in hand."

Paul Denman, bass player with Sade, grew up on the same council estate in Hull, albeit a few years later: 'Michael had ambition, very much like myself. I'm pretty sure if he was here now he'd say: "Yeah, I can't wait to get out of Hull", and neither could I. I used to get the shit kicked out of me every day, just walking to the bus stop, and I'm pretty sure Michael had a rough time of it as well, it was that kind of estate. So he was driven and he wanted to get out, he wanted to be out there, and be part of a bigger world. Fortuitously he met Bowie, he saw this kid is going to be something, and he can help the something be more. You have to understand as musicians we're shit-scared, we're really insecure. So for him to put himself from the Rats, which was basically a cover band, for him to push himself from that into David Bowie's insane universe and go, "I'm gonna do this", it is a big step up, but he did make the step up.'

Mick handed in his notice with Hull City Council Parks Department and told his bandmates. Having been the band's singer for seven years, Benny Marshall knew it was the end of the line: 'That was the end of the Rats. We didn't bother after that. There was nobody could take his place really. It wasn't really worth looking.' It was a blow for Woody Woodmansey too when Mick left. Mick was apologetic and assured him he "would sort something out", leaving Woody with the clear impression that they would definitely be playing together at some point. That point was to come sooner than he expected, but for the moment it was a pause in Woody's music career. On 13 February, *Hull Daily Mail* reported on Mick's imminent move to London with the headline 'Ex-Rat gets his chance in big time':

> After three years as guitarist for the Rats in Hull, Michael Ronson's break for the big-time comes on Monday, when he sets course for London to work in a new group formed by pop-

Bowie, Hype and The Man Who Sold the World: 1970

idol David Bowie, whose disc 'Space Oddity' hit the Top Ten last year. For 23-year-old Michael his chance has not come too soon. 'My parents know that this is the only thing I have ever really wanted to do, and I have often felt like banging my head against a brick wall through wondering why I wasn't getting anywhere', he explained. Michael's chance as a pro with the new group, which is called The David Bowie Hype, came through another Hull musician already with Bowie in London – John Cambridge, who lived at 9 Brisbane Street off Hessle Road. John went to the big city eight months ago and worked with Junior's Eyes before Bowie asked him to be his drummer. John promptly mentioned Michael's name to Bowie, and since then, as Michael says, 'It's just all happened. I've been offered jobs in London before,' said Michael, 'but nothing as secure as this. I didn't want to go back there and find myself in debt with my equipment again, and the money from this job means I shall be able to live properly. The Hype has a record, 'Prettiest Star', for release shortly and after that we shall be off on bookings up and down the country,' added Michael. 'The main thing for me now, what I'm really after, is just to get myself known.'

Appearing the day before Valentine's Day, the article also announced Mick's engagement to Denise Irvin: 'It will be quite a weekend for Michael, who lives at 8 Milford Grove, Hull, and who today says "goodbye" to his work with Hull Parks Department and tomorrow announces his engagement to Denise Irvin, who, like Michael, lives on Greatfield Estate.' Although Denise would bear Mick's son Nicholas a year and a half later, they never married. The article also mentioned: 'David Bowie will be in Hull this weekend looking for some additions to his antiques collection and will take Michael back to London with him on Monday.'

Bowie's visit, which was the only occasion he spent significant time in the city, was prompted by John Cambridge: 'David Bowie did come and stay at our house down Brisbane Street in early 1970. The reason he came was because he'd just bought a Rover and he was going to get it serviced. I said, "Why don't you bring it to Hull?" I said my mate "Muff", who was a roadie in the Rats, I said, "I'll get him to service it for you probably hell of a lot cheaper than you getting it serviced in London."' Pete Murfin duly obliged: 'Where I worked was Turner & Sellers, back

The Mick Ronson Story

then in Hessle Square, it's still there. He came by himself and we just did a complete service on it. It was a Rover, a Rover 100. It was a pretty old car and I thought, "He's a rock star and he's got a pretty old Rover here." The thing that did surprise me was how small Bowie was, he wasn't very tall. He was a nice enough guy – I got along with him pretty well.'

According to Jim Simpson, Bowie was not averse to getting other things fixed in the cheaper 'mates rates' world of Hull. Jim's day job was refrigeration engineer and at some point after Mick had moved down to London, Jim had a complete stranger turn up one night. With a fridge. 'I'm sat at home, knock on the door, and the driver's there with a fridge, a blue tabletop fridge. I said, "What's that?" He said, "It's Bowie's from Haddon Hall and it's not working.' I thought *What!?* He said, "Can you fix it? Will it be ready tomorrow?" So I said, "Yeah, of course it will." Anyway I brought it in the house and I opened it up and had a look. And tied to the side of the cooler box, the freezer box, was a piece of marijuana taped there, cannabis, which I guess was my payment! I just shook the fridge about a bit, and sent it back the next day and never heard another thing."

John Cambridge was Bowie's 'tour guide' during his visit to Hull: 'David and Angie stayed at mam and dad's, and Tony Visconti and his girlfriend Liz Hartley at the time came and stayed at my girlfriend's house, now my wife Angie's, and they all stayed for four or five days, something like that. I took them in pubs for a drink, so I know the pubs he was in, but this is like before he was massive.'

They also paid a Sunday lunchtime visit to the Phoenix Club on Hessle Road, with Jim Simpson and his father. Jim recalls: 'I don't think Bowie had met anybody from the north before, so he just found it all fascinating. He said he'd like to go to a working men's club. Phoenix Club was up the road, so [I said] we'll go there. The guy on the door, however, took exception to Bowie's appearance. "You can't come in like that with that hair!" Bowie did have quite long hair then, and they're just not used to that then on Hessle Road, so they just said, "Sorry, you can't come in."' Jim Simpson's father knew the club chairman and went to have a word: 'My dad said, "You know he's a popstar, don't you?" He says, "No, I don't care." He says, "Look, he's a popstar, and they've got to look like twats!" And the bloke says, "Oh, let him in."' Once in the club Bowie played bingo, which according to John Cambridge 'David thoroughly enjoyed!'

John's father Tom got on well with David, even though Bowie 'smoked all of his fags' and ran up a big phone bill at their house while

Bowie, Hype and The Man Who Sold the World: 1970

trying to get some northern gigs booked for Hype. He managed to secure just one booking at Hull University, for 6 March. *Hull Times'* 'Teen Scene' reported on Bowie's visit to Hull:

> Last week we mentioned that two Hull lads, Michael Ronson and John Cambridge, were now working with David Bowie, whose record 'Space Oddity' rocketed up the charts last year. David was in Hull last weekend. What did he think of the city on his first visit? 'It's ok,' he said, 'and with two Hull lads in the group I may make it a second home.' He was particularly impressed with a local fish and chip restaurant! David stressed that the group containing Michael and John, to be called Hype, is not a backing group, but that he and the group would retain their separate identities. Hype are to start work next month on their own LP and David will probably start on one himself with the group about the same time.

Underneath a photo of Bowie, the article also states: 'His hunt for antiques proved unsuccessful.'

Mick moved into Haddon Hall in London, joining Bowie, his girlfriend Angie, John Cambridge and Hype's roadie Roger Fry. Visconti and his girlfriend Liz Hartley were looking to move out to their own flat but were still living there at this point. Benny Marshall would come to visit, and his trips down from Hull continued through the recording of *The Man Who Sold the World* in 1970 and *Hunky Dory* the following year. Benny has strong memories of Haddon Hall: 'You walked in the front door, there was a big double staircase going up to a gallery, a massive stained glass window at the back of the staircase. To the left was the kitchen, next was the front room where the boys were sleeping at that time. First door on the right was Bowie's bedroom, second door was Tony Visconti's bedroom. There was a downstairs, that was like the practice room, and you went out the back and it was a veranda. There was the big garden with a bit of like woods at the bottom, that was the setup of it. Eventually he [Bowie] wanted the front room back, so he moved us all back up onto the gallery and we was sleeping up there. His mother used to make us a dinner if I was there on a Sunday, she used to make a Sunday dinner for everybody.'

Mick's overriding impression of Haddon Hall was its size: 'It just seemed big! It seemed big, coming from where I come from – Hull, up north – it seemed like a big fancy place really. It was nice. I have fond memories of all that stuff. It was great.' Coming from a city with a reputation for straight-talking, Mick was instantly drawn to and connected with Bowie's clarity of purpose and ambition: 'He was very straightforward, he knew what he wanted to do and got on and did it. That's what I remember most about him. And he was quite a giving sort of person too, very kind person and that's what really struck me about him. You knew you weren't here messing about. He was going to be somebody. You can kind of tell that from some people and you don't get that off other people. He was one that you definitely got that vibe with. He was going to be a star or something, you know, right away.'

Mick's first public gig with Bowie and Hype was at the Roundhouse in London on Sunday, 22 February, as part of Implosion Festival. They were back in Hull playing Hull University on Friday, 6 March, the gig that Bowie had arranged during his stay in the city. Benny Marshall joined the band onstage that night to play harmonica on 'Unwashed and Somewhat Slightly Dazed'. The gig coincided with the UK release of Bowie's new single 'The Prettiest Star'. It was also the day that Decca, his former recording label, released the album *The World of David Bowie*. Cashing in on Bowie's 'Space Oddity' success, the record was basically a rehash of his first album with the addition of some previously unreleased recordings. A further release that day was Michael Chapman's album *Fully Qualified Survivor*, so it must have felt satisfying for Mick to be playing a home gig on the same day a record appeared with his name on the credits. Whatever celebrations took place, they were likely to have been low-key, as they were playing Regent Street Polytechnic in London the next day.

Hype played a second gig at the Roundhouse on 11 March as part of the Living Theatre's week-long Atomic Sunrise Festival, in what has become known as the first ever glam rock gig. Hype's support act were Genesis, an unsigned band at that point, fronted by Peter Gabriel with Mike Rutherford, but without Phil Collins, who joined later that year. Genesis' stage shows increasingly became known for their theatricality, but that evening it's unlikely they trumped anything costume-wise offered up by Hype, as John Cambridge describes: 'Bowie gave us all names. Mick was Gangsterman, and he's wearing a gold suit. Bowie was Rainbowman and he's wearing silver lurex tights, knee-length boots and a flowery silver blouse. Tony Visconti was Hypeman, so whereas Superman would have an S on, he had an H for Hype and a cape. I was Cowboyman. They just sewed some frills on my shirt, and they give me a cowboy waistcoat, brown suede, and of course a cowboy hat. And I still

Bowie, Hype and The Man Who Sold the World: 1970

have the hat! And that was the gig.'

Reminiscing on the BBC's *Bowie 5 Years On* programme broadcast in 2021, Tony Visconti recalled the audience's response to their visuals that night: 'We looked really silly. People just laughed at us, till maybe the second song and they started taking the music seriously. Marc Bolan was in the audience watching us taking it all in like a movie camera, so it was a very important night.' There were some heckles and homophobic comments from the audience and during the gig the band's clothes were stolen from the dressing room, so they had to travel back to Haddon Hall that night in their superhero costumes. Hype's performance was also marred by sound problems according to a review in *Disc and Music Echo* from March 1970: 'This show was a disaster. He needs an expert on sound balance who should effectively solve the teething problems of the new line-up.... The volume on Mick Ronson's lead guitar was so high that not only did he block out David's singing, but also completely overpowered John Cambridge's drums. The volume also cleared the seats in a direct line with his speaker.' Mick's tendency to pump up his amp volume would be a recurring issue, but his sense of the whole gig that night, was probably affected by something else: 'I never really took drugs or anything, and I was backstage at the Roundhouse and we're in London like, at the Roundhouse and really hip sort of place with all these hip people backstage, and this guy said to me, "Here you are man, take a few puffs of this joint, it'll steady you down, you know." And I never really smoked or anything, and I picked this joint up, took a few puffs of this joint and I got so stoned, I have never been that stoned in all my life. So from there it got pretty confusing. I remember being onstage and not knowing what I was playing, you kind of forget what you're playing. It was funny afterwards, but I got very confused, all my lips stuck together and everything. Oh dear, I was glad when I came down off that one.' Two nights later at the Locarno Ballroom in Sunderland they took once more to the stage in costume, but the mixed reception led them to ditch the dressing-up idea for good. The world was not yet ready to embrace it, and though Bowie took to wearing a dress later in 1970, it was Marc Bolan and T Rex's album *Electric Warrior,* released in 1971, that brought glam rock into the mainstream.

Mick's first studio session with Bowie and Hype was at Trident Studios on 23 March. Hype were recording a single version of 'Memory of a Free Festival' from the *David Bowie* album of the previous year, but with some changes. Bowie had hired a Moog synthesiser for the session on the assumption that Mick, as a pianist, would play it. When it came to overdub the Moog part, Mick couldn't play it in tune. By chance another musician Ralph Mace was in the building and he retuned the Moog and then went on to play it for the recording. The session at Trident was booked for overnight from 11 p.m. to 4 a.m. and there was still studio time remaining, so they started on 'The Supermen', a new song that David and Mick had been working on at Haddon Hall. Hype had played the song at the Roundhouse, so John Cambridge was familiar with it, but in the interim Mick had developed it to include a new section with a tricky drum fill. During their songwriting sessions at Haddon Hall, Mick and Bowie had made it clear to John that he wasn't included in their creative deliberations, so he was now having to play it in the time-pressured context of the recording studio without any prior knowledge or rehearsal of the changes. He kept getting the drum fill wrong. Mick was possibly still feeling a bit under pressure from the episode earlier with the Moog, or perhaps over-focused on the need for immediate creative results, as this was his first recording session with Bowie. Either way he uncharacteristically lost his cool and took out his frustration directly on John Cambridge. With his face pushed up to the drum booth window, he told John in no uncertain terms that it's 'fucking easy'. Bowie intervened and suggested he and John take a break, so they had a drink in a nearby club while Mick and Tony stayed in the studio. The break eased the tension and when John returned they completed recording 'The Supermen'.

On Wednesday, 25 March, Bowie with Hype recorded tracks for Andy Ferris' *Sounds of the 70s* BBC Radio 1 show at the Playhouse Theatre, London. The following Monday, the 30th, they played the Star Hotel in Croydon – which turned out to be John Cambridge's last gig with Hype. Bowie and Visconti had already talked privately about possibly replacing him, but both were surprised that Mick wanted this too, as Visconti described in his autobiography B*owie, Bolan and the Brooklyn Boy*: 'Mick confided in David and I that he knew a far better drummer in Hull – the one that had replaced John when he went off to join Junior's Eyes. David and I were considering replacing John anyway, but this was a surprise coming from Ronson. We liked John very much, his presence was very uplifting, but he wasn't the adventurous drummer we needed to go to the next level.'

On 6 April, John was at Haddon Hall perched on top of a ladder painting the ceiling, when he heard David and Angie pull up outside in their car. The overheard snippet of conversation left him in no doubt that he was the subject of their animated discussion. Bowie came inside and immediately told John he was looking for a new drummer. It was almost a year to the day that John had been sacked from the Rats, and now Bowie was telling him he was no longer needed in Hype. He was devastated. That evening Andy Ferris' *Sounds of the 70s* with Hype performing was broadcast on Radio 1. John Cambridge had no stomach for staying in at Haddon Hall to listen, and spent a miserable evening on his own at the local pub.

The next day he set off early back to Hull, without a word exchanged with Mick or his former bandmates. Mick had stayed silent that morning, keeping his face fixed resolutely to the wall of their shared room, while John noisily cleared his belongings. He drove home and tried to work out how to restart his life. He joined the Mandrakes, but without its star singer Alan (Robert) Palmer. His career on the national music scene had been curtailed, a promising trajectory cut suddenly and ruthlessly short. In the absence of explanations, he suspected that Mick was the instigator, and felt deeply hurt. Mick was his friend. It was bad enough that this was the second time Mick had sacked him. Worse, it was John who had made this opportunity happen for Mick in the first place. The sense of betrayal cut deep.

Back in Hull, Jim Simpson had been working with John Cambridge's father on plastering jobs before John had moved down to London to play with Hype: 'I was working with his dad for some months, when John just turned up again, and he wouldn't really talk about it. I didn't push him, 'cause I knew it would upset him, although he would never show it. It's only now after 50 years that he's told me how much it hurt him, how much he was hurt by it all. He was upset and quite rightly so.'

With John out of the picture, arrangements were put quickly in place. Mick's suggestion of Woody Woodmansey as a replacement was taken up and Bowie gave him a call. Having just been offered a promotion at the factory where he worked in Driffield, Woody was caught in the same dilemma that Mick had experienced two months earlier: take a leap and follow his dream, or sit tight with a well-paid job for life. It took a further call from Mick to convince Woody to join him and Bowie down in London. Soon after his arrival at Haddon Hall, Woody posed for promotional photographs alongside Mick and Tony. The three Hype band members signed a contract with Phillips, witnessed by Bowie and backdated to 3 April. The contract gave the band a £4000 advance, which they used to buy a new PA system. The intention all along had been that Hype would be Bowie's band, but as with Junior's Eyes beforehand, it would also retain its own identity and capacity to do gigs without him.

The contract also confirmed – as if there were any doubt left in the matter – that John Cambridge was no longer part of the Hype or Bowie scene. Bowie was at a stage in his career where he valued and needed Mick's creative input. Mick had been highly resistant to the idea of another move to London, but having made that leap, he now felt he had to make it work. John's friendship with Mick, was effectively severed and for the next 20 years they had little or no contact. Their friendship was only rekindled and the split healed when John phoned Mick not long before his death in London in April 1993. Benny Marshall continued his trips down to Haddon Hall, now with Cambridge out of the scene: 'I was in one of the sessions when Woody had just took over and Bowie said they sound like a different band and he was sort of happy with it all. That's the way it goes, I suppose, that's the cut-throat music business. If you don't fit, you're out.'

On 17 April, a few weeks after John Cambridge's departure, recording for the album *The Man Who Sold the World* started, alternating between Advision and Trident studios in London. With Visconti in the producer's seat, this marked the start of Mick's apprenticeship in studio production skills, which would serve him well in the years ahead. In a 1980 article for *Beat Instrumental*, Mick recalled: 'When I was working with David, Tony Visconti used to be down at the studio, and I'd say to him, "Can I come and watch what you're doing?" and he'd say, "Sure". I was really impressed with what Tony did – I thought he was great. I still think he is. He's got a really good ear for sound. I thought to myself 'I could do that as well.' Visconti had an equal respect for Mick and they formed a strong partnership in the studio, as Visconti described in an interview with the authors of *The Spider with the Platinum Hair*: 'Working with him was incredible. He was one of the greatest musicians I have ever worked with. Even though he had recorded one album before us with Michael Chapman, it still didn't add up to a lot of studio experience. He acknowledged that I taught him a lot of things about how to record and score. He was asking me questions incessantly, *how do you do this?* and *how do you do that?* and he was such a good student on that level.' At the same time, Mick was tutoring Visconti in the art of rock bass guitar: 'I wasn't that great a musician then and Mick certainly was. As a consequence of playing every weekend with the Rats before he came down to play with Bowie, he had a lot more rock stage experience than me. So Mick was teaching me how to be bold and bodacious on bass and I was teaching him all the finesse in the studio, how you get all the special effects tricks and all that.' Mick suggested Visconti replace his

Bowie, Hype and The Man Who Sold the World: 1970

Fender bass with a Gibson EBO, the same bass that Jack Bruce played, and encouraged him to bend the bass strings. Along with a heavier bass sound in the mix, particularly on tracks such as 'She Shook Me Cold', this produced the sound Mick was aiming for: 'He made me sit down and listen to Jack Bruce of Cream, saying, "You've got to sound like this." He figured if he was going to go down on record as being the guitarist in this band, it was going to be on his own terms.'

Mick played a pivotal role on *The Man who Sold the World*. Having made the break from Hull and the Rats, and with Woody in place as the drummer he wanted in Hype, Mick clearly felt this was his chance to make his mark. He had bonded well with Bowie and the two had spent hours working together developing Bowie's embryonic songs. Once in the studio, Mick then became an invaluable ally to Visconti, who increasingly came to rely on him to deliver what was needed, particularly as he felt that Bowie was not fully engaged in the process. In love with his new wife Angela, Bowie was spending a lot of valuable studio time entwined with her on the sofa or absent altogether. Mick, Tony and Woody would lay down the various tracks, and then Bowie would come up with the lyrics at a very late stage and record the vocals with the studio clock ticking. Visconti's frustration led him to split with Bowie once the album was finished, and he acknowledges how crucial Mick was in the whole process: 'There wouldn't be any songs if we didn't pre-record those tracks based on David's chord changes. It was so frustrating because the guy [Bowie] was mentally absent for most of it. It did lead to David and I breaking up. In the end I said, "Look, man, I just can't make an album under these conditions." I have to really go down on record in saying if it wasn't for Mick and his desire to show the world that he was a great guitarist, who knows what would have happened.'

The album was released in the States in November 1970, but not until April the following year in the UK. It didn't sell well until its reissue in 1972 on the back of the *Ziggy* success. At the point of completion at the end of May 1970, it stands as a remarkable testament to the influence of Mick Ronson on the development of David Bowie as an artist. Bowie's transition had started with Junior's Eyes, but *The Man Who Sold the World* marks the substantial shift from his period as an acoustic folk or folk-rock guitarist, putting him firmly in the mould of a heavy rocker. The album sounds close to Cream or Led Zeppelin, with tracks featuring extended guitar solos and sections of almost prog-rock grandiosity. Mick brings a driving rock sensibility absent from previous Bowie albums, whilst Bowie brings an obvious songwriting ability lacking in Mick's earlier bands such as the Rats. 'After All' stands out as a quintessential Bowie ballad that feels like a precursor to 'Hunky Dory'. The Bowie-Ronson partnership is perhaps best evidenced by the title track, which integrates Mick's distinctive guitar hooks with Bowie's strong rock-pop melody and intriguing lyrics.

On 21 May 1970 Bowie with Hype played the Penthouse at Scarborough, which marked Woody's first live performance with Hype and their first live gig since John Cambridge's departure. In June Mick was briefly back in Hull and went with Benny Marshall to an all-nighter at Burton Constable Hall. Rick Welton had teamed up with Barry Nettleton to form Hull Brick Company and following the successful event a year earlier they staged another on 12 June, called All Night Again. Soft Machine and Free headlined, with the line-up also featuring Michael Chapman, with Rick Kemp on bass. Benny Marshall recalls: 'We weren't playing. Mick had come up from London and Michael Chapman had a gig there that night. So he said, "Would you come and play one or two of the album tracks?" So Mick says: "Oh, I didn't bring my guitar with me", so he says: "You are alright, we've actually smuggled it in." So [Michael] had actually smuggled the guitar in so that he [Mick] could play the gig with him.'

Chapman was riding on the success of *Fully Qualified Survivor* and the producer Gus Dudgeon asked both Michael and Mick to record for Elton John on his album *Tumbleweed Connection*, which Dudgeon was also producing. The album was recorded over the same period as *The Man who Sold the World* and Mick played on the song 'Madman Across the Water'. The track was subsequently re-recorded using Davey Johnstone and Chris Spedding on guitars with strings by Paul Buckmaster. It wasn't included on *Tumbleweed Connection* released in October that year, but was held over to become the title track of Elton John's next album released in 1971. The original version with Mick's impressive guitar work is around three minutes longer and powerfully demonstrates his ability to create stunning guitar solos that complement rather than dominate the existing tune. This version wasn't released until the 1990s.

With recordings for *The Man who Sold the World* complete, Mick was getting restless and increasingly frustrated at the lack of tour dates. Bowie and Hype did a few one-off gigs, but the momentum was stalling. Hype was contracted separately from Bowie, so they could have gone on the road as an independent band, but without Bowie and his songs, the band at this point simply had no material to play. Besides, with the record deal money all spent on equipment, there was little spare cash to

Bowie, Hype and The Man Who Sold the World: 1970

fund a tour. Visconti moved out of Haddon Hall in July and by the end of August signalled his complete split with Bowie. His experience on recording *The Man who Sold the World* had left him disillusioned, and he was keen to focus his efforts on producing the up-and-coming Marc Bolan. Earlier in the Summer Ronson had written to Benny Marshall in Hull, strongly hinting at a future career option without Bowie which would involve reforming the Rats.

Bowie's career was at a crossroads. He had ended his relationship with manager Ken Pitt and was looking to strike a new publishing and record deal. This was currently in limbo and was dependent on his new manager, Tony Defries. Defries would come to play a crucial role in Bowie's subsequent success, but at this point was focused more on trying to secure Stevie Wonder as an artist under his management. On 1 August Mick accompanied Bowie at a Rock with Shelter charity gig at Southend, which also had Michael Chapman on the bill. A few days later the band was due to be playing with Bowie at Leeds. Mick and Woody travelled separately with the band's gear, while Bowie drove up with Angie. Seeing the road sign pointing to Leeds in the west and to Hull in the east, Mick and Woody made a spontaneous but significant decision: they headed east to their home city, leaving Bowie to do the Leeds gig on his own. Following the example set by Visconti, they too were breaking with Bowie, with no guarantee that they would ever be working together again.

6 From Ronno to Ziggy: 1970–1971

From Ronno to Ziggy: 1970–1971

In Hull, Mick went back to his family home on Greatfield Estate and Woody moved in with his girlfriend June in her rented flat. Having split from Bowie, the pair immediately recruited former Rats singer Benny Marshall on vocals: 'I'm sat in the house, knock on the door and Mick and Woody stood on the doorstep and he said, "We've left him. We've left Bowie. We're going to keep going as Hype." He says, "Do you want to do the vocals?" So I says, "Yeh, I wouldn't mind."'

With the benefit of hindsight and the massive success that was to come with Ziggy, it seems almost unfathomable that Mick and Woody were prepared to break from Bowie, and embark on their own separate journey with Visconti on bass and Benny Marshall on vocals. But at this point Ziggy lay in the future and Bowie was still the one-hit wonder with 'Space Oddity'. Bowie's second album with Junior's Eyes hadn't made any big impression and *The Man who Sold the World* wasn't yet available in the record shops. With Bowie's career in limbo and Hype gigs thin on the ground, it made sense from Mick and Woody's perspective to get things moving under their own steam. Hype had their own record deal with Phillips, independent of Bowie, and Mick had forged a strong partnership with Visconti, who at this point probably looked a safer career bet than David. The pressure of trying to make a living in London was probably also in their minds, given that they could base their activities out of Hull on a fraction of the cost. Mick had been living in the capital for six months, and Woody four, so a move back to Hull offered the temporary prospect of a much cheaper place to live, the chance to take stock and recharge creative batteries and, for Mick, the enjoyment of some home cooking and comforts. There was, however, a money issue for Benny over the contract with Phillips, as the record company was not prepared to offer him an advance: 'So I said, *Well, I'm not signing the contract then*. So what Tony Visconti did, which was good of him to do, he arranged for me to get session money for all the time I was there, so I got paid session money for the work that we did.'

Visconti remained in London, now increasingly busy as a producer, particularly after the success of Marc Bolan's 'Ride a White Swan' single that autumn. As Visconti was unavailable for regular touring with Hype, Mick decided to pull in Hull musician and bass player Trevor Bolder. Mick knew Trevor from the Jelly Roll Blues Band (later Flesh), which had also included Ched Cheesman and then John Bentley. Trevor played bass with Hype at live gigs, but Visconti played the bass parts on the band's studio recordings. In a throwback to the Rats days, Hype rehearsed at Woodmansey village hall. Their touring potential was limited by the lack of an active manager and confusion over the band's relationship with Bowie. Bookings were made through the Bronze agency owned by Gerry Bron, who launched his own record label in 1971. Hype were still under contract with Phillips, so Bronze were understandably reluctant to maximise the full potential of a band signed to another label.

With Woody, Mick and now Trevor on board, this was the embryonic line-up of the future Spiders from Mars. Benny was a strong rock and blues singer but unlike Bowie, he couldn't deliver in one crucial area – he wasn't a songwriter. Mick's experience with Bowie had led him to completely reverse the position he'd taken earlier in the Rats: cover versions of songs were now out. He wanted Hype, now renamed as Ronno, to produce original material, as Benny describes: 'Mick used to come up with the riffs and the chords and I used to write songs to it, or tried to. Nobody else wanted to write. Woody wouldn't write, and Trevor wouldn't write. It was, *You're the singer – you've got to write the words.* Mick was always in a hurry, it was like, *Write songs to order.* He'd maybe give me three riffs and I had to have words the next day type of thing, and it just didn't work like that, you don't write songs like that. The reason Ronno failed was there was no songwriter in the band, we couldn't write a song to save our lives really. We were just not songwriters, or we didn't have enough time to be songwriters, 'cause everything had to be done yesterday – We've got gigs to do. Come on we've got to be on the road. That was how it was – hurry, hurry.'

That November Ronno were back in London recording at Advision Studios, but the lack of songwriting ability and new material left them with little to show for it. Visconti provided the track 'Clorissa' and Benny with Mick wrote a Black Sabbath-style number called 'Power of Darkness'. The most appealing song was '4th Hour of My Sleep'. Benny recalls: 'The track was written by a friend of Tony Visconti, a guy called Tucker Zimmerman. Everybody thought that Bob Dylan had wrote it, 'cause all it says under the title is Zimmerman. He was like an acoustic folksinger and he played it to us and then he went off for the day. During the day we put it all together – solo, and harmonies on the solo. He come back and he says, "I left you a song and I've come back and I'm knocked out – absolutely fantastic." He was really pleased with it.' Ronno were filmed playing the song at the Marquee Club, with Visconti and Bolder sharing the stage, Tony playing rhythm and Trevor bass. The film was shot for a Swiss TV music programme. In January 1971 Phillips released '4th Hour of My Sleep' as a single on their Vertigo label with 'Power of Darkness' as the B side. The single failed to make an impact and any

Below: Mick playing at the Chestnut Cabaret, Pennsylvania, 8 November 1989.

Right: Photobooth pics of Mick and Keith 'Ched' Cheeseman, November 1968.

MILFORD GROVE

Left: Milford Grove on Greatfield Estate. The Ronson family lived at number 8 up to 2017.

Opposite Bottom Left: Ronson Close named in honour of Mick on Greatfield Estate.

Below: Mick in London in 1966, when he realised the streets were defintely not paved with gold.

Above: Rats gig poster for December 1967, Malton, North Yorkshire.

Below: Rats 1966 line up. L-R Benny Marshall, Geoff Appleby, Mick Ronson and Jim Simpson.

Above: The Rats East Park Free Concert, 24 August 1969.

Below: Flyer for East Park Free Concert, 28 September 1969.

Above: Former Hammonds Department Store whose music department was run by Rick Kemp and frequented by Mick.

Left: The original Fairview Studios in Keith Herd's house on Great Gutter Lane where Mick recorded with the Spiders.

Right: The later purpose-built Fairview Studios behind Keith Herd's house on Great Gutter Lane.

Below: Woodmansey Village Hall, where Mick often rehearsed with the Rats and later as Ronno.

Above: John Cambridge telling the 'Rats on Holiday story' live at the show 'Turn & Face the Strange'.

Left: Ched playing Mick's Les Paul guitar at BBC Radio Humberside.

Below: Dave Bradfield, drummer in three bands with Mick.

Above: Keith 'Ched' Cheesman with some Rats promo.

Right: Rats drummers John Cambridge and Jim Simpson.

THE happy STAR HOTEL ★ W. CROYDON
296 London Road, Broad Green
Monday, March 30th **DAVID BOWIES HYPE**
LIGHTS
SOUNDS ＋ **UGLY ROOM**
We are changing our night to Fridays and are pleased to begin with
BLACK SABBATH on FRIDAY, APRIL 3rd

Above & Left: Hype promo.

Below: Drummers John Cambridge and Woody Woodmansey meet on 4 August 2018 at Humber Sesh Festival.

Below: Montage of Hype in stage costumes 1970. L-R Tony Visconti, John Cambridge, Mick, Bowie.

Above: Princes Avenue Music Legends Mural.

Right: Mick Ronson mural on Greenwich Avenue shops, by the former Co-op where Mick worked.

Above: Mick with the Rats at Withernsea.

Above: Mick in tune and ready to play.

Left: Mick tuning other musicians guitars onstage.

Opposite Top: Gina Labrosse (Riley) with her photo of Bowie, Jeff Beck, her father Leon Riley, Mick and Dana Gillespie at the Cafe Royal party.

Opposite Bottom: Trevor Bolder who played in the Spiders and on Mick's two solo albums, playing later in Uriah Heep.

Above: Ian Hunter and Mick.

Opposite: Kevin Cann, Mick and baby Joachim, May 1991.

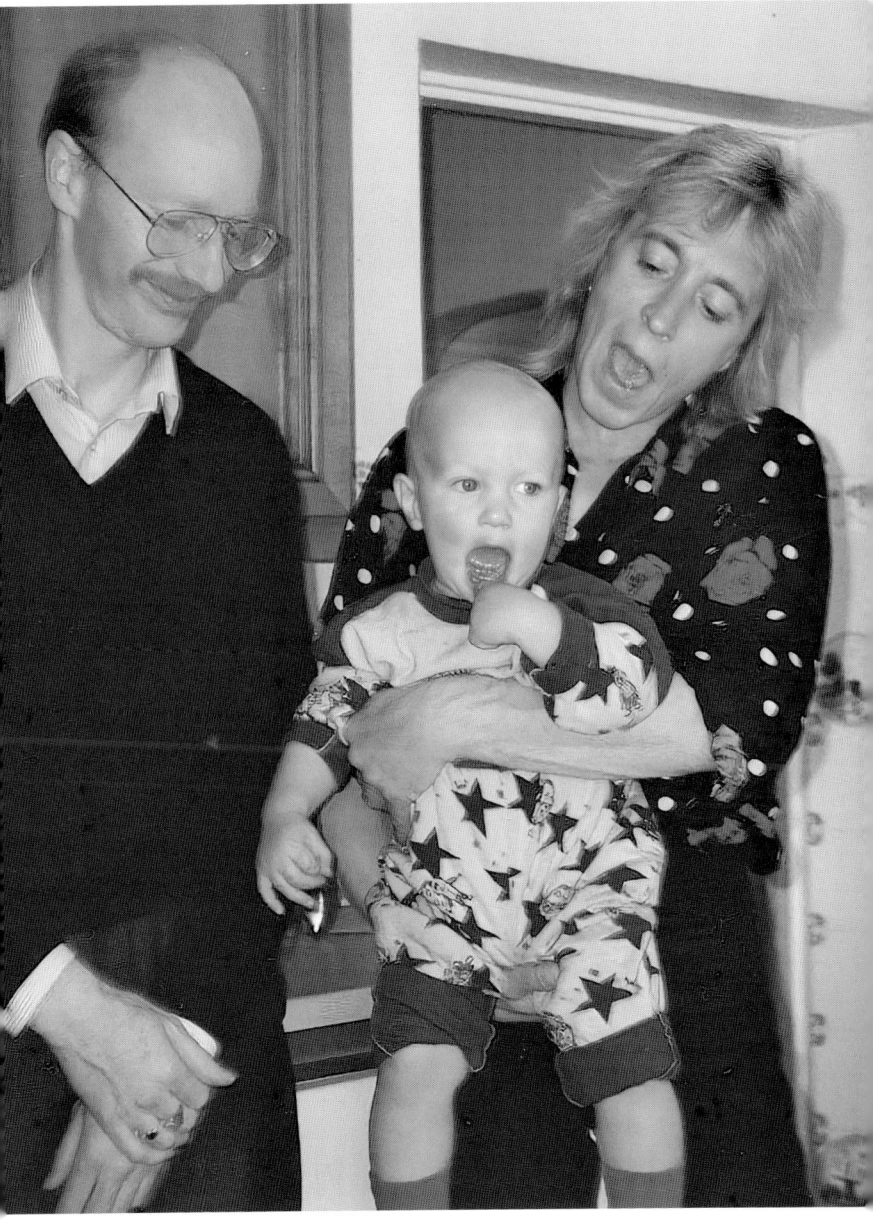

Above: The Spiders from Mars Plaque, Paragon Station, Hull.

Top Right: East Park where Mick worked as a gardener and where the Rats played in 1969.

Bottom Right: Mick Ronson Memorial Garden in East Park.

Below: Maggi Ronson with Guitar Sculpture artist Janis Skodins, June 2017.

prospect of a Ronno album was shelved.

As the months of 1971 went by, Mick's music career was stalling once again. His eponymous band was touring, but without Bowie or another songwriter in the mix, there was little future potential, according to Benny: 'It would have been great if we were just doing the album, 'cause we could sit and pull things to pieces and put things together. But when you have to go on the road and play – I mean we were playing venues like the Cavern Club and places like that, and you couldn't go into them places playing second-rate music, which is what we were playing. All the instruments were played brilliantly, but what they were playing with them wasn't very brilliant.'

On 10 April 1971, *The Man Who Sold the World* was finally released by Mercury in the UK, ten months after it had been recorded. Its cover showed Bowie wearing a flamboyant dress designed by '60s fashion designer Michael Fish. The album has gained considerable status retrospectively, but at the time of release it didn't sell well, perhaps failing to appeal to an audience of rock fans due to the cover. All that was to change – in September, Marc Bolan and T. Rex would release what became the bestselling album of 1971, *Electric Warrior*; Ziggy Stardust would make his first appearance the following year – but for now the world was not yet quite ready for an androgynous rock and roller. Mick must have felt some satisfaction with the record finally in the shops: it's the first album on which he performed on all tracks, and the first on which he played a pivotal creative role. He was not, however, credited as arranger, despite doing the arrangements with Visconti for most of the songs.

On 7 May Ronno played at the Temple Club in London and Bowie went with a group of friends to see them. Within a couple of weeks Bowie was on the phone to Mick in Hull suggesting they restart their collaboration. Mick said in later years that this period was the lowest point in his career and that Bowie was offering him an escape route at exactly the time he needed it most.

Within days he was back down at Haddon Hall with a mandate to put a new band together for Bowie. Perhaps wanting to keep all options open and aware that the split between Visconti and Bowie wasn't going to be healed at this point, Mick approached his old Mariners bandmate Rick Kemp and his regular playing partner Ritchie Dharma as potential bass player and drummer. Rick Kemp remembers them both going down to Haddon Hall, but instead of auditioning, they just had a chat with Bowie: 'His main interest seemed to be wanting to know if I was a relative of a mime artist called Lindsay Kemp.' The duo didn't get the gig. Mick brought back drummer Woody and Trevor Bolder on bass. Thus the three musicians from Hull came to join Bowie in the line-up that was to be later immortalised as the Spiders from Mars.

There are clear reasons why Mick, having jumped ship from Bowie just nine months earlier, now leapt at the chance to be back on board. The experiment with Ronno had failed: their single '4th Hour of My Sleep' made no impact on the charts, and their one attempt to record an album bombed due to their lack of songwriting skills. Visconti was even busier as producer now that Marc Bolan's career had taken off, and he was unlikely to be giving any further time to Ronno, whether in the studio or on the road. Mick probably realised that what he needed, only Bowie could offer: leverage and profile in the music industry, and most importantly the ability to write original songs. Mick knew he could bring all the elements that Bowie lacked and wanted: a creative music collaborator, gutsy rock 'n roll, and a band that could deliver it. At this stage in their respective careers, it made absolute sense for them both to give it a second go. Mick also knew that staying in Hull was not ultimately going to advance his music career; he needed to be in London. He was still in a relationship with Denise Irvin and their son would be born in October. There is no evidence of any plan or date for a wedding, despite the public announcement of their engagement over a year earlier. It is not known how, or indeed if, the pregnancy played any part in Mick's decision to return to London.

On 29 May 1971, Ronno the band played the Brickhouse in Hull, in what was probably their final gig. The Brickhouse was a short-lived alternative arts and music venue set up by Barry Nettleton and Rick Welton, which opened in April that year in a former Methodist Chapel on Baker Street in the city centre. It hosted a range of music, theatre and alternative arts events along with a Saturday café and market stalls. The Hull-based performance art collective COUM Transmissions, with Genesis P-Orridge and Cosey Fanni Tutti, performed there, as did Hull Truck Theatre Company with an early show. Jeff Parsons remembers seeing Ronno play the Brickhouse and he wasn't overly impressed: 'I remember going to see them there, kind of expecting to see something pretty special. This was when I was in a band of my own and I remember feeling a little bit, *They're not that great*, because I didn't think their material was that great. Mick was still a great player, but I remember thinking *It's not that great*. They played a song in which the line "it all depends on the pleasure man" was repeated ad infinitum.' It may seem

From Ronno to Ziggy: 1970–1971

surprising, given how relatively early this is in Mick's career, but the 1971 Brickhouse gig was probably the last time Mick Ronson ever played in his home city of Hull.

Bowie was booked to record on John Peel's radio show *In Concert* on 3 June, leaving little time for Mick, Woody and Trevor to assimilate the new numbers that Bowie had written and intended to perform. Trevor travelled down to London under the impression that Herbie Flowers was going to play bass on this session, but on arriving Bowie asked him to play. Like Mick the previous year, Trevor now had just a couple of days to learn and rehearse the tracks, flying by the seat of his pants during the 'as live' recording session. The experience was no doubt made even more surreal for him when Bowie entered the studio wearing his Mr Fish dress, which he had worn for the cover of *The Man Who Sold the World*. Performing with friends Dana Gillespie, George Underwood, Mark Carr-Pritchard and George Alexander, they performed a number of tracks that would appear on the subsequent *Hunky Dory* album. The band returned briefly to Hull after the session, then moved back down permanently to London, living first at Haddon Hall and then moving to their own flat in Beckenham. The band Ronno was defunct from this point on, and Benny Marshall found himself out of the running for a second time. Bowie clearly didn't need another vocalist and despite his assurances to Benny that he would try and sort something out with his manager Tony Defries, the recording of the *Hunky Dory* album put any further collaboration with Benny out of the picture: 'It was hard 'cause I'd given things up to be part of it. I always thought that it would be alright later, but Mick never actually came back. But that's the music business – you're in it for yourself and anybody else doesn't really matter. That's how the music business works.'

The US release of *The Man Who Sold the World* the previous November had generated enough airplay in the States for Mercury to organise a promotional trip to America for Bowie in January and February 1971. Once there, Bowie encountered a whole set of people and influences that was to kick-start a new phase in his music. On his return, he installed a piano at Haddon Hall and this became the main instrument for developing his new songs. It began with 'Oh! You Pretty Things', which was released as a single in April by Peter Noone of Herman's Hermits, reaching No. 12 in the UK charts by June. Tony Defries had meanwhile failed to secure a management deal with Stevie Wonder and Bowie was again his main focus. He started a campaign to negotiate a better record deal than the current one with Mercury, which was due to run out in June, or ditch them for a different label altogether. Bowie seemed to have found a more purposeful and positive attitude to his career and was re-energised and focused by the time he started recording the new album, *Hunky Dory*, on 8 June. Mick and Woody had recorded with Bowie before, but for Trevor it was a new and challenging experience: 'When we were working together Mick was an excellent, brilliant friend. He helped me a lot and looked after me, showed me what I should and shouldn't do. I was inexperienced in those days about what went on in studios. I think we learned a lot together.' Hull-born Trevor was also learning to navigate the new world of the cosmopolitan capital, including nightclubs frequented by Bowie such as the Sombrero Club, where to his surprise and consternation he realised, 'Everyone there was gay!!'

The pattern of work for recording the new album often meant Mick, Woody and Trevor would operate as a trio, building on Bowie's foundations of the song and nailing the track down before Bowie recorded the vocals. It was often done in just two takes to keep it spontaneous. Mick had the primary role as band leader and arranger, but also took on the responsibility for string arrangements, which had previously fallen to Tony Visconti. Despite his classical training in piano and violin, this meant Mick had to learn a new skill of scoring for an ensemble of string players, and then directing the assembled musicians in the recording studio. As Mick described when interviewed at the Hammersmith Odeon, it was a leap in the dark for him, and a leap of faith from Bowie. 'When Tony left, I kind of filled that spot writing arrangements and string arrangements. I'd never written string arrangements before but I could always write and read music, and I used to watch Tony writing this stuff out in his basement. I would help him write things out here and there, and I thought *If he can do it, so can I. I can read and write music, why couldn't I do some arrangements, why can't I do some orchestration?* We went out for dinner and we was with Dana Gillespie and Dana wanted some tracks recording, and some of them needed strings. And David said, "Oh, that's alright, Mick does string arrangements and he's going to do it." And I'm just sat there thinking like, *Gulp, I've never done one before in my life*, and I had to go home and do it.'

Back home in Hull the piano his mother Minnie had bought became an essential tool for working on the arrangements. At one end of the country was Bowie developing songs on his piano in Haddon Hall, and at the other Mick was doing the same with arrangements in the less

From Ronno to Ziggy: 1970–1971

grandiose setting of the family council house on Greatfield Estate. Mick took some music theory lessons from his sister Maggi's piano tutor, Mrs White, who lived in East Hull. In her day job Mrs White would play the piano in school assemblies for the gathered throngs of reluctant hymn-singing teenagers, who would soon be grooving to Ziggy and the Spiders from Mars, oblivious to the fact that their school assembly pianist had been tutoring one of them. Mick was more than willing to put in the effort and dedication needed to acquire this new skill. It was a further example of how the partnership with Bowie was based on shared creative risk-taking: 'It was like ploughing in head first. Back then you didn't have a synthesiser, you couldn't play it on a synthesiser and sequence it and it would play it all back to you – you kind of had to do it out your head, or pick up the guitar or check it on piano. It was a very good way to get into it. It was kind of like being thrown head first into it. David was really good at that too: he was always good at kind of pushing you forward to do something. And that's one of the greatest things about him, that he would let that happen. I mean, I could think of a million people that would say, "Oh no, he can't do that", and automatically dismiss it and get somebody who can do it. I always remember David for doing them things – he would always push you forward.' Paul Denman was impressed by Mick's readiness and ability to take it all on board: 'You have to remember the arrangements he was doing, and the string structures and parts he was writing, he'd never done that before. At least, there was no evidence that he had. None. Suddenly he steps up, he sees a gap, he sees that Bowie can't do it, so *I'm just going to go and do it*.'

On trips back to Hull Mick would also spend time with a younger friend, Kevin Hutchinson, who was keen to collaborate on new songs: 'At that time they were doing *Hunky Dory* and Michael didn't know if it would be a big success, he didn't even know if he was going to have a job. So he was looking to do other things, and he was looking to produce a lot, produce Dana Gillespie and a band called Milkwood. So we were starting to write songs together, Michael and I. So I'm in his house quite a lot, and I'm only this 16-, 17-year-old."

Kevin recalls how the arrangement came about for one of the album's iconic tracks: 'One day I'm in his house and he's explaining about this new song that David had written. I didn't even remember the title being "Life On Mars", but he played it to me on the piano. It sounded wonderful, because he was a good piano player, was Michael. He then said, "I've got to do an arrangement for it and I've got to make it sound like this." And he goes to the record player and puts on the record, "Wild Eyed Boy from Freecloud". "That's what I need on this song, this big orchestra, all this noise, I want it on this song and that's what I'm doing now." He had this score spread out on the piano and he said, "This is what I'm writing for this song." We finish that day, and the next morning I knock on his door, because I was a pest. I remember it was in the morning, and Mrs Ronson opens the door: "Oh, hello, Kevin." "Is Michael in?" "Yes, he hasn't been to bed, he's been up all night writing this score. He hasn't been to bed at all." When I went in, he didn't look tired or anything, he was fine and we got back to where we left off writing these songs.'

A few months later, in December, *Hunky Dory* was released. Kevin Hutchinson bought a copy at Star Disc record shop in Hull and met up again with Mick. 'I mentioned to him, "Oh, the 'Life On Mars' track, brilliant Michael, it's fantastic, done a great job." He said, "No, I messed it up, I totally ballsed it up. The string arrangement – I got it all wrong. We had all the musicians in the studio and it just wasn't right. So I had to scrap one section because it was totally wrong, and get recorders in to play that. And this other section I had a guitar part going on but there should have been strings there, and I'd ballsed that up as well. So basically it was a total balls-up." To me it has to be the greatest balls-up in rock music! You've got the fantastic tune, you've got Bowie's fantastic voice, then you've got the arrangement and you've got the guitar solo. Without the arrangement and the guitar solo, which are brilliant, that song would only be half as good as it is. It's amazing.'

'Life on Mars' was recorded on 6 August, on the last day of the sessions for *Hunky Dory* at Trident studios. Rick Wakeman played the piano part on the same Bechstein grand played by Paul McCartney on 'Hey Jude' and later by Freddie Mercury on 'Bohemian Rhapsody'. Mick introduced himself to the assembled group of BBC string players by taking his time rolling a cigarette, thus calming his own nerves and establishing his authority in his own inimitable style. They were so impressed by the song and the arrangement that they offered to do a third take which they felt they could improve upon on earlier ones, and this was the take used on the album. So whatever misgivings the famously modest Mick had shared with Kevin Hutchinson, there was no doubt that the BBC session musicians gave it their seal of approval.

Soon after recordings were complete, Hull musician John Bentley paid the band a visit at their flat in Beckenham. John had also moved down to London to pursue his music career and was living nearby, sharing a house with Arthur Brown: 'Trevor, Woody and Mick were

From Ronno to Ziggy: 1970–1971

living in a house just down the road from me, and they were just about to release *Hunky Dory*. They'd recorded it and Trevor phoned me up at home 'cause we still kept in touch and he said *Why don't I come over to the house*, 'cause it was literally walking distance from where I was living in Beckenham. So I walked over to the house and knocked on the door and I hadn't seen him since he'd joined the Spiders from Mars. The door opened and there was this alien with sort of green sideburns and orange hair. I knew it was him as soon as he went, "'Ello, John" 'cause he still had the accent. Anyway I went in and the whole band was there with David. They'd just got an acetate of the album *Hunky Dory*, so we all sat together and listened to it. It was an amazing experience, it was just incredible. At the time I was just hanging out with old mates from Hull and I remember listening to it and thinking what a fantastic album it was. They were all really, really chuffed with it, commenting on the sound, commenting on the mix and what could be a single. It was just an absolutely incredible experience, to be there at that time."

Earlier that year in the summer, Mick had done a few performances as a duo with Bowie. On 20 June they performed at Glastonbury Festival with Mick alternating on bass and six string guitars. The festival was in its infancy then and didn't have the celebrity cachet it has now. In 1971 it was much more of a low-key hippy affair and with the constant slippage of the performer schedule, Bowie and Mick ended up taking to the Pyramid Stage at 5 a.m. in the morning. Mick was not impressed and said in 1983: 'I hated Glastonbury. It was so cold and I had to try and sleep in a little tent on the grass. It wasn't much fun.' If Mick was still awake that evening, it's likely he got more pleasure from listening to the session they'd recorded for John Peel a few weeks earlier, which was broadcast that same day.

On 21 July, the duo performed at the Country Club at Haverstock Hill in London, with Rick Wakeman accompanying on piano. Bowie asked Wakeman if he would join the band. Rick agreed instantly but Bowie suggested he take some time to decide. By the next night Rick had been asked to join the band Yes, which he accepted. It's fascinating to speculate what the Spiders from Mars would have been like as a four-piece with Wakeman on keyboard.

On 11 August Bowie and Mick were back again at the Country Club. In the small audience were cast members from Andy Warhol's show *Pork*, which had opened at the Roundhouse in London earlier that month. It was stage-managed by Leee Black Childers and the cast included Cherry Vanilla and Tony Zanetta, who would all play a promotional role the following year in Tony Defries' MainMan management drive to make Bowie a megastar in America. Mick was exposed to the full force of the entourage's 'shock 'em dead' tactics when Bowie introduced them that night from the stage. Cherry Vanilla promptly displayed her bosom in acknowledgement. Leee Black Childers recalled: 'All of that kind of stuff really wasn't Mick. That wasn't the way he was and it really embarrassed him. If he could have blushed under that snow-white Hull skin, he probably would have!' Mick and Bowie saw *Pork* at the Roundhouse, and afterwards went to the Sombrero Club, where Cherry Vanilla came on strong to Mick. He was accustomed to female attention but her approach was more direct and forthright than he was used to – in her words: 'I was practically attacking him sexually!' On a more aesthetic level, this connection to the Warhol crowd was the start of a two-way transatlantic exchange of ideas, style and music that would come to fruition with Ziggy the following year and lead to collaborations with Lou Reed and Iggy Pop.

By August Tony Defries had contractually become Bowie's manager and that month flew to the States to negotiate a new record deal with a list of potential companies including United Artists and RCA. Back in London Mick and the band still hadn't any formal contract as such, but were on enough money to pay the rent on their flat, enjoy life in London and record in the studio. In September Mick flew to New York with Bowie and Defries to sign and promote the newly secured record deal with RCA. It was Mick's first trip to the States and most likely his first ever flight on a plane. The boy from the council estate in Hull, still only in his mid-twenties, was clearly going places, and this was the first of many transatlantic flights over the course of his career. In New York they teamed back up with the *Pork* crowd, who showed them the nightlife of the Big Apple, and Bowie finally got to meet Andy Warhol, along with Iggy Pop and Lou Reed. Bowie still owed Mercury a third album under the previous deal, but Defries had negotiated aggressively with the company. He agreed to pay back all the costs of recording and promoting *David Bowie* (aka *Space Oddity*) and *The Man Who Sold the World* in return for Mercury releasing Bowie from his commitment to deliver a third album. This not only secured Defries the rights on those previous albums, it also meant that *Hunky Dory* was already lined up for release by RCA.

Back in London Mick and Bowie performed again as a duo, recording on 21 September a session for Bob Harris' *Sound of the Seventies* radio show broadcast on 4 October. The band's first public gig

From Ronno to Ziggy: 1970–1971

with Trevor Bolder in the line-up was at Friars Club in Aylesbury on 25 September. It started with some Bowie solo acoustic songs, then built over the set with increasing rock guitar energy from Mick, ending with 'Waiting for the Man'. It wasn't yet Ziggy and the Spiders from the Mars, but it was moving in that direction.

A more momentous event in Mick's personal life took place on 14 October 1971 when his fiancée Denise Irvin gave birth to their son Nicholas at Hull Royal Infirmary. Nick's arrival into the world came in the short gap between recording the *Hunky Dory* and *Ziggy Stardust* albums, right at the point when Mick's music career was about to take off. In a few months he would embark on what would turn out to be almost a year and a half of continuous touring throughout Britain, America and Japan. It wasn't the most appropriate context in which to be a first-time father, and the relationship with Denise and his son would end.

By the close of October, Mick and the band were busy at Underhill rehearsal studio in Blackheath rehearsing material with Bowie for what would become the *Ziggy Stardust* album. The recordings proper began on 8 November at Trident studios and would continue for a week, with Mick's stunning solo for 'Moonage Daydream' recorded on 12 November. Bowie's songwriting output that year was remarkable, with recordings for the second album starting before Hunky Dory was even released, on 17 December.

Hunky Dory marked a shift in musical emphasis from *The Man Who Sold the World*. Mick's strong influence on the previous album is clearly identifiable with its heavy rock sound and extended guitar solos. *Hunky Dory* has a much gentler, piano-driven set of tracks that are highly melodic and at times almost commercial pop songs, but with Bowie's original quirky twist. Mick's influence on this album was to underpin and enhance the songs through his arrangements, rather than making his guitar work a dominant factor. For the first time Mick received an album credit both as a performer and arranger, and his string arrangements on 'Kooks', 'Quicksand', 'Fill Your Heart', and the sublime 'Life on Mars' are a fundamental part of the album's quality and appeal. The only track that harked back to Mick's work on the previous album is 'Queen Bitch', which was also a precursor of what was to come with Ziggy Stardust.

As far as his music career was concerned, Mick ended 1971 in a much stronger position than he'd started the year. He now had two albums under his belt and a third was in the making. He was earning a living from his music without having to juggle or compromise his ambitions with the demands of a day job. Although money was by no means plentiful, he was living within his means, and in the 1975 interview with *Hit Parader* he looked back on the tougher times he'd lived through up to this point: 'For about five years I had one pair of shoes a year, if that, and I used to get one pair of trousers. I've really been through all that. I was really scraping a bit. I was doing that for a long time and I thought, Well, I'm getting older, is this ever going to end? At the time it's so depressing. Sometimes I sat down and cried because I thought, What am I going to do, and Why can't I do this, and Why won't this happen? Then it just happened."

His creative partnership with Bowie was solid, and in the year ahead the two careers would align ever closer. Mick would become the essential sideman to David Bowie, both in the studio and onstage. He would achieve a level of fame and recognition as vivid as in those dreams he'd enjoyed as a teenager in a council house in Hull. In place of the Stones, it would be the Spiders. The dream was about to become real.

7 Ziggy Played Guitar:
1972

The Mick Ronson Story

On 4 January, 1972, Mick and the band were back in London with Bowie after the Christmas and New Year break to rehearse the remaining songs for *Ziggy Stardust*. On 7 January, RCA released the single 'Changes' from *Hunky Dory*, but the band's focus was very much on the new *Ziggy* album and upcoming tour. Defries had delivered an early acetate to RCA, who felt the album was lacking a single, so Bowie obliged by writing 'Starman', which was recorded at Trident along with 'Suffragette City' and 'Rock 'n' Roll Suicide' on 4 February. As many commentators have observed, it seems remarkable the iconic 'Starman' was such a late addition to the album, replacing the Chuck Berry cover 'Around and Around'. It also underlines how the whole Ziggy concept was a work in progress with a degree of retrofitting of ideas to an emerging set of songs, rather than a fully formed concept from the outset. Some of the songs had their first public airing on Bob Harris' BBC radio show *Sounds of the Seventies* at the end of January, including 'Hang On to Yourself', 'Ziggy Stardust', and 'Five Years'. With recordings complete the band felt they were on to something, that Ziggy was going to make an impact, as Trevor describes: 'When we finished the *Hunky Dory* album, I really liked it, but it didn't feel particularly special, not like it was going to be a big-selling album. That did happen with *Ziggy Stardust*, though. When we finished that album, everybody knew something was going to happen. Especially when we heard 'Moonage Daydream' coming out of the speakers after it was mixed. There was something magical starting to happen.'

Ziggy Stardust represents Bowie's full transition from folk-rock singer-songwriter to a hard-edged rock and roller, and Mick Ronson was central to the success of that transformation. The music was the prime element, but it was also a package combining social ideas, science fiction, image, fashion, ambiguous sexuality and theatricality. Through Ziggy, Bowie was not only reinventing himself, he was creating a brand. Defries' strategy to make Bowie an international star involved the established mix of a touring show, exposure in the press and on radio and TV, and the release of a single in April, building momentum to the release of the album in June. What set it apart was that Bowie, his alter ego Ziggy and the Spiders from Mars, not only offered great music and entertainment, they generated and then rode a wave of cultural and social change. It was music to be enjoyed on its own terms, but it was also controversial, challenging, risky and subversive and it transformed society. It changed the way things were.

The Ziggy persona allowed Bowie to explore the idea of a singer-

Ziggy Played Guitar: 1972

performer as a character, enacting a story journey through the sequence of live songs. This didn't require dialogue, interaction between actors, or a structured sequence of dramatic scenes, let alone a coherent plot or storyline. It didn't imitate musicals or opera. It was still rooted firmly in a live band playing a gig, but incorporated theatrical elements such as expressive movement and mime, choreographed sequences, costumes, lighting and stage set design. These were all employed with the aim of enhancing the meaning of the songs and the total experience of the live music event. If the concept served the band, and the band were good, the format was stunning, but it was not without risk: it carried with it the perils of camp theatricality, pomposity and pretentiousness, of the sort parodied to great comic effect in the 1984 film *This is Spinal Tap*. Bowie, however, was able to align content and form: Ziggy Stardust was a fictional rock star with a band, bringing a message to his audience and the world through the medium of rock music – and the music was terrific. Bowie's performance, allied with Mick Ronson's guitar and the driving force of Woody and Trevor, were all stunning components. The ace in the pack was the element of risk and danger, which came with Bowie's androgynous, ambiguous sexuality. Breaking sexual rules had always been at the heart of rock and roll, but this took it to a whole new level: this was transgressing perceived notions of gender identity and revelling in it. For Mick and the other Spiders from Hull, this was out of their comfort zone. Whilst confident with the music, they were on a somewhat scary rollercoaster ride with Bowie, which challenged their own attitudes to male sexuality, image and identity. In Bowie's world they had to do what his song instructed – turn and face the strange.

Back in the autumn of '71, Bowie had encouraged the band to expand their cultural horizons. He was keen for them to see theatre productions and appreciate the role played by theatre lighting, with a view to how they might incorporate it in their gigs. They'd built up a friendship with the cast of Warhol's *Pork*, and Bowie knew that theatre could be cool and was not restricted to the tired models of traditional repertory. In November they saw Alice Cooper perform at the Rainbow in London – with John Bentley's Beckenham housemate Arthur Brown on the same bill. Alice Cooper used a live snake in the shock rock show and had his band dressed in tight, sequined, glam rock costumes. Bowie was later dismissive of Alice Cooper's theatricality, but now he was clearly checking out the competition, and did the same again later that June when Alice Cooper played the Empire Pool Wembley.

Bowie's personal image makeover for Ziggy began with his hair.

The Mick Ronson Story

The long flowing locks of the Pre-Raphaelite troubadour were pulled back and recoloured on the album cover image for *Hunky Dory*. Then in January 1972 he had it cut short with the distinctive Ziggy mullet. The style was created by local Beckenham hairdresser Suzi Fussey, with the distinctive colouring added later that year once the band were on tour. Suzi was taken on as part of the tour entourage and would become Mick's girlfriend, wife and mother to his daughter Lisa.

The second element for Ziggy was stage costume. In December '71 the film *A Clockwork Orange* was given a UK release and Bowie and the Spiders all went to see it. The film was a big influence on the image Bowie wanted for Ziggy and the Spiders. He copied the droog-style, one-piece costumes with their collarless bomber jackets and tuck-in trousers. He also mimicked the bovver boots, opting for brightly coloured patent leather wrestling boots. Designer and Sombrero Club regular Freddie Buretti suggested colourful fabrics in place of the white cotton boiler suits used in the film, to lessen any suggestion of violence. Angie Bowie scoured local shops to source the material. The band were taken by the idea of being a gang but were appalled when they saw what was being suggested at a costume meeting at Haddon Hall. Bowie wanted Trevor to wear a blue one-piece, Mick a gold one and Woody pink. Woody remembers the reaction it provoked: 'Mick actually left one day. It was the day when David asked him to put on the gold suit. He just used too many swear words to repeat. He packed his case and was at the station. He said, "You must be joking, I'm not going out like that." Bowie asked me to go and sort him out. "We need him back." I went to the station and sat on the platform with Mick and talked. He came back and eventually he got into it.'

Bowie and the band played their first try-out Ziggy gig in costume on 29 January at Friars, Aylesbury, which was attended by an expectant crowd of Bowie fans with an excited buzz in the air. The band went down a storm. In the audience were Freddie Mercury and Roger Taylor from Queen: 'We were blown away. It was so fantastic, like nothing else that was happening and so far ahead of its time.... I hate to gush but he did have it like no one else did at the time.' Kris Needs who would go on to be a rock journalist and editor of *ZigZag* magazine was at the Aylesbury gig: 'That night lit the fuse on everything – the 70s, glam, punk rock and all that came after. Here was the future, though it was grounded in old-school Judy Garland showbiz, the theatre and New York's underground as directed by Andy Warhol, Lou Reed and Stanley Kubrick. Like the Stones before him, Bowie's impact would extend much further and deeper than the music, straddling image, pop culture – and social taboos.'

Mick, Trevor and Woody's initial resistance to the way Bowie wanted them to look onstage, gave way to a grudging acceptance and then total embrace. Bowie had his hair dyed orange by Suzi Fussey and the Spiders followed suit. Woody had his hair bleached blonde, Trevor had his dyed jet-black and his sideburns sprayed silver, while Mick, whose long blond hair was already a head-turner for the girls, simply needed a bit of highlighting and styling. Mick would mirror Bowie and bare his trim torso on stage, and Trevor and Woody became accustomed of sorts to their blue and pink outfits. They were a gang, albeit of an extraterrestrial order, and certainly not the kind of gang you might find on the backstreets of a Hull estate. The final hurdle was make-up and that barrier was breached in June.

Before appearing on *Top of the Pops* that summer, Bowie and the Spiders performed 'Starman' on the ITV Granada children's show *Lift Off with Ayshea*. In the dressing room Bowie brought out a bag of make-up and began to apply it, suggesting the others should do the same. Their 'No way!' reaction was cleverly countered by Bowie, who said that under the studio TV lights their faces would look green, so they duly complied. It was then a small step to wearing make-up onstage for gigs. Within weeks it would lead to the amusing situation where Mick was in the dressing room before a gig and completely lost his cool with the others, accusing them of stealing his mascara. A northern sense of wind-up humour soon encompassed their new alien look. That year Rick Kemp joined Steeleye Span and, keen to appear in the style of how he thought the folk-rock band would look, turned up for their first rehearsals in London wearing mediaeval hippy clothes. Mick met up with his old Hull bandmate along with Trevor and Woody, all in their Spiders glam rock gear because they were in the middle of a photo shoot with Bowie. The Pythonesque encounter of a mediaeval-garbed Rick Kemp and a bunch of alien glam rockers prompted Mick's dry Yorkshire humour: 'Are you going out tonight?' he asked Rick. 'Yes.' 'What – dressed like that!?'

The territory that was far more problematic for the three Hull Spiders, came with Bowie's public announcement that he was bisexual. Before the Ziggy tour had started, he declared in an interview published on 22 January in the widely read *Melody Maker*: 'I'm gay and always have been.' The article was intelligent rather than sensationalist, and writer Michael Watts contextualised Bowie's announcement both in terms of the rock and roll tradition of shock and outrage, as well as contemporary social mores: 'The expression of his sexual ambivalence establishes a fascinating game: is he, or isn't he? In a period of conflicting sexual identity he shrewdly exploits the confusion surrounding the male and female roles.' The Ziggy persona had yet to make a public appearance, but Watts had already identified the androgyny and sexual ambiguity at its heart. He also differentiated between Bowie as a skilled artist playing with these ambiguities, as opposed to a mere drag-act. Mick and the Spiders struggled, though: they were a gang with a shared stage image, so were uncomfortable with the implication by association that they too were gay or bisexual. At the same time they were all aware that Bowie's statement was progressive, subversive and liberating.

Homosexuality had been decriminalised just five years earlier with the Sexual Offences Act of 1967, but this only legitimised same sex acts in private. Gay men were still being arrested and charged for committing acts of gross indecency, and in the decade following the 1967 Act, prosecutions under this law trebled. In 1972 being gay meant being ridiculed and stigmatised by large sections of the British public. Or worse – violently assaulted. Mick later described Bowie's 'self-outing' as 'a very brave thing to do', but it clearly challenged him at the time, as he made clear in a 1975 interview for the American music magazine *Circus*: 'I took it quite seriously because he wasn't kidding. I didn't like it at first, but then you get used to it. You got used to so many people around being bisexual that you got used to it for yourself. But it shook me up. I felt, "Wow, what are people going to say."'

Perceptions of male identity had been changing ever since the advent of long hair with the Beatles and the popular culture of the flower power hippies in the 1960s. Indeed, Mick with his long blond hair was, as far as his appearance went, already in that territory of male-female crossover. But it's one thing to look like a cool rock star. Looking like anything else might play less well. What would be the impact on his family? 'When David came out and said he was gay, that's a pretty shocking thing to say at the time. It was very outrageous then. I was kind of a little bit in shock really. And it wasn't a very good thing to say, especially up north. My family got a lot of flak for this. I gave my mother and father a car and somebody threw paint all over it.' According to Woody the car was daubed with the words 'Ronson is a poof'. Suzi Ronson believes a line was crossed just once by Bowie in relation to Mick: 'David wanted Mick to pretend that he was gay. He wanted Mick to announce that they were this bisexual bureau. Mick got really really, really cross and said, "No

Ziggy Played Guitar: 1972

fucking way!" He stormed off. I think he went back up to Hull. David had to talk him into coming back down to London. It was never asked of him again.'

Mick knew his own boundary, but as with the issue of stage costumes and make-up, the longer you were in the world of Bowie – and the tour was pulling in huge audiences, including scores of adoring females – the easier it became to assimilate what was unfamiliar and uncomfortable at the outset. By the summer of '72 the Spiders themselves were having a joke on men who felt threatened by their appearance. They would wind up studio engineers and technicians, invariably male, who expressed any wariness in their presence or were unnerved that they might not be entirely straight. The Spiders would throw out comments such as *That one's got nice legs* and *Not as nice as his*. They'd learnt to outface the strange. Despite the success of the Ziggy tour, they were still exposed to homophobic abuse: shouts of 'Queers!' followed them aggressively. Mick's former Rats roadie Stuey George was hired as personal security on the tour.

On 8 February Bowie, Mick, Trevor and Woody watched their first television appearance as a band on Bob Harris' *The Old Grey Whistle Test*, which had been recorded the previous night. Wearing their glam rock, droog suits they performed 'Five Years' and 'Queen Bitch'; 'Oh You Pretty Things' had also been recorded but was not broadcast. Back in Hull, Mick's friend Steve Magee had a foretaste of how the city's older generation would react: 'I'd be sat in watching *Old Grey Whistle Test* and there was Bowie and Mick Ronson on. And the door would go and me dad come in. "I aren't watching that bloody rubbish!" And that was it. I'd say, "I was watching that!" "Who pays the bloody licence? When you pay the licence, you can watch it!" It was "all those bloody poofters" and that's the way it was.'

The official UK tour of Ziggy began on 10 February at the Toby Jug in Tolworth. It was the start of a 45-date tour ending in mid-July at the Friars Club in Aylesbury where they had started with their try-out gig. Although the tour began with a low-key mix of pubs and small venues, its growing success led to increasingly larger venues being booked and the addition of more theatrical elements to the show. By the end of the tour the gigs would be sold out, Bowie would be a star, and the Bowie/Ronson partnership would be on a par with that of Jagger/Richards. As with the Roundhouse gig two years earlier, Mick was still prone to the charge that his playing drowned out the rest of the band. In a neat reversal of the classic *Spinal Tap* scene, where guitarist Nigel Tufnel shows the extra volume number added to his amp, Bowie's roadies secretly adjusted Mick's Marshall amp so the volume level was below what it was registering on the dial.

At the end of April, 'Starman/Suffragette City' was released as a single in the UK and a month later in the US. Early sales were slow, reaching only No. 41 in the UK charts, although by May the tour dates were selling out. Then came the groundbreaking appearance on *Top of the Pops* in July, which sent the single racing back up the charts.

In the same month, Bowie produced the single 'All the Young Dudes', recorded by Mott the Hoople. Mott enjoyed a big following for live shows but their records, including four albums by this point, simply didn't sell. After a dispiriting tour of Switzerland, the band decided to fold. Bass guitarist Pete Overend Watts approached Bowie to see if he needed a bass player, and on learning of the intended demise of the band, Bowie offered them 'All the Young Dudes'. The single was released in July, reached No. 3 in the charts and became a rousing anthem for the youth of the time and ever since. Bowie effectively saved the band and propelled them in the direction of glam rock, sporting platform boots and spray-can hair colours. Bowie also produced the album of the same name, which reversed the band's history of album failures, reaching No. 21 in the charts. Mick Ronson added a string arrangement for the track 'Sea Diver', written out on the back of a cigarette packet. Ian Hunter paid him the 'mates rates' fee of just £20. It was the start of what would grow into a lifelong friendship between Mick and Ian.

Bowie's growing profile on the back of the tour, along with Defries' relentless promotion in the runup to the album release, saw Mick recording two radio sessions at the BBC for *Sounds of the Seventies* in May: the 16th and the 23rd. He also made his second promotional trip to the States within a year with Bowie and Defries. Then finally, on 16 June, *The Rise and Fall of Ziggy Stardust* and *the Spiders from Mars* was released by RCA. The much-hyped album didn't fail to disappoint. In the first week it sold 8000 copies in Britain and was in the Top 10 album chart by the second week. It continued selling well throughout the year and peaked at No. 5 in the UK charts in February 1973. It went platinum in the UK and gold in the States. An indication of the enduring appeal of the album was its return to the UK charts in 1981 during the New Romantic period. It is the second highest-selling album from Bowie's entire catalogue, surpassed only by 1983's *Let's Dance*.

Bowie's story concept for Ziggy tells of an omnisexual alien sent to Earth to deliver a message to humanity that has only five years of

Ziggy Played Guitar: 1972

existence remaining. The message of hope foretells the coming of a Starman who will save Earth, but the messenger Ziggy is himself destroyed by his own rock and roll excesses. Or something like that. What mattered wasn't so much any plausibility of the story, but the way it could function as a scaffold on which to hang a terrific set of rock and roll songs, that packed a visceral punch with memorable tunes. The Ziggy concept could also be endlessly analysed, discussed and reflected on by fans and pundits, young or middle-aged, while Bowie's lyrics give enough imaginative space for listeners to formulate their own interpretation of their meaning. The rich mix of rock and roll, and its liberal all-embracing attitude to sexual expression and personal freedom, made it a winner, especially for a younger generation that was exploring and expressing their personal and tribal identity. Mick's influence is significant, ranging from stunning guitar solos to skilled string arrangements, and his overriding talent for enhancing Bowie's songs with memorable riffs or a driving rock rhythm. The album is a perfect synthesis of Mick's heavy rock of *The Man Who Sold the World* and Bowie's melodic songwriting of *Hunky Dory*.

On 17 June the Ziggy promo machine notched up a gear when photographer Mick Rock captured the infamous 'guitar fellatio' moment at the performance at Oxford Town Hall. With Mick's back to the audience and Bowie between his legs, mouth at the height of Mick's guitar, it gave the impression that Bowie was giving Mick a blow job. Defries paid for the photograph to be published in an advert in the following week's issue of *Melody Maker*, thus gaining further notoriety, increased ticket sales, and another prod to Mick's anxieties about how far he should be going along with the bisexual theatricality of the Ziggy circus.

With 'Starman' hitting the UK singles charts, it gave them an entrée to *Top of the Pops* – the Holy Grail for any band wanting commercial success. Bowie hadn't enjoyed a chart hit since 'Space Oddity' three years earlier, and as far as the majority of the audience watching on the evening of 6 July 'Starman' could easily be mistaken at first as the follow-up. As the camera panned back from Bowie's direct knowing gaze to reveal a multicoloured, crotch-tight, figure-hugging one-piece costume, it became instantly obvious that something startling had happened to the permed-hair, hippy folksinger from a previous age. The message was hammered home with the band strutting in blue, gold and pink costumes and brightly coloured boots. This was not the Bowie of before, nor was it the denim jacket and jeans of old school rock and roll. In a louche gesture that was both friendly but intimate, Bowie draped his arm round Mick Ronson's shoulders, ensuring a drop-jawed response of either delight or disgust in the living rooms of Britain. The gesture could be read as a bloke acknowledging a mate or getting up close with his lover. A few moments later Bowie looks directly at the camera singing the line, 'I had to phone someone, so I picked on you' and his pointing finger left little doubt in the mind of anyone watching that he was talking directly to you. Looking back at the clip half a century later, it seems tame and innocuous, but then it sent shockwaves through the country. It was beaming out a message that could be read two ways. For those who were receptive, particularly the younger generation, it was saying: 'I've got your back. Whoever you are, however you swing, come and join me.' But as Paul Trynka observed in his book *Starman*, parents would read it differently: it was time now to lock up not only your daughters but also your sons!

Many people mark this prime-time broadcast as a life-changing rite of passage moment, either prompting them to become a musician or speaking to their sexuality, or helping to define their own sense of identity. Paul Denman: 'Every pop star I talk to from my generation – you know, Boy George, even George Michael, and I knew them all – they go back to Ziggy. They go back to the arm around the shoulder. You have to remember at the time men did not touch men, no way, you did not touch. So when David is putting his arm around Mick on *Top of the Pops*, he might as well have been saying, "Hello, world, this is my girlfriend!" It just wasn't done and I remember looking at the telly going, "Oh my God!!! What happened!" It was a game changer.'

Whatever the response individually, there was a clear split down generational lines. The song's chorus was strikingly similar to and evocative of Judy Garland's 'Over the Rainbow', with an octave jump on the word 'Starman' akin to 'Somewhere'. It was as if Bowie was taking the emotional memory of an older generation, reclaiming and re-channelling it as a message for contemporary youth. It was a double whammy, offering the empowering shock of the new for its receptive youth audience and simultaneously giving the two fingers to their outraged elders.

Bowie carried the duality of his onstage persona into his real life, but Mick kept the two distinctly separate, as Suzi Ronson describes: 'When Mick was onstage he was like an evil doll with his make-up and hair and facial expressions. Then when he came off he was just a real nice lad.' For viewers in Hull like Paul Denman, the disparity between

Ziggy Played Guitar: 1972

the talented local lad that everyone knew as charming and polite, and the images that were beaming across their television screens was startling: 'This kid lived across the street from me on Greatfield. I'd seen him mowing the lawns on Bilton Grange estate. And it seemed like the week after that, he was on *Top of the Pops* with Bowie. It was astonishing. He took a lot of stick. "He was a fag and a poof and a queer", but he wasn't. None of them were. Me and my mate put make-up on and went out in the town and got the shit kicked out of us. It wasn't that kind of town. You couldn't be effeminate.'

The generational split occurring throughout the country was certainly evident in Hull, as Lynne Mitchell recalls: 'I thought it was wonderful, but my dad... He said, "What the hell's he got on?!" I said, "Dad that was the lad that was on the Co-op van, don't you remember?" He said, "Well, he looks like a right nancy." He was a bit straight-laced, he was an old navy man, was my dad, and Lycra belonged on girls. He said, "They should've got dressed up properly for coming on telly!" In my dad's eyes, there was something the matter with them.' Mick's Hull friend Les Morfitt also recalls: 'Mick turned up at my mother's and he had his long hair and it was just after 'Starman' had been on Top of the Pops. My mum loved him to bits, but my dad was straight-laced: *Get your bloody hair cut!* You know, that sort of thing. My dad said to him, "Don't ever knock on my front door again, walk round the back. You look like a poof!"'

While Mick was enjoying new heights of success and recognition in the national media, his anxieties about the response back home in Hull and the impact on his family were proving justified. Sister Maggi got abuse from teenage girls referring to 'her poof brother', and mother Minnie was for a time sent to Coventry at her workplace at Imperial Typewriters: 'People were really jealous round here when he made it on the telly. They snubbed me because they thought I was rich, they sent me to Coventry.' The homophobic taunts that culminated in the vandalism of the family car were indicative of the culture of the time and not unique to Hull, but were naturally upsetting for the Ronson family. They could of course take solace and satisfaction in the fact that their son and brother was fast becoming a star, that his achievement was based on his remarkable musical talent, and no amount of bigotry could ever detract from that. To many in Hull Mick was a local hero, the estate lad 'done good', and for some, Mick and Bowie were articulating what had previously been unspoken or unrepresented on mainstream media. For Hull teenager Graham Jenkinson, it offered a route to self-realisation and empowerment: 'You couldn't really come out and go to school with your hair dyed red and say: "I'm gay" in my time at school. I wasn't particularly sure of my sexuality at that stage and Bowie shone out like a beacon. The lyrics were often pretty direction-giving for people who might be lost between phases of sexuality. It was just so life-changing that I wasn't the only person in the world that had those feelings. I think it was just an affirmation that I don't have to be hidden. I don't have to be forgotten or bottom of the pile, or abused or obscured by people with more power than you. That was a unique talent that Bowie had, engendering personal power in people, giving them confidence to believe in themselves. It was a beacon of hope for everybody, for getting through that gloomy period of politics to a better world that I think we all wanted at that time. Sexual politics were changing and it went hand in hand with that.'

The first leg of the UK Ziggy tour ended in July. While Trevor and Woody flew with David and Angela Bowie to holiday on Cyprus, Mick flew to Toronto to work in the studio with American country rock band Pure Prairie League. The trip set a precedent for his many future collaborations with scores of musicians and bands across different continents.

That August Ziggy was scheduled for two shows at the Rainbow Theatre in London, with a third added due to demand. Bowie took the opportunity to develop the theatrical elements of the show, incorporating a multilevel scaffold set, projected images and a troupe of androgynous dancers choreographed by Bowie's former mime mentor Lindsay Kemp. The shows were a commercial and critical success with a high level of media exposure.

Mick and Bowie alternated rehearsals at the Rainbow with co-producing Lou Reed's album *Transformer*, recorded in just ten days in August. Bowie was a fan of the Velvet Underground, penning 'Queen Bitch' on *Hunky Dory* as an homage to Lou Reed, and performing 'Waiting for the Man' and 'White Light/White Heat' both onstage and in radio sessions. Defries was adding Lou Reed and Iggy Pop to his stable of artists and brought them both over to Britain that summer. Lou Reed guested in early July with Bowie and the Spiders at a Friends of the Earth gig at Royal Festival Hall. On 14 July he performed solo for the first time in the UK at Kings Cross Cinema, and Mick and Bowie both attended. Mick's role on *Transformer* was hugely significant, being co-producer, arranger and primary session musician, and playing lead guitar, piano and recorder. He also provided the arrangement for 'Perfect Day' and

Ziggy Played Guitar: 1972

without his memorable piano and strings, it's hard to imagine the song being anything other than average. The original demo featured just the vocal from Lou Reed along with his choppily strummed and slightly out-of-tune acoustic guitar. It needed Mick Ronson's arrangement to make it something special. As Paul Denman describes: 'Lou Reed wrote those songs, then Michael thought, *I can do something with that*, and that was his skill. His skill was *I can add to this great song*. He was a song helper rather than a songwriter, and that is a fantastic skill to have. It's as good as songwriting. Given the right material he could elevate it into something wonderful, something that Bowie or Lou Reed probably didn't expect that it could be elevated to. That's the genius of the bloke.'

Mick remembered the recording sessions as focused and fulfilling, and with his usual modesty, downplayed his own contribution: 'Working with Lou Reed on *Transformer*, that was a very good experience, a really great album to work on. It was great. It seemed to go real quick and real easy. We'd bring the musicians in whatever the song was going to be that day, we'd go in there, record it and leave. It was kind of as simple as that.' Mick also painted an amusing picture of Lou's laconic style: 'Lou was so laid-back. He'd kind of walk into the studio and go *Hey* – sort of sit down in the chair and put his guitar on. It would be all out of tune and he'd go *Are we ready?* and this guitar's way out of tune. I'd tune it up, and Lou used to look at me – he didn't really care whether it was in tune or out of tune really, he just wanted to sing the song. Lou used to say some funny things like *Can you make it a little bit more grey* or something. I mean then to me, *What the hell's he talking about?* I guess he was just trying to explain things in a more artistic way, I suppose. It was kind of going over my head a bit, but it was great you know and, as I say, it was done very quickly.' *Transformer* was released that November and reached No. 13 in the UK charts, along with the classic hit single 'Walk on the Wild Side/ Perfect Day'.

Bowie and the Spiders undertook a second mini tour of the UK from the end of August, but the main event that autumn was Ziggy's first tour of the States. Defries opened a New York office of MainMan, staffed by the 'trio terrible' of Tony Zanetta, Leee Black Childers and Cherry Vanilla, who were now on the payroll to promote the tour, travelling to cities in advance of the show. After a turbulent flight home from holiday in Cyprus, Bowie avoided any future air travel. He travelled to the States by boat, sailing from Southampton on the *QE2*, while the rest of the band made the transatlantic flight, arriving on 18 September. The tour entourage included Suzi Fussey on hair and make-up, Mick Rock on

The Mick Ronson Story

tour photography and film, and Stuey George along with Tony Frost as security. In New York Mick auditioned jazz pianist Mike Garson, who got the gig and began what would be a lifetime of playing with Bowie. The Ziggy tour travelled the States by bus and train, with the band not only performing 22 shows between late September and early December, but also developing many of the songs for the next album, *Aladdin Sane*, with some being recorded in the States. The slower travel by bus and train offered an immersion into Americana, which Bowie and the Spiders fully embraced and used to good effect on the album. The tour crossed America, playing Cleveland, New York, Chicago, Detroit, Phoenix, Philadelphia and Los Angeles amongst other cities.

Defries' aim was to make Bowie a star in the States, and to bolster that illusion he encouraged the whole entourage to live the star lifestyle, charging everything to hotel room service whilst getting RCA to pick up the tab. The tour was actually losing a significant amount of money due to its large crew and a lack of dates in the schedule. Some venues sold out but others were only half-full. Defries managed to keep the whole circus both literally on the road, and on the road to stardom with the energetic media exposure generated by MainMan, including a front cover image of Ziggy in the November edition of *Rolling Stone* magazine. In Phoenix Mick got sunburn lazing by the hotel swimming pool and made things worse by diving into the pool with his bleached blond hair, unaware that the pool was treated with chlorine. As a consequence his hair turned bright green, which along with his red skin gave him an alien appearance well beyond the norm even of the Spiders. In early November RCA reissued the two former Mercury albums in the UK and the States. 1969's *David Bowie* was retitled *Space Oddity*, and 1970's *The Man Who Sold The World* replaced the original album cover of Bowie wearing a dress with an image of him as Ziggy. On 24 November RCA then released the lead single 'Jean Genie' for *Aladdin Sane* while the band were still in America. Promoted as 'Written in New York. Recorded in New York. Mixed in Nashville', the single reached No. 2 in the UK charts, making it Bowie's highest-selling single to date. 'Jean Genie' started life as a Spiders tour-bus improvisation based on the Bo Diddley track 'I'm a Man'. Although its lyrics and riff are firmly rooted in America, the original Bo Diddley track had been covered in England by the Yardbirds with Jeff Beck, then in turn covered by the Rats as part of their set list back in the '60s. As with countless songs it had crossed the Atlantic back and forth between American and English musicians, with Mick Ronson being one of the key links in the chain, culminating in Bowie's take with 'Jean Genie.' In the stage show 'Turn and Face the Strange', Ched Cheesman demonstrates how the Rats version of 'I'm a Man' morphs seamlessly and imaginatively into Bowie's 'Jean Genie'.

The US tour ended in Philadelphia on 3 December, but Mick and the band stayed on with Bowie in New York for a further week to record more tracks for *Aladdin Sane*. They all reconvened for a sell-out homecoming gig at the Rainbow in London on Christmas Eve, before the Spiders headed home to Yorkshire for a much-needed break before two final, end-of-year gigs in Manchester on 28 and 29 December. Over Christmas Mick could enjoy with his family the Christmas Day repeat broadcast of 'Starman' on *Top of the Pop*s, and a Boxing Day broadcast of 'Queen Bitch' on *The Old Grey Whistle Test*.

1972 had been a phenomenal year of success for Bowie and it's unlikely it would have happened without the creative input and musicianship of Mick Ronson. After three years without a hit, Bowie had four singles in the UK charts that year: 'Starman', 'John, I'm Only Dancing', 'All the Young Dudes', and 'Jean Genie'. The *Ziggy* and *Dudes* albums had both charted, as had Lou Reed's *Transformer*, co-produced by Bowie and Ronson. The Ziggy album alone sold over 95,000 copies in the UK and the same in the US. The Spiders with Bowie had been on the road for 11 months that year, with over 90 performances. Mick Ronson was firmly on the map as Bowie's essential sideman, arranger and all-round creative musical partner. The years of perseverance, dedication and sheer hard work had finally delivered. The estate kid from Hull was living his dream,

8 Ziggy's Rise and Fall:
1973

Ziggy's Rise and Fall: 1973

On 5 January 1973, the *Hull Daily Mail* published an article celebrating Mick's phenomenal rise to success. The local lad had done more than just good – he was now a fully-fledged rock star: 'Hull housewife Mrs. Minnie Ronson will next week receive from her son a special piece of bric-a-brac to place on her mantlepiece – a gold disc. Her elder son is 26-year-old Michael Ronson, guitarist with the David Bowie set-up which is currently taking the pop charts by storm. This week the group were presented with a gold disc for the sales of their recent LP *Ziggy Stardust and the Spidermen* [sic], an award which will go straight into the front room of Mrs. Ronson's Greatfield Estate home. 1972 was a great year for Michael, a former member of the Hull group The Rats, and his mother envisages 1973 being even greater. World-wide success looms for David Bowie and Michael, who combine to present one of the most audacious acts on the pop scene.'

Mick's high octane rise to stardom was showing no sign of slowing, with a second tour of America scheduled, followed by a tour of Japan. Bowie appeared for the first time on a TV chat show that January, interviewed by Russell Harty, with the Spiders performing 'Drive-In Saturday'. Studio recordings for *Aladdin Sane* were completed by 24 January, and the next day Bowie sailed from Southampton for the States, with the usual pattern of the Spiders flying a few days later. Bowie increased the band line-up for the Stateside shows, including Mike Garson on piano and additional musicians on guitar, sax, flute and backing vocals. Countering press comments that they were 'adding Spiders' Bowie gave an interview to the *New Musical Express* at the end of January: 'I'd like to get one thing straight: these aren't additional Spiders. The Spiders are still Trev, Mick and Woody. We've got some back-up men on tenor saxes, piano and voices. It's three Spiders, back-up musicians and me.'

The extra musicians added to the impact of the shows in America, which were playing to much larger venues than on the first tour. Bowie also went further down the route of developing the theatrical elements, incorporating mime sequences, heavier make-up, and several costume changes, wearing oriental-themed costumes by the Japanese designer Kansai Yamamoto. Musicians' positions onstage were marked and cued as part of the overall show design and choreography. Bowie opened the first show on 14 February at Radio City New York, suspended in the air in a steel cage which was lowered during the opening song. The second half started with the Spiders ascending through a trapdoor on the stage, top-lit for maximum dramatic effect. The show went down a storm.

The Mick Ronson Story

The second tour lasted a month, taking in 17 shows in 6 cities, including New York, Philadelphia, Nashville, Memphis, Detroit and ending on 12 March at the Hollywood Palladium in Los Angeles. The majority of gigs were sold out with additional early evening matinée shows added to the schedule. Bowie and the Spiders were now a massive draw, with all the attendant media focus and hype that it entailed. The Spiders were living in a touring bubble, from hotel to bus to tour venue in a *Groundhog Day* existence, with all the associated rock and roll elements of free booze, groupies, and drugs for those who wanted them. The Spiders relationship with Bowie began to change, as he increasingly became more distant. Where they'd once been a 'gang of four', the team was dividing into the Yorkshire contingent and Bowie, with the band allocated their own suite, and the star often travelling separately and sometimes staying in a different hotel. A fracture was occurring, as Bowie seemed increasingly to mirror and then inhabit the internal mental world of his alter ego. The situation wasn't helped by the fact that Defries had forbidden any press interviews with the Spiders, in order to control the star's PR and maintain Bowie's crown position with the media.

A flashpoint occurred after a conversation between Woody and Mike Garson, where Woody realised he and Trevor were being paid only a fraction of Garson's wage for the tour, which the two felt was deeply unfair, given that they'd both been with Bowie from the start of the Spiders. They talked with Mick, who at first was supportive of his bandmates and shared their sense of injustice. He set in train discussions for a possible record deal for the Spiders, separate from Bowie's with RCA. When Defries heard about it, he summoned them all to a meeting with Bowie, which turned aggressive and confrontational. Woody demanded a pay rise for himself and Trevor, which Defries countered with the scathing put-down that he didn't think they were worth paying any more than the roadies. At that point Woody threatened to pull out of the remaining gigs. It was of course a bluff; he had no wish to leave the band or fail to fulfil his professional obligations. The ploy worked insofar that Defries backed off and agreed to increase their pay, but he was already discounting Woody, if not Trevor as well, in any future plans. Woody remembered Mick being quiet throughout the meeting, and in retrospect came to realise the reason for Mick's silence was that Defries had secretly offered him a career route post-Ziggy, with a plan to promote him as a MainMan solo artist and star. For the moment, however, the conflict appeared to be resolved. Under the surface, and

Ziggy's Rise and Fall: 1973

unknown to either Woody or Trevor, plans were being made to retire Ziggy for good.

In March Bowie sailed from Los Angeles via Vancouver to Honolulu, and then on to Toyko. The Spiders flew home to Britain, then regathered at Heathrow Airport to fly out to Japan in early April. The flight had a refuelling stopover in Moscow, where the three Spiders were taken under armed escort to a waiting lounge and kept isolated from other members of the public. The guards explained that as the band had caused riots in other countries, it was not permissible for them to be seen by any Russian citizens. The band arrived in Tokyo on 6 April, the same day that 'Drive-In Saturday' was released as a single in the UK, reaching No. 3 in the charts.

During the band's hugely popular tour of Japan, Mick Ronson gained a nickname in the Japanese press and media as Ricky Monsoon. The band performed eight shows in five cities, playing in Tokyo, Nagoya, Hiroshima, Kobe and Osaka, and during their tour *Aladdin Sane* was released, on 13 April. It went straight to No. 1 in the UK charts, remaining there for five weeks, and peaked at No. 17 in the US charts. It was Bowie's most successful album commercially in both countries up to that time. Mick was again credited with all song arrangements and according to Mike Garson, whose jazz piano was a new distinctive element on the album, Mick played a key role in the making of the record: 'Mick had a lot to do with the creation of that album, there's just no question about it. The stacking of the guitar parts, the arrangements, he was right in there. He was very astute and clever to help guide me through what to play. Of course, the final production of me playing the solos on "Lady Grinning Soul" and "Aladdin Sane" did come from the old mastermind David, but on the mechanics, in the studio and in rehearsals, Mick was taking charge.'

Aladdin Sane was the third and final album of Bowie with all three of the Spiders from Mars. Conceived and part-recorded during the first American tour, it bears the strong influence of their time there. Essentially it is Ziggy in America, from the retro doo-wop style of 'Drive-In Saturday' to the Hollywood themes of sex and 'past your sell-by date' stardom in 'Cracked Actor'. Mick's driving rock guitar is prevalent on 'Watch That Man', 'Panic in Detroit', 'Jean Genie' and the Rolling Stones cover 'Let's Spend the Night Together'. They sit alongside some highly original genre-mixing songs such as 'Time' with its Brecht-Weill cabaret influence, 'Lady Grinning Soul' and the album's title track, all pinned by Garson's rich piano playing.

The popularity of the Japanese tour reached a frenzy on the final gig in Tokyo on 20 April. The fans went wild, cheering and rushing the stage, and on the third encore, their enthusiastic stomping caused the front area of the audience floor to collapse. The band ran from the stage and the following day the police declared that the tour entourage were responsible for inciting a riot. With the possibility of arrest warrants being issued, a hasty departure was arranged for Angela and Zowie Bowie and Tony Zanetta. Mick with the Spiders flew back to London while Bowie embarked on a 6000-mile trip by boat and train on the trans-Siberian express to Moscow and then on to Britain.

While in Japan, Bowie and Defries met with Mick to outline their plans for the future. RCA were unwilling to put up any further money for a proposed third tour of the States after being landed with the costs for the first two. Bowie wanted to take a break from Ziggy, to give himself time to recharge his creative batteries and consider the next stage in his career. They decided the best option was to retire Ziggy at the end of the imminent UK tour, after which Bowie would take a break, and Defries would promote Mick as his next big solo star. Trevor and Woody were kept in the dark. Mick said later in 1984: 'I knew that David was going to retire when we were in Japan. I had to swear to keep it to myself.' Mick attended Bowie's homecoming party at Haddon Hall on 5 May, where Tony Visconti was reunited with Bowie for the first time since their split in August 1970. It was the end of an era as far as Haddon Hall was concerned, as Bowie and Angie looked for alternative accommodation soon after, to gain some respite from the ever-increasing army of fans who were camping out in the gardens.

The second and final leg of the UK tour lasted from May to July 1973, playing 41 dates almost non-stop across the country. Ziggy-mania was at its height and a number of venues were vandalised. Some fans were hospitalised at gigs, leading Bowie to publicly confront overzealous security staff directly from the stage. On 22 June RCA capitalised further on Bowie's back catalogue by re-releasing 'Life on Mars' from *Hunky Dory* as a single, where it reached No. 3 in the UK charts.

On 28 June the Ziggy tour played Bridlington Spa, which was the nearest performance to Mick and Trevor's home city of Hull, and Woody's home town of Driffield. In the audience was Graham Jenkinson, who vividly remembers the night: 'I went on my own to see Bowie at Brid on that Ziggy Stardust tour. I don't know how I managed to get there, I was only about 17 and that was just an incredible, life-changing night. You've got your musical idol, your personal idol performing in front of

Ziggy's Rise and Fall: 1973

you… absolutely overwhelming and gobsmacking. It was an absolutely incredible evening that seemed to go by in the click of a finger.'

Mick always made sure his family and friends received the full VIP treatment at gigs and Bridlington was no exception, with the family seeing the show and staying over at a hotel in nearby Scarborough. Mick and his family's generosity would often extend to fans, some of them complete strangers, as a young Allan Abbey found out that month. He had bought a ticket to see the show at Leeds University on 2 June, but the gig was cancelled at short notice: 'This was obviously a huge let-down and I was gutted. I was so disappointed that I decided to write to Mick Ronson to tell him how disappointed I was and ask him why the gig had been pulled only six hours before it was due to start. In those days, telephone directories contained addresses and I was able to look up Ronson's family address on Greatfield Estate and wrote to him care of this address. I don't remember exactly what I wrote in the letter but I told him how I felt he'd let his fans down. I felt better having vented my disappointment, but I wasn't expecting what happened next.' A few days later Allan received a phone call from Mick's mother Minnie, who offered him a free ticket to the show at Bridlington Spa later that month, along with the opportunity to meet Mick afterwards. 'There was no way I was going to miss out on that! We went to the gig and afterwards I met up with some of Ronson's family and friends to board a coach that took us on to the hotel in Scarborough where Ronson and Bowie were staying. Looking back on it, it was a surreal coach journey. I was a shy teenager with long hair and wearing my best greatcoat, on a coach with Mick Ronson's family on my way to meet Mick! At the hotel we sat at a long table and were served food. I don't remember a lot about what happened apart from being asked if I wanted to go through and meet Bowie, which I declined because I was more interested in being with my guitar hero. We then retired to the bar where I was too shy to talk much to Ronson. It was all like a dream and I don't remember anything I actually said to him. He signed a large Aladdin Sane poster for me and posed for me so I could take a couple of photos on my cheap camera. What I do remember, though, is how much time he seemed to have for a strange young boy who he'd never met before and he probably didn't have any idea why I was there.'

Also at the Bridlington Spa gig was 15-year-old Hull-born Gina Riley, now Gina Labrosse. Her sister had got her two tickets, so Gina went with her friend by coach from Hull. As they queued up to get in, a massive surprise was in store: 'The doorman stopped me and told me

The Mick Ronson Story

I was the 100,000th person to see the Ziggy show. They said I would be meeting David Bowie, so before the show started I was taken backstage on my own and shown into Bowie's dressing room. I remember he was putting his make-up on and he had his leg on the dressing table. He was busy getting ready, he didn't say much to me, he was talking to other people in the room. I was so excited and really nervous. Mick was also there. He was very friendly and chatty, he took the time to talk to me, he was trying to put me at my ease. He asked me where I was from. I told him I was from Orchard Park. He said: 'Oh the estate of fences!', making a joke of it – he knew Orchard Park. I was then taken to the front of house to my friend and we went in to see the show. I think it was during the interval they made an announcement that I was the 100,000th person to see the show. They called my name out and invited me onto the stage. I was presented with some LPs and they said I would be getting free tickets to see the final show at Hammersmith Odeon in London. My friends from school were all cheering. I remember thinking I wasn't a total Bowie fan at the time. I liked him but I didn't go into the whole dressing up thing or putting on the Bowie look, so I remember feeling a bit guilty, 'cause the place was packed with fans who had dressed up and were obviously total David Bowie fans. It was a brilliant concert. I really enjoyed it – great atmosphere. On the coach back everybody was talking about it. Some of the girls were really jealous about me winning the tickets. At school the next day some girls wouldn't talk to me because they didn't think I deserved getting the tickets!'

The cancelled Leeds University gig was rescheduled at Leeds Rollarena for the day after the show at Bridlington Spa, and 13-year-old Lou Duffy-Howard travelled from Wetherby to see it: 'It was an amazing experience. It blew my mind basically. Ronno with his amazing guitar sounds, the costume changes, I just couldn't believe it. It was quite alien. It was exciting, loud, vibrant, colourful. Costumes that I had never seen before, these guys with glitter in their hair and boots stacked high. It was packed with people, all these people around me all dressed in eight button baggies and star shirts and a few brushed haircuts. It was a huge theatrical show that I'd just never seen anything like it before in my life. It was electrifying it really was. And I thought I want to do that. I had a vision that it was something that I wanted to do.' It set Lou Howard on a path to becoming a professional musician, playing with the successful '80s Hull band the Red Guitars, and still playing today.

On one of Mick's visits home, he met up with his Hull friend Les Morfitt and asked him to join the tour for the remaining dates: 'Mick

Ziggy's Rise and Fall: 1973

came home for a short while and we met him. He was in the middle of the tour and he'd just come home to see his family. He said, *They're coming to the end of the tour, if you want to join up and mosey along with us. We can do with a bit of help, it's getting bigger* type of thing. I joined him somewhere like Leicester De Montfort Hall. There was about 10 or 12 gigs left. We weren't hired help, we were just there helping out. We didn't get paid or anything like that, I was just part of a crowd but there was nothing we wanted for. Everything was there for us, it was fun. We were just helping out at the side of the stage, like roadies but we weren't the roadies, we were just there."

The final concert of the Ziggy tour, on 3 July at Hammersmith Odeon, has gone down in rock music folklore. The playing was tight and raw, with that extra edge of energy that comes from an artist and band at the height of their powers, knowing this is a special night with the added bonus of a well-earned break coming up. That month all five of Bowie's RCA albums were in the UK Top 40 chart, with three in the Top 20, and the gig was inevitably sold out. The three-and-a-half thousand capacity venue was crammed with an expectant audience of fans and celebrities, including Mick and Bianca Jagger, Rod Stewart and Ringo Starr. In the tight circle of those who knew what was coming, including Mick of course, the night had a special frisson. For those who didn't, particularly Woody and Trevor, it was to be an evening that started with excitement and adrenaline, but ended with a deep sense of shock, bitterness and betrayal.

The concert started with a solo spot on piano by Mike Garson, who played a medley of Bowie songs. It kicked off proper with a rip-roaring rendition of 'Hang on to Yourself' and continued its high-powered rock and roll culminating in Mick's phenomenal solo on 'Moonage Daydream'. Les Morfitt was at the side of the stage and appears briefly in the D.A. Pennebaker film of the show: 'During the concert when Mick's doing his "Moonage Daydream", I'm just stood at the side of the stage and I think Stuey George was stood with us. I just happened to be at the front and Mick was getting rather close to the crowd at the front and I'm sure it was Stuey or somebody behind me, pushed me forward and said, "Grab him, pull him back!" I grabbed hold of Mick and pulled him away from the crowd, and that's it, that's my two seconds of fame!"

In the audience that night at Hammersmith Odeon was Gina Riley. Being just short of her 16th birthday Gina was classed as a minor and it was a requirement of winning a ticket that she had to be accompanied by an adult, so she travelled down to London to see the show with her father Leon Riley. Gina and her father were not only getting complimentary tickets to see the show, their travel down to the capital was being paid for, along with accommodation at the same hotel in London where the band were staying. Gina remembers: 'I think we had seats on the balcony. We were sat next to Brian Connolly, singer with the Sweet. During the show Jeff Beck played guitar with his teeth. It was a really amazing show. They announced my name over the tannoy, that Gina Riley, a young girl from Hull, was the 100,000th person to see the show and that I was there tonight. I couldn't believe I was there to be honest. I absolutely loved it, it was electric.'

Mick's own memory of the gig was vivid years later. In an interview recorded in 1992 in the same Hammersmith Odeon auditorium, he said: 'We did a whole tour of England before we did this concert, and it was a pretty wild tour. I mean places were mobbed, screaming fans, it was great, it was a great tour. This last night, it was a great last night too, I mean there was a lot of energy there. It was pretty sad in some ways too, 'cause it was kind of the end of that period. I don't know what people saw it as, but I have been told it was great, the way David was onstage, and the way that I was onstage. For me when I was onstage I was doing what I had to do. I think a lot of people saw it as a counterfoil, me and David, 'cause David was more like delicate, you know the dressing and a little more woman-like, or something, and I was kind of like stomping along on the side there, a bit more like – I can't really say bricklayer, but that's kind of what I mean.'

After a slower quieter sequence with Bowie performing solo on acoustic guitar, the concert picked up its energetic pace, leading to a guest appearance towards the end of the show from Mick's lifelong guitar hero Jeff Beck, who played on 'Jean Genie' and the Chuck Berry classic 'Around and Around'. Mike Garson remembers the sheer magic of the two guitar players sharing the stage that night: 'They were great together. I mean Jeff is a great, great guitar player. Jeff had a certain influence on him and Mick had a lot of respect for Jeff, so you could feel that on the stage. They were just back and forth, it was just a great, great jam. Wonderful. It's hard to emphasize the emotion that Mick was able to put through his guitar.'

After Jeff Beck left the stage, Bowie stepped up to the mike and made the announcement that would dumbfound the audience, and send thousands of fans across the country into a state of mourning: 'This has been one of the greatest tours of our lives... Of all of the shows on this tour, this particular show will remain with us the longest, because not only is it... not only is it the last show of the tour, but it's the last show that we'll ever do. Thank you.' The concert ended with 'Rock 'n' Roll Suicide', a remarkable alignment of artist, song and statement, and a consummate expression of Bowie's showmanship. He was going out in style. He was not only ending the tour, he was killing off Ziggy and the Spiders from Mars. Mick left the stage without speaking to his bandmates. Woody and Trevor were in disbelief and shock, not certain if it was true or if Bowie was just pulling another stunt. Les Morfitt recalls the immediate aftermath: 'We went backstage afterwards but there was a lot of commotion going on, there was a lot of reporters and people. It was one of those sorts of episodes where... *what's happened? What has actually gone on? Is that right, what he's just said?* And then by that time Bowie had sort of done one, like he always did at the end of the concert and just left the stragglers and hangers on really to clean up the mess – and what a mess he left!'

As a characteristic Ronson coda to what had been a remarkable night, Mick had made sure that his old Hull mate John Close received free tickets for the Hammersmith gig, and had also paid for John and his wife to stay at the same London hotel as the band, along with an invite to the after-show party the following night. 'So we were waiting in the foyer of the hotel, just having a couple of drinks at the bar and this maître d', or whoever it was, came along and he said: "Mr Close?" I said: "Yeah", he said: "Your car's here." So we went out and there was a chauffeur-driven limo there, and we gets in the car and it was surreal. It was at the Café Royale, Regent Street. It was the now infamous Last Supper as everybody called it, after he folded the band. There was just press and fans everywhere outside down Regent Street, and we were escorted through all this crowd of people up into this birdcage... they had this fantastic ornate birdcage lift and a guy in top hat and tails, and they took us up and it was just a big room full of these circular tables with white tablecloths with buckets with magnums of champagne.'

Gina Riley was there with her father Leon: 'I was at the same table as Mick Jagger and Labi Siffre. There was food and my dad said: "Have the lemon sole" – he knew his fish cause he'd worked on the fish dock in Hull! Labi Siffre was lovely. I spoke with Angie Bowie – she was very friendly and nice, I liked her. I felt a bit odd being there. I was from Hull, a 15-year-old drinking champagne!' John Close remembers: 'I was sat at a table, Ringo Starr was on the table, Lou Reed was certainly around, Mick was there obviously, quite a lot of other A-list megastars, and I'm just a kid from Greatfield Estate, you know, with my wife, and that was all down to Mick and it didn't cost us a penny!'

Over the coming days and weeks, the full impact of Bowie's onstage announcement would sink in for Woody and Trevor. They were being sidelined. Woody had proposed to his girlfriend June while on tour in Japan, and the wedding date was set for two days after the Hammersmith Odeon gig at Bridlington, with a second service for friends in Sussex on 7 July. Bowie and Mick were both invited, but didn't attend. That afternoon, Woody received a phone call from Tony Defries and was told he was sacked from the band. It was a devastating blow for the Spider who had been part of the whole Ziggy journey. As before, Mick preferred to keep a low profile, avoid direct confrontation and follow his ambition as a musician. Trevor was extremely angry at Woody's treatment and confronted Bowie: 'I went to see David at his hotel and created a bit of hell with him. Mick told me to keep my mouth shut or I wouldn't be working, because David would get rid of me as well. David had actually said to me, "If you don't like it, you can clear off and we'll get another bass player." When everything had calmed down, David said: "Come over here, I've got some songs to play you", and he played me all the songs he was going to do on *Pin Ups*.'

Trevor was placated to the extent that he did agree to play on the album that was recorded that July in France, but for him it wasn't a rewarding experience: 'It was really bad, the band thing had gone then. Once you pull any member out of a band, it changes. It was sad not having Woody there.' It was the end of the line for the trio from Hull. Mick had a future solo career in the pipeline, but the Spiders from Mars had reached the end of their particular road.

For Mick, there was a further closure, not in his professional career but in his personal life. He'd started a relationship with Suzi Fussey and at some point during the two years of intensive touring with Ziggy, Mick's relationship with fiancée Denise Irvin had come to an end. After some early trips down to Haddon Hall, where their baby Nicholas played with Bowie's son Zowie, Denise moved back with their son to her parent's home on Greatfield Estate, not far from the Ronson family home. Benny Marshall remembers the earlier times when Mick would bring his baby son Nicholas round to visit him in Hull. 'He used to bring Nicky down to the flat I used to live at on St. Georges Road. He was only a toddler, just walking, when he used to come round. Mick did go down to London and he never had any part in Nick growing up. Denise moved to Malton.' Christine Park, married at that time to musician Rick Kemp and living in Hull, remembers, 'I went down a few times to see her (Denise) with this little boy, little blond-haired boy. And then she left and went to live out of Hull, and that was the last I heard. She said she was moving out of Hull to start a new life. I think it was just a private thing with the family. A very private thing.'

9 From Sideman to Frontman:
1973–1974

From Sideman to Frontman: 1973–1974

Mick left with Bowie and his group of musicians for France on 9 July 1973 to record *Pin Ups*. Aynsley Dunbar replaced Woody Woodmansey on drums. Mick was supportive of Trevor Bolder staying on to play bass, but he was probably only there after Bowie's first choice, Jack Bruce, declined. The album was recorded at the Château d'Hérouville, where Marc Bolan had recorded *The Slider* and Elton John *Honky Château* a year earlier. Bowie would return there in 1976 to record *Low*. Set in the peaceful French countryside around an hour's drive north of Paris, it offered musicians an idyllic residential retreat where they could chill and record at any time of day or night without the clock-driven pressure of cost, unlike the London studios that booked and charged by the hour. Recording in France also offered the advantage of avoiding British tax liability.

Pin Ups was co-produced by Bowie and Ken Scott, with Mick credited with the song arrangements. The album was a pragmatic way of Bowie fulfilling contractual obligations to RCA, as well as paying tribute to his and Mick's music heroes from the 1960s. It was an album entirely of covers, including tracks by the Pretty Things, the Yardbirds, the Kinks, the Who and Pink Floyd. It was unashamedly feel-good rock and roll of the old school variety, featuring bands who inspired Mick during his long years as a jobbing musician with the Rats in Hull. He had followed them all, and even seen some live at Hull City Hall or the Skyline Ballroom. Mick reminisced in a 1988 article in *Music Maker*: 'That album was great to do because the songs were our favourites when we were teenagers. I started to play guitar because of Duane Eddy, and shortly after that you got the Beatles, the Stones, the Yardbirds. The best music is the music that gets you so excited that you want to pick up and learn to play an instrument by yourself. With *Pin Ups* we got to record all those songs ourselves.' *Pin Ups* was recorded in just three weeks, with finishing touches by Ken Scott after the end of July, barely a month following the Ziggy farewell concert, so it would be ready for an October release.

With the album completed, Mick took a holiday break in a villa near Rome where his relationship with Suzi Fussey blossomed. They were back at the Château d'Hérouville at the start of September where Mick spent the entire month recording his first solo album *Slaughter on 10th Avenue*. He retained the core of musicians from the *Pin Ups* sessions, including Mike Garson on piano, Aynsley Dunbar on drums, and his Hull mate Trevor Bolder on bass, trumpet and trombone. With Bowie absent, Trevor felt the shadow of recent events begin to fade: 'I enjoyed doing *Slaughter on 10th Avenue* with him. I played all the brass on it as well. We had real good fun actually, it was quite a laugh. We had a good time doing that album because David wasn't there and Mick's a lot more open and friendly. I'd known him for such a long time it was like two mates making an album together.'

For the first time in his career Mick had complete control over the content and production of an entire album. He was producer, arranger, string conductor, musician and singer. He was the main man, enjoying the freedom and funding that Tony Defries had bestowed under his masterplan to make Mick his next big star. What Defries and RCA perhaps didn't calculate, was that given this freedom, Mick chose to explore and experiment with a rich range of music genres rather than follow the crowd-pleasing and income-generating path of an album delivering blistering rock guitar tracks. On the notes for his second solo album Mick wrote: 'After being with David, the first thing I didn't want to do was go and do a guitar solo album, along the same lines as the things that I had been doing with him. I wanted to do what I wanted to do. I've never been singing before, so I wanted to do songs, and find out how my voice worked. It was like a big experiment, that first solo LP.' The songs on *Slaughter* range through ballads, jazz, showbiz orchestral, with just the occasional straight rock and roll track as in 'Only After Dark'. Mick's three-year period alongside Bowie had nudged his creative instincts way beyond the Rats days of staying cocooned in the cosy world of rock and blues covers. He was now at a stage where he was prepared to pin his imminent solo career on an album defined by experimentation. Whilst it demonstrated Mick's high standard of musicianship, it didn't offer the makings of a hit record by a pop star being groomed to inherit the mantle of Bowie.

On the album Mick co-wrote two tracks, 'Only After Dark' and 'Pleasure Man', with Scott Richardson, the singer of Detroit band SRC, who were fans of British bands such as Cream and the Pretty Things. Mick was intended to form a new band, the Fallen Angels, with Scott Richardson on vocals, Trevor Bolder on bass and Aynsley Dunbar on drums, but the idea foundered when Richardson objected to Defries wanting a substantial percentage of their future record income. The track 'Hey Ma Get Papa' was written by Mick with lyrics by Bowie, and is the sole Bowie-Ronson song credit from their entire period working together. Bowie also provided the track 'Growing up and I'm Fine'. Mick was a fan of Annette Peacock and covered her song 'I'm the One', with Mike Garson's piano enhancing the strong jazz influence. Mick

From Sideman to Frontman: 1973–1974

also covered the classic Elvis Presley song 'Love Me Tender' and did consider a version of Lou Reed's crowd-pleasing rocker 'White Light/White Heat', which had been recorded during the *Pin Ups* sessions and had been a perennial Ziggy encore favourite. In the end it was omitted, appearing on Mick's next album *Play Don't Worry*.

The album's title track 'Slaughter on Tenth Avenue' was originally a ballet with music by Richard Rodgers and choreography by George Balanchine, and featured as an episode at the end of Rodgers and Hart's 1936 hit Broadway musical *On Your Toes*. It tells the story of an African American hoofer, a soft-shoe tap dancer who falls in love with a dance hall girl, who is then shot and killed by her jealous boyfriend. In retaliation the hoofer then shoots the boyfriend. Subsequent adaptations of the story, notably by Gene Kelly, had variations on the ending where the hoofer gets shot by the boyfriend. The track had been covered by the American instrumental guitar band the Ventures in 1964, and also by the Shadows in Britain, released in 1969. Mick's 'Slaughter on Tenth Avenue' was a powerful piano-guitar dominated instrumental, combining all the skill of his solo guitar playing with a jazzy middle section and an impressive orchestral arrangement. Mike Garson remembered the recording session: 'Mick decided to use that song but do his own arrangement. We worked on the piano part from midnight to six in the morning. He just wanted me to get it perfect. He really wanted it right, so he just kept doing take after take, refining it repeatedly. He was a very good producer, something I remember very, very clearly.' Mick's arrangement of the song suggests he might have pursued a career composing film scores, like Mark Knopfler for *Local Hero* or Eric Clapton for the series *Edge of Darkness*. Critics have speculated that Mick might have felt more comfortable and natural moving into a space inhabited by the likes of these musical peers, rather than the teen idol, sex symbol direction he was now being driven down by Defries and MainMan.

The final touches to the *Slaughter* album were completed back at Trident Studios in London and work began on pre-publicity, including a proposed photo shoot by Leee Black Childers on Tenth Avenue in New York. This eventually turned into a promo video directed by Macs McCarey, with the shoot organised by Cherry Vanilla. The film was shot in an actual bar on Tenth Avenue with locals appearing as extras. It showcases Mick and Suzi as the two dancer-lovers from the original dance-show storyline. Mick wore the striped sailor top and white neckerchief that was now his branded image as a solo star, and would feature on the cover of *Slaughter*. The promo is pure melodrama, devoid of any intentional irony, and Mick's voice-over with his strong Hull accent, contrasts incongruously with the New York context and the film's Chandleresque intent. RCA were not particularly enamoured with the finished result of the *Slaughter* album and put back its release to March 1974, allowing Defries time to do more of what he had previously done with great success for Bowie – promoting Mick as a ready-made solo star before he was one.

Despite Ziggy being retired that summer, the momentum of its phenomenal success continued through the autumn of 1973. At the end of September Bowie practically swept the board in *Melody Maker*'s annual readers' poll, coming top in the categories of British Singer, International Singer, Best Single (first with 'Jean Genie' and second with 'Drive-In Saturday'), International Producer and International Composer. Always the sideman to Bowie, Mick won only joint second place in the category of Arranger. On 3 October, the single 'Sorrow' from *Pin Ups* was released reaching No. 3 in the UK charts, followed by the album release on 19 October. It went straight to No. 1 and stayed in the charts for another 21 weeks. At that point Bowie had a total of six albums in the UK charts, and Mick had played a crucial role on five of them.

Pin Ups reached No. 23 in the US charts, but with sales not as healthy as in the UK, and any chance of a further American tour pulled by MainMan in the light of RCA's refusal to underwrite it, a compromise was reached: Bowie would perform a recorded television special for broadcast in the States. NBC agreed to air the show on *The Midnight Special* programme presented by Wolfman Jack. The show was recorded live that October at the Marquee Club in London, where Mick had met Bowie for the first time nearly four years earlier. The show was performed to a small enthusiastic audience of celebrities and invited members of Bowie's fan club, backed by the *Pin Ups* band of Mick, Trevor Bolder, Mike Garson and Aynsley Dunbar. It was to be the last appearance of Mick as sideman to Bowie as Ziggy, and he wouldn't perform again with him until his 1983 cameo appearance in Toronto on the Serious Moonlight Tour. Post Ziggy, Bowie would make comments that were sometimes critical of Mick, but Minnie Ronson said of her son in 2016: 'Michael remained very loyal to David throughout his life.'

Bowie was writing new material in preparation for what he hoped would be a stage musical based on George Orwell's *Nineteen Eighty-Four*. Orwell's widow Sonia declined permission, but Bowie had already started to compile the new songs, and had written classic tracks which would eventually lead to the *Diamond Dogs* album, including 'Rebel

From Sideman to Frontman: 1973–1974

Rebel' and '1984'. To circumvent Sonia Orwell's objection Bowie christened the project 'The 1980 Floor Show' punning on the Orwell book title, and went ahead with the design and staging of what was to become a largely unmemorable final Ziggy appearance. In some respects Bowie was trying to recapture that interesting borderline territory between rock music and theatricality which he had explored so effectively on tour with Ziggy, but the deadening effect of the small screen television format, coupled with some cliched cabaret and choreography tropes, rendered the effect self-indulgently camp. Trevor Bolder was not impressed by this final outing with Bowie: 'You had David who was now acting like the big rock and roll star. A man you couldn't get near to, who used to drive you to gigs at pubs – now you couldn't even get to talk to him. Then you had Mick who was all dressed in white and he was going off to do his solo venture and be the star. Then you had me in the background dressed in black with the rest of the band. You've got all these other musicians playing and it's not the Spiders anymore. It was finished then really, that was it.'

Wearing an eye-grabbing, all-white suit designed by Freddie Buretti, Mick is clearly being lined up as a star, sharing the front of the stage on an equal footing with Bowie. The most effective moments are when Bowie and Mick duet on 'Space Oddity' and when the band are playing with the same live energy and passion you would expect at a large rock gig, particularly on 'Jean Genie'. In a mirror-image throwback to the *Top of the Pops* broadcast of 'Starman', Mick casually drapes his arm round Bowie's shoulder during a chorus of 'Jean Genie', now totally at ease. Perhaps the worst moment of the show was Bowie duetting 'I Got You Babe' with a stoned Marianne Faithful dressed as a nun. Trevor could at least lurk thankfully in the shadows at the back.

Mick and David parted on good terms, but Mick was now on his own in uncharted territory. His challenge was not only to assimilate a range of disparate musical influences, much as Bowie had done, but to project a distinctive sound and a charismatic musical identity of his own. The pressure was on from MainMan and RCA to retain commerciality, and for Mick this meant being the frontman, with all the pressure it entailed. He was finally going to be a big rock and roll star in his own right. There had been setbacks on the way, but his profile was now at its peak. All that was needed was the talent, which he had by the bucketload, the charisma and self-belief to carry it off.

In 1974 glossy teen magazines featured Mick on their covers as a beautifully groomed, shirtless, sex symbol, while huge billboards

The Mick Ronson Story

advertising Mick's face adorned the lofty towers of Times Square. A year later in an interview for *Circus* magazine, Mick described how he really felt about his projected image: 'I looked like a doll on there, like a doll you would buy in a store with bright red rosy cheeks. I thought it would be a photograph, but it was this painting. I remember looking up at it from the cab window and thinking it looked funny.' MainMan were in promo warp-drive, with a show launch at The Rainbow in London on 22–23 February 1974, the release of *Slaughter* on 1 March, followed by a UK tour in April and a likely Stateside tour to follow. The line-up for the Rainbow gig included Trevor Bolder on bass, Mike Garson on keyboards, Mark Carr-Pritchard on second guitar and Ritchie Dharma on drums. It also included vocal backing from the Thunderthighs, a five-piece horn ensemble, and string players from the London Symphony Orchestra. Despite all the hype and anticipation, the reviews of the show were disappointing and highlighted the fact that automatic entry into the realm of superstardom was not guaranteed. Charles Shaar Murray of the *NME*, though a loyal Bowie champion and full of praise for Ronson's musicianship, offered this advice: 'Mick Ronson is an exceptionally gifted man. His album proves that he can sing and that he has a coherent and convincing musical identity of his own, and his live work with Bowie demonstrated that he is an exciting and original guitarist as well as a fine live performer. But Friday's show proved that he cannot hope for super-stardom by divine right, which is what all MainMan's hype and flummery was trying to set him up for ... What's needed now is a lot of hard work.' Chrissie Hynde saw Mick at the Rainbow and wrote a further review for the NME after seeing the April gig at the Hammersmith Odeon: 'The band is tight and Ronson's in control this time – unlike the Rainbow gig when he looked about as lost as some wino who'd wandered in off the street.' Woody Woodmansey saw the Rainbow gig and whilst applauding Mick's consistent flair on guitar solos, felt that his former Spiders colleague looked nervous as a frontman.

The 13-date UK tour saw Mick and the band gig through England and Scotland, retaining the Thunderthighs and the brass section, but dropping the orchestra. Reviews improved steadily as the tour progressed, and by the end the feeling was that Mick had made an awkward but respectable start, whilst not yet setting the world alight. The tour's set list was predominantly songs from the *Slaughter* album, but it was notably the encores of 'Moonage Daydream' and 'White Light/White Heat' that got the fans out of their seats. A young Kevin Cann saw

From Sideman to Frontman: 1973-1974

the show at Hemel Hempstead: 'It was great – I thought he was terrific – I thought he was definitely a star and delivered a great show. It didn't go wild, cause he wasn't really like that and Hemel itself wasn't really that type of audience – but it was still a great buzz.' Mick still had traction from the success of Ziggy, and *Slaughter on 10th Avenue* reached No. 9 in the UK charts, but his first solo album was possibly trying to touch too many musical bases when what most fans really wanted was simply more of the Ziggy-style rock and roll.

In July '74 Mick was back in the studio, recording his second solo album *Play Don't Worry*. Was the title a reflection of the internal dialogue he was having at that point, or a tacit admission that he needed to get back to doing what he really enjoyed? Maybe, but it also harked back to his days in the Crestas, a decade earlier, when singers Eric Lee and Johnny Hawk would allay the young musician's pre-gig nerves with the repeated mantra of 'Play don't worry!' Either way the pressure was back on Mick to deliver, as the relatively low level of US sales for *Slaughter* had led to the proposed American tour being scrapped.

Play Don't Worry marked a shift back towards less musical experimentation and more traditional guitar-based rock and roll. It was also the first album on which Mick wrote lyrics to some of the songs. As with *Slaughter* Mick produced, arranged, conducted and played a host of instruments on the album. He also brought in a number of additional musicians, including Ian Hunter to complement the reliable stable of Trevor Bolder, Mike Garson, Aynsley Dunbar and Ritchie Dharma. The album's rocking tracks included the eponymous 'Play Don't Worry', 'Angel No. 9', 'Girl Can't Help It', 'Woman' and Lou Reed's 'White Light/White Heat', inherited from the *Pin Ups* recordings. It also included the ballads 'This is For You' with its distinctive Garson piano, and 'Empty Bed', an Italian song with re-penned lyrics by Ronson. The album's single 'Billy Porter' is one of those Marmite tracks that divide Ronson fans into those who really rate it, and others who hate it as a mockney novelty track akin to Bowie's 'The Laughing Gnome'. Many fans agree, however, that 'Angel No. 9' with its hallmark power chords and signature solos is a Ronson classic. The album was released in January 1975 and reviews were mixed, some offering praise, some scathing and some opting for the middle ground, suggesting the album was like a fire that smoulders but never really ignites. According to Ian Hunter, Mick was in the studio with him, about to record a guitar part on the song 'Truth, The Whole Truth, Nuthin' But the Truth', when he read a damning review of *Play Don't Worry*. Mick's reaction was to blush, then launch into a characteristic blistering and brilliant lead solo.

By the time *Play Don't Worry* was released, Mick had effectively given up on his career as a frontman. Despite still being promoted by Defries as a solo star, Mick had not enjoyed the pressure the role entailed: 'I was starting to feel very uncomfortable within myself. I knew that other people would spot that in the audience and I didn't want that. I just couldn't wait to get it over with. Everything kind of happened in such a rush, I just got very confused. It just all happened so quickly that I didn't have time to work it out or why I was doing it.' Unlike Bowie, Mick didn't take a career break. He had gone from 18 months of continuous touring with Ziggy straight into recording *Pin Ups*, followed immediately by recording *Slaughter on 10th Avenue* and then into his live solo career. According to Suzi Ronson, 'Mick was slung out there before he was ready. Mick has always worked better with somebody else. I think he missed having that other key person.'

In an interview on *The Old Grey Whistle Test* in November 1974, Mick told Bob Harris, 'Being on your own all of a sudden, it's a bit strenuous you know, 'cause you've got no one else to talk to about it, you've only got yourself to talk to. So you end up asking yourself questions, and you answer your own questions, and it's really a bit strange. When you're working with other artists, or a combination say such as a group, each member of a group has certain ideas of their own as well, which makes it a little bit easier on you. I find I like the company of other musicians, and I also like to hear what other musicians have to say. I trust the judgement of other musicians.' Cherry Vanilla takes this view: 'Tony Defries pushed Ronson in the wrong direction. Defries tried to put the same treatment onto Ronson that he did onto Bowie. To make him a pop star in the only way he knew how. I think Ronson would have been better taking the route of writing arrangements and movie soundtracks and not trying to be the flashy pop star, because his persona was too much of a real person. He was too sweet. I think he liked being in partnerships. He enjoyed that.'

In September 1974 Mick joined Mott the Hoople. He was back doing what he enjoyed most – playing guitar as part of a band. Though he was still under contract to RCA and still managed by Tony Defries, his days of pursuing a solo career were effectively over. And yet, unlikely as it seemed to anyone involved at the time, let alone the fans, the days of Mott the Hoople were likewise numbered.

10 Musician and Producer for Hire: 1974–1977

The Mick Ronson Story

Mick knew Ian Hunter and Mott the Hoople from 1972, when Bowie gave them the hit single 'All the Young Dudes' and Mick arranged the track 'Sea Diver' for their album the same year. Mick had an easy relaxed friendship with Ian, but knew the band members less well. He could have joined Mott the Hoople in 1973 when lead guitarist Mick Ralphs left the band to join Bad Company with Paul Rodgers and Simon Kirke from Free. At that point, though, he had his sights set on a solo career and was not available due to his contractual obligations to RCA and MainMan. Mick Ralphs' replacement was the former Spooky Tooth guitarist Luther Grosvenor (aka Ariel Bender), but after only a year with the band he decided to leave. So, by the late summer of 1974, the idea of joining a band and collaborating with Ian Hunter – friend and strong performer, and a songwriter to boot – was an attractive option for Mick.

Lynne Mitchell, a childhood friend of Mick, remembers seeing him on the top deck of a Hull bus, heading home after an 'audition' for the band: 'I got on at East Park, I'd been out with my friends, went upstairs and he was sat on the bus and he shouted: "Hiya" to me. I went and sat next to him and said: "Where have you been?" and he said: "I've just got back from London. I've just been for a –" and he called it an interview, he didn't call it an audition. He said, "I've just been for an interview with Mott The Hoople." I said, "Do you think you've got it?" He said, "I think so." He was just like the lad next door again. There was no side to him at all, there was no big-headedness or anything. He just had a pair of jeans on and a jacket, he wasn't fancy at all, just normal. He had his long hair, though, which made people look. It was the middle of the day, it was full of old lady shoppers, so they wouldn't have known him from Adam. So despite all his fame with Bowie, he was on a Hull bus, sat upstairs. He didn't even get a taxi.'

The music press announced that Mick was joining Mott the Hoople in September 1974. The band's members were all genuinely excited that Mick was on board, as he brought not only his phenomenal guitar-playing but also skills as a producer and song arranger. For the band and its fans it was a dream-team partnership, a win-win for all involved. Joining an existing band meant there was now no role for his long-time bassist Trevor Bolder. Mick told him as much at the MainMan office in Fulham.

Trevor now called Woody Woodmansey, who had visited Mick in his new apartment near Hyde Park, and laid to rest any grievances over what had happened at the end of the Ziggy tour. That autumn the two former bandmates combined forces to reform the Spiders from Mars.

Musician and Producer for Hire: 1974–1977

They asked Mick if he wanted to join them, but with commitments elsewhere and perhaps a sense of not wanting to repeat the recent past, he declined. The new Spiders from Mars recorded one eponymous album, released by Pye Records in 1976, but it failed to make any impact. Trevor went on to join Uriah Heep that same year.

Mick's first task on joining Mott the Hoople was to learn their current repertoire of songs before embarking on the band's European tour, starting on 10 October. He also went into the studio to record their new tracks 'Saturday Gigs' and 'Lounge Lizard'. Ian Hunter was supportive of Mick throughout, but from early on, tensions began to build amongst the other band members over aspects of Mick's engagement. Mott was a highly democratic band, used to making decisions based on a group consensus, but Mick's arrival brought with it factors that were beyond their agreement or control. What started out as shared enthusiasm soon led to suspicion and disillusionment. It started with some of the band being excluded when Mick was recording in the studio, and then resentments grew over a *Top of the Pops* recording that in the event wasn't even broadcast.

Once on tour, divisions got worse. A lot of the problems centred on the fact that Mick was contracted to RCA and under Tony Defries' management, whereas the band were separately contracted to CBS records. Unknown to the band members, Defries had arranged with CBS for Mick to be touring with Mott for no payment, in exchange for expenses and the benefits of gaining media exposure and profile for his imminent second solo album release. The set-list included mainly Mott songs but also some tracks from *Play Don't Worry*. That wasn't a problem in itself, but Mick had all the trappings of MainMan's hype and promotion strategy, where he was given the star treatment and existed in a world devoid of cash payments. To the bandmates it seemed weird and somewhat standoffish that he wouldn't accept any payment for being in the band, and yet seemed able to dine at expensive restaurants, when their earnings obliged them to seek out cheaper options. Mott felt they were very much a band of the people, on a par with their audiences, whereas Mick's touring lifestyle appeared to them suspiciously superior and arrogantly distanced from the experience of their fans. The irony was that Mick was very much grounded as a personality, and on an equal level with fans, but the impact of Defries 'star-making' strategy made it appear the direct opposite. The situation wasn't helped by the two record companies vying for supremacy over who got the most media exposure. This led to situations where one limo was hired for the band,

and a separate one just for Mick and Suzi. Mott's bassist Pete Overend Watts was at one point evicted from Mick's designated limo by an RCA promo woman. It all led to poor communication, growing resentment, bruised egos and an increasingly 'us and him' dynamic, with Ian Hunter caught in the middle.

Back in England with the European leg of the tour finished, Mick was interviewed on 5 November by Bob Harris on *The Old Grey Whistle Test*. He emphasised the positives of playing in Mott the Hoople and was clearly relieved to be free of the pressure of being a front man: 'I'm enjoying it. It's been good fun because I can just pick up a guitar and walk around the stage and play.' If he was aware of the tensions within the band, he tactfully steered clear of the subject and was enthusiastic about the future: 'It'll be nice when we record a new album, because then I'll probably feel like I've added more. I'm looking forward to doing fresh material where I can feel like more of a part of Mott the Hoople, rather than just being another guitar player coming in and learning the set numbers.'

During that week's break between the European tour and the planned UK tour, Ian Hunter flew to America and was taken seriously ill with physical and mental exhaustion. The UK tour was rescheduled and Mick was despatched to the States to support Ian. The more they talked, the more they realised they shared much in common. Ian was as tired of the burden of being Mott's frontman as Mick had been with his short-lived solo career. Ian was weary of trying to manage the band's dynamics and tired of being the bad guy in the middle. Mick later described his short period with the band in a 1984 interview with Kevin Cann for *Starzone*: 'Mott the Hoople was really just something else to do, but I liked Ian, really more than I liked the band. It was Ian that I did it for; the band talked me into joining them, which was just for about three weeks. I got disillusioned real fast. It was partly my fault, I suppose; it just didn't gel. Ian was also getting tired of that situation too, so it was a good excuse to work together. He asked me if I would do an album with him if he left Mott and I said "Sure" and that was it.' Mick and Ian's decision to free themselves from the politics and pressures of the band, meant the remaining members of Mott were left with the option of carrying on without them, or folding the band. By the end of December, Mott the Hoople was no more.

Out of the wreckage emerged a stronger professional and personal bond between Mick and Ian, which formed the basis for many music collaborations and a lifelong friendship. In January 1975 they worked

Musician and Producer for Hire: 1974–1977

together at Air Studios in London, recording Ian Hunter's first eponymous solo album. They recruited Dennis Elliott on drums, Pete Arnesen on keyboards, and former Rats musician Geoff Appleby to play bass. Geoff was delighted: 'The whole experience was brilliant and great fun. The magic between Ian and Mick was in their communication, the respect for each other, but most of all their love and friendship. I loved working with Mick, he's the best guitarist I've ever worked with and one of the best friends I've ever worked with.' Mick shared producer credits with Ian, was credited with song arrangements, and also had a co-writer credit for the song 'Boy'. The album has the energy and confidence of accomplished rock and roll with great guitar work from Mick on 'Once Bitten, Twice Shy', 'The Truth, the Whole Truth, Nuthin' but the Truth' and 'Lounge Lizard', which Mick had worked on during his brief stint with Mott. It demonstrates once again how Mick was musically far more at ease working alongside a skilled songwriter, sharing the creative process of developing the songs.

In January 1975 'Billy Porter' was released as a single in advance of the February release of Mick's second solo album *Play Don't Worry*. By then Mick had stepped away from the solo spotlight and his focus was fixed firmly on doing further work with Ian Hunter. In March they embarked on a two-week UK tour as Hunter-Ronson. The former Mott pianist 'Blue' Weaver replaced Pete Arnesen, who was unable to do the tour. The set-list was a mix of songs from Ian's new album and Mick's two solo albums. It was a great combination, and the professional enjoyment that had eluded Mick over the past two years began to re-emerge. The creative elements he valued were all now in place with the right people who could accomplish it live and in the studio.

Joe Elliot first saw Mick live on this tour at Sheffield and Mick Rossi, who would form the band Slaughter and the Dogs, would be a regular attendee at gigs. Ronson fan Steve Parry saw the Hunter Ronson Band at Leeds City Hall on 27 March 1975: 'It was an incredible set, but it is not the music I remember most that evening but the sheer humanity of Mick Ronson. It was a cold winter night in Leeds. After the performance a few of us had gathered at the stage door hoping to meet our hero. Mick came outside and proceeded to sign autographs, pose for photos and numerous other requests. He appeared genuinely pleased, humbled by the fact we loved the music and had bothered to hang around after the gig to say hello. He was also concerned that we might catch our death of cold. Worried about our well-being he invited us onto the tour bus and entertained us by chatting for almost an hour. I recall fondly a rather shy, gentle, modest person, unblemished by fame, keen to compliment other people.'

In April 'Once Bitten, Twice Shy' was released as a single followed by the Ian Hunter solo album. On 11 April, the band were booked to perform on *The Old Grey Whistle Test*, but Ian was obliged to leave for the States shortly before to fulfil his American visa requirements. Geoff Appleby remembers the session: 'That was very memorable. It was originally scheduled as a Hunter-Ronson set to promote Ian's solo album, but Ian had to shoot off to America, so we did it without him.' The band played two tracks off Mick's solo album – 'Play Don't Worry' and 'Angel No. 9' – with Mick totally at ease and confident, not only on guitar but also with his role as frontman on lead vocals. Working the right way with the right people was now delivering the creative outcome that the hype of MainMan had failed to achieve.

From mid-April to early June the Hunter-Ronson band, including Geoff Appleby on bass, toured the States. From the summer of '75 Mick and Suzi relocated to a rented flat in Hudson Street in the Meatpacking District of Manhattan in New York, between Chelsea and Greenwich Village. Mick and Ian were writing together with every intention of recording a Hunter-Ronson album, but their respective record companies, RCA and CBS, couldn't agree to a deal that would allow this to happen. Ian Hunter felt that Tony Defries was partly responsible for the impasse, and was frustrated that both were still caught between competing agendas: Ian could do a solo album and so could Mick, but they couldn't do an album together. To add to Mick's frustration, RCA had no real enthusiasm for a third Ronson solo album but still held him to their contract without any commitment to financing or promoting a record. According to Kevin Cann: 'MainMan gave Mick no guidance after the release of *Play Don't Worry*. Defries was now based in New York and focused on Bowie and busy with many other projects. Mick's records weren't selling that well either, which didn't help matters. So Mick and Suzi moved to America because nothing was really happening for them in England.'

What Mick and Ian could do, was enjoy each other's company and hang out at the local Greenwich Village bars and clubs where top artists played and socialised. At one such club, the Bitter End in Bleecker Street, renamed the Other End in 1975, Mick met Bob Dylan. Mick had gone to the club with singer-guitarist Bob Neuwirth and according to one account, Mick got hassled by the bartender, which resulted in him being thrown out. Bob Dylan came out onto the street and suggested

Musician and Producer for Hire: 1974–1977

he and Mick go elsewhere for a drink. That night Dylan asked Mick to join his Rolling Thunder Revue Band, which was scheduled to tour that autumn. Mick readily agreed, heard nothing for a month and then got a phone call from Dylan saying they were starting rehearsals the next day.

Mick had never been a particular fan of Bob Dylan and wasn't interested in playing folk music. Much of Dylan's early material was dominated by acoustic guitar and harmonica, and unlikely to have registered on Mick's musical radar when he was playing in the Crestas, the Mariners or the Rats. Dylan had 'gone electric' in 1965 at the Newport Folk Festival and by the mid-'70s was firmly in folk-rock territory, so asking Mick Ronson to perform with him was not in itself out of the ordinary. What probably was startling was the cultural juxtaposition of the American icon of inscrutability with the dry Yorkshire wit of Ronson. Dylan like Lou Reed before him, found Mick's thick Hull accent hard to understand and Mick thought Dylan sounded like Yogi Bear, the Hanna-Barbera TV cartoon character.

The Rolling Thunder Revue was Dylan's 60-date cross-country road trip, featuring friends and legends such as Joan Baez, Ramblin' Jack Elliott and Roger McGuinn, and a stream of guests including Allen Ginsberg, Kinky Friedman, Joni Mitchell, Leonard Cohen, and Arlo Guthrie. A backing band called Guam was assembled and included Bob Neuwirth, T Bone Burnett, Rob Stoner, Dave Mansfield, Steven Soles, Ronnie Blakley and Howie Wyeth. In October 1975 Mick was in New York rehearsing with Dylan and an assembled throng of many of these legendary musicians. Mick could hold his own musically with any big star and had years of experience playing with Bowie and other top musicians, but there in that rehearsal room he had a 'boy back at school' feeling of anxiety and nerves: 'We went in and did like 150 numbers in 10 hours straight through. I thought there'd be a set of numbers and we'd try to get them right, but there were so many, there was no way. I was a bit worried, but they gave me encouragement by not saying anything. If I'd been playing a few notes and everybody's eyes had gone to me, I would have died on the spot. But everybody was so easy-going. I'd look to T Bone Burnett for chords and sometimes *he* wouldn't know.'

Over the course of the ten hours' continuous rehearsal, they covered the bones of a huge number of songs from Dylan's massive back catalogue. The rehearsals were really more like jam sessions, as musicians were invited to run through the songs with Dylan and 'keep up' with him as he chose the key, the time signature and whatever version of the lyrics he fancied for that day's particular interpretation.

The Mick Ronson Story

John Bentley remembers a chance meeting with Mick in London sometime after Mick had finished the Rolling Thunder tour: 'I was asking him what it was like and he said, "When we rehearsed with Dylan, you wouldn't have time to run through all the songs, so what he'd do is he'd just do a verse and a chorus of each song, so you could get through everything. It's still quite a long day sort of running all these songs." They'd been probably doing it for I don't know how many hours, just doing the verse and chorus of each one, and then he got to the end of the rehearsal and Dylan turns round to everybody and goes, "Is everybody OK with all that?" And everyone's going, "Yeah, yeah, that's cool, Bob." Mick just retains a fantastic sense of humour and it's very unique to Hull, and this would have gone completely over Dylan's head, but Ronno turns to Dylan and says: "Yeah I'm alright with that, but er, you know that song about the wind?' and Bob Dylan goes: "'Blowin' in the Wind'?" and Mick Ronson says: "How's it go again?"'

The first leg of the Rolling Thunder tour ran from October to December 1975, with a second leg from April to June 1976. As in rehearsals, they would play the songs live in an unpredictable key or tempo, with varying structures or stop points, with the set-list as such being open to the point of random. For the band of musicians less familiar with Dylan's repertoire, Mick in particular, this required a high level of musical proficiency and an ability to improvise in the moment with skill and spontaneity. In *Classic Rock* magazine Bob Neuwirth described how Mick responded to the challenge: 'Ronson was a great lead player and he just jumped into it. I fell in love with his guitar playing on the spot. There were seven guitarists in the band at one point, but Mick's brilliance was the way in which he adapted to what everyone else was doing around him. He played every style of music, too – Beck, Hendrix, you name it. Mick Ronson was, quite simply, a tour de force!'

Mick made a big impression and charmed some of the most iconic figures on the tour, including Joan Baez. In a classic tour image, she gazes adoringly at Mick, coolly clad in a hippy bandana with his long platinum hair and arms raised aloft. A recent graduate of the David Bowie school of hair and stage make-up, Mick took an impromptu responsibility for some of the male grooming and the spooky painted faces that Dylan and the others wore on stage. The tour introduced Mick to a score of American musicians, leading to countless future collaborations in the studio and on the road. Even before the Rolling Thunder Tour had finished, Mick worked with Roger McGuinn in the gap between the autumn and spring touring schedules, playing on and

Musician and Producer for Hire: 1974–1977

producing his solo album *Cardiff Rose*, released in May 1976. The Rolling Thunder Revue also led to a live album, *Hard Rain*, on which Mick plays on the track 'Maggie's Farm'. It also spawned a film by Dylan, *Renaldo and Clara*, in which Mick plays a cameo role as a security guard, his first acting since the *Slaughter on 10th Avenue* promo film. In June 2019 Martin Scorsese released Rolling *Thunder Revue: A Bob Dylan Story*, a filmed record of the tour in which Mick is prominent in many scenes.

Over the Christmas 1975 holiday, Mick was back with his family in Hull on Greatfield Estate. An 18-year-old Paul Hudson, an obsessive Bowie fan, got to hear that Mick was home and plucked up the courage to ask Mick's brother David if he could get the chance to meet him, and was told to come round to the house. 'I went to the pub first to have a few pints to get a bit of Dutch courage. I walked past the house several times before I plucked up the courage and knocked on the door. Dave said: "Yeah, come in, come in" and I went into the living room and Mick was just laid on the floor. I'm sure he had a white towelling dressing gown and he was smoking roll-ups and drinking snowballs. Of all the things, he was drinking advocaat and lemonade! I'm pretty sure he was playing a game with his Dad, called Mastermind.' Mick chatted with the star-struck teenager, by which time his pre-visit courage-booster was starting to kick in: 'By now I was busting to go to the toilet, but 'cause there's Mick Ronson there, I daren't, you can't leave the room, but after a while I was in that much pain I couldn't stand up straight. I practically crawled up the stairs. I went to the toilet and came back down again. After a while I said: "Would you sign my albums for me?" and he said: "Yeah, yeah no problem." So I run home back to my house, I could have probably beaten Mo Farah that day, running back to my house and back to Milford Grove. He signed my albums, he signed both of them, and I've treasured them ever since.' What struck Paul and has stayed with him was the startling juxtaposition and disparity between Mick's massive profile as an international rock star, and how unassuming and ordinary he and his family were as people: 'If you'd have walked into the house and somebody said this is Mick Ronson's mother's house, I don't think you would have believed it. It was just a basic family home. You got the feeling he really was just chilled out, rolling the odd fag now and again, and relaxed to be back at home with his family, away from whatever he was doing at that time. It was for me the chance of a lifetime.'

With the Rolling Thunder tour over by the summer of 1976, Mick decided to make some changes in his professional career. With no prospect of a further album with RCA, Mick opted to finish with Tony

Defries and MainMan, and chose Barry Imhoff as his new manager. He and Suzi also decided to move out of Manhattan and bought a house in the Woodstock area. The district was still bathed in the afterglow of the legendary festival from August 1969, held in Max Yasgur's dairy farm at Bethel, a small village 64km (40 miles) from the actual town of Woodstock. With its attractive rural setting only a two-hour drive north of New York, numerous musicians and producers had settled in the area, creating a laid-back community of post counter-culture musos. Albert Grossman, the manager of Bob Dylan, the Band, Janis Joplin and Todd Rundgren, had started a small recording studio at Bearsville, which offered someone like Mick the ideal environment. Alongside his frequent continental trips to work in England and Europe, it gave him the freedom to practise his craft, producing songs, both for himself and for other artists, without having to travel. That summer he started the Mick Ronson Band with himself on lead guitar and vocals, Mick Barakan on guitar, Jay Davis on bass and Bobby Chen on drums. They did some recording sessions and a short tour in December of dates across New York State. The band failed, however, to secure a potential record deal with Atlantic, so the recorded material from the studio and live shows didn't surface until 1999, when some of it appeared on Mick's posthumous albums *Just Like This and Showtime*. In the spring of 1977 Suzi was pregnant with their daughter Lisa and in March, Mick and Suzi married in Woodstock. Lisa was born in August that year, and quickly became the apple of her father's eye. Suzi recalls: 'He loved little Lisa, that was his girl. She is very much like her dad, two peas in a pod. They're very similar in looks, as well as personality. She is a darling girl and he adored her.'

That year *The Old Grey Whistle Test* with its presenter Bob Harris visited the Bearsville Picnic, an annual 'backyard' music festival held in the area, with the programme broadcast by the BBC the following year, on 2 May 1978. Numerous local musicians, as well as celebrity performers such as John Sebastian, Paul Butterfield and Todd Rundgren, played sets outdoors or in the local Bearsville Theatre. Amongst those filmed was a very relaxed Mick Ronson, who was clearly at ease in the chilled-out vibe of the event and the locality. Interviewed by Bob Harris, Mick flagged up his intentions to do more production work later that year back in England: 'I want to check out a few people around London, different musicians, you know, I want to see what's going on. The last time I was in London I was with Van Morrison and London was real kind of busy. Every time I turned my head around I would see somebody else and I was getting to do some playing and stuff, and it was real nice, there was a lot of action going on.'

Still only just in his 30s, Mick had already achieved more than most people manage in a lifetime, but his focus was still on maintaining the momentum of constantly working, whether on the road touring, or producing in the studio. That pattern was fixed for the remainder of his life. The estate kid had well and truly broken free from the small-town boundaries of a northern industrial city. He'd not only left Hull, he'd left the UK, and was now living in the States and working internationally wherever the music took him. He was also beginning to hit the bottle.

11. The Long Road Home: 1977–1993

The Long Road Home: 1977–1993

As a young man Mick rarely drank, and as friends and band members would always assert, he wasn't one for the pubs, other than as a place for playing or listening to music. Mick knew that anything more than a half pint would make him tipsy and affect his playing, so he steered clear of alcohol apart from in small quantities. Even on tour with Bowie he avoided the wilder excesses of rock and roll party culture. But once settled in America, he put aside the abstemious lifestyle and began drinking spirits, sometimes in voluminous quantities. He was an incredibly hard-working musician and producer, but with the music business being a wholly liberal milieu, there were few or no constraints in the workplace. After a heavy session a big English breakfast would see him through, and many colleagues were amazed at his ability to be up and functioning in the morning, when they were still pretty much out of it. It did, however, sometimes affect his work.

In 1976 he was back in England in the studio with Michael Chapman, who wanted him to play on *The Man Who Hated Mornings*. He was looking for some more of the magic that Ronson and his electric guitar had brought to '*Fully Qualified Survivor*' six years earlier. In an interview with the authors Chapman recalled he was not impressed: 'Mick turned up at the sessions with his blond Les Paul and a bottle of vodka. He was in a bit of a state and sounded terrible. Even I could have done better.' Chapman was noted for wanting to be in and out of studios as quickly as possible, as he felt the time spent recording was robbing him of touring gig income. As Mick got progressively worse throughout the day, he was about to write the whole session off. 'Then all of a sudden he just seemed to come alive on one tune, ironically "I'm Sober Now", before going back to playing shit again!' Mick's solo on that track is precise and accomplished, but it is the only song featuring him on the entire album. A more successful session that year was on Roger Daltrey's solo album *One of the Boys*. Mick was one of several top guitarists to play on the album, including John Entwhistle, Eric Clapton, and one of Mick's early heroes from the Shadows, Hank Marvin.

In 1977 Ched Cheesman, Mick's former Rats bandmate, met up with Mick in London in the Marquee Club: 'I was in a band with Geoff Appleby called the Monitors and we did a support gig to Chris Spedding in Hull, and it turned out his tour manager was a guy from Hull, so he got us to support Spedding at the Marquee Club. So we went down there to do a gig and I guess Geoff Appleby must have been in touch with Mick and told him we were playing, so he came down to see us. Most of the night I would have been onstage and playing, but

The Mick Ronson Story

I remember having sat at the table just having a general conversation. Mick wasn't doing anything at the time, I don't think he had a band, and I remember saying to him: "You should get a really good rock band together. Surely now you should be able to get just about anybody you want in a band", but he didn't really respond to me, he just kind of stared at me as if he didn't know what to say about that.'

In the autumn of '77 Mick was back in London checking out various bands and musicians with whom he could potentially work as a producer. Punk had exploded on the music scene with its raw sound and DIY attitude. Mick met up with Glen Matlock, former bassist with the Sex Pistols and now with the Rich Kids. In 1978 Mick produced their only album, *Ghosts of Princes in Towers*, with guitarist Steve New, drummer Rusty Egan and vocalist Midge Ure. He also worked with Mick Rossi of Slaughter and the Dogs, an ardent Ronson fan, who had seen many of his gigs and named the band after his favourite Ronson and Bowie albums. Mick played on the tracks 'Quick Joey Small' and 'Who Are the Mystery Girls?', which appeared on the band's first LP *Do It Dog Style*. In a characteristically generous gesture Ronno gave Mick Rossi his Les Paul guitar and it went with Rossi to the States when he moved there. By a circuitous route it ended up back in Britain in Manchester, when it was purchased by guitar collector Alan Maskell. It returned temporarily to Hull when Alan kindly offered it to be exhibited, and performed by Ched Cheesman, for *Turn and Face the Strange* in 2017.

In 1978 Mick also produced the Dead Fingers Talk album *Storm the Reality Studios*. DFT had started life in Hull in 1969 as the band Bone, influenced by late '60s rock and psychedelic bands. Founder members Jeff Parsons and Rob Eunson, aka Bobo Phoenix, had both seen Mick play in the Rats. Bone folded after a year but then reformed in 1975 as Dead Fingers Talk, by which time singer Rob Eunson had become keen on Bowie and bands such as the New York Dolls. The pair's musical influences were thus a part mirror-image of Mick's own career. Drawn by the punk scene, DFT moved to London in 1977 and secured a record deal with Pye. Aware of Mick's work with Rich Kids and Slaughter and the Dogs, the record company suggested the new-wave Hull band team up with fellow Hull musician and producer Mick Ronson, so they worked together for several weeks recording the album. Rob Eunson: 'I just remember him like, he didn't put on any airs and graces. He didn't brag, he didn't name-drop, he didn't do any of that kind of bollocks. We were musicians and he was there to help us and that was it.' Jeff Parsons recalls: "My memory of him was of a real nice, down-to-earth guy who's

The Long Road Home: 1977–1993

just like one of your mates. We had a lot of fun talking about the old days, talking about Bowie and Dylan. Maybe we just got on a bit too well and it was a bit too free and easy. We weren't well disciplined and in some ways I think if he'd have been a little bit more of a taskmaster maybe we would have got better results.' After several weeks in the studio, the record company wanted their product, so the album was somewhat rushed in the final instance. Despite the album perhaps failing to fulfil its potential, Jeff Parsons is in no doubt as to Mick's contribution: 'Mick had this real musical gift, so he knew what sounded good and why it sounded good and he had that ability to make things work in the studio. He knew instinctively what would work and he would put in these little touches, which is one of the things about being a producer. It's about hearing a song and being able to hear stuff in there that adds to the song. Whereas some people just want to put their sound all over a song, especially guitar players, he served the song and that is the big thing. Serve the song, do what the song deserves, what the song needs, and he could do that.'

Mick's ability to collaborate in the studio with many different musicians across a range of music genres took him that year from punk rock to avant-garde jazz, when he worked again with Annette Peacock. Her music spanned a wide range from innovative electronic music, using an early prototype Moog synthesiser, to jazz ballads. Mick rated her debut solo album *I'm the One* from 1972 and had re-recorded its title track along with her arrangement of Elvis Presley's 'Love Me Tender' on *Slaughter*. He also recorded her song 'Seven Days' and released it as the B-side to the 'Billy Porter' single. Annette had signed with MainMan and relocated to London, where in 1978 she recorded her second album *X-Dreams*. Mick played on four tracks: 'My Mama Never Taught Me How To Cook', 'Questions', "Too Much in The Skies', and 'Don't Be Cruel'.

In October '78 Mick began working again with Ian Hunter on his fourth solo album *You're Never Alone with a Schizophrenic*. Recording started in London but then moved to New York, engaging some of Bruce Springsteen's E Street Band. The title for the album came from Mick spotting it written on a New York toilet wall. The moment he mentioned it, Ian wanted it as the album title, trading it for a joint songwriter credit on the LP's single 'Just Another Night'. Mick played his usual stunning guitar on the album and was co-producer with Ian. The record was released in March 1979 and became Hunter's best-selling album to date.

Mick worked almost exclusively with Ian over the next two years. The wrangles with record companies meant their extensive tours were billed as the Ian Hunter Band featuring Mick Ronson. Fans didn't mind because the partnership was as strong as ever onstage with terrific live performances. The band headlined their own shows and also played support at various times to the Kinks and Blue Oyster Cult. The success of *You're Never Alone with a Schizophrenic* prompted Chrysalis to follow it up with a double live album *Welcome to the Club* recorded during the November '79 gigs at the Roxy Theatre in West Hollywood and co-produced by Mick and Ian. The live album provided a strong showcase of the power of the Hunter-Ronson partnership with its combination of Ian's songs alongside Ronson's powerful guitar. Mick's own tracks such as 'FBI', harked back to his love of the Shadows, and the constantly reworked instrumental 'Slaughter on Tenth Avenue' was arguably far more powerful live than the studio version on the original album. 1979 saw the band playing across Canada and the States with around 90 gigs, culminating in just one show in London at the Hammersmith Odeon. The incessant touring continued into the '80s with shows from April in Germany, filmed at the Rockpalast gig in Essen, and in Paris, with yet another extensive tour of the States from May through to July. A rough tally of their performances over the two years leads to a total of around 120 gigs together, a phenomenal stint even by rock and roll's standards. Mick then co-produced, with Mick Jones of the Clash, Ian's fifth studio album *Short Back 'n' Sides*, which was released in 1981. Mick Jones' punk-reggae influence can be clearly heard on the album. The song 'Lisa Likes Rock & Roll' was Ian's tribute to Mick and Suzi's daughter.

That year Mick formed a new band with Mick Barakan, touring the States in August as the New York Yanquis. He also played on Meatloaf's second album *Dead Ringer*, which reached No. 1 in the UK. Mick also composed music for a film titled *Indian Summer*, which didn't progress to shooting; it took another 20 years before the music appeared on an album of the same name released in 2001.

In October '81 Ian Hunter was on the road again, but without Mick Ronson, when his keyboardist Tommy Mandel suffered a stroke. Hunter phoned Mick's then manager Sam Lederman to ask if Mick would step in, which puzzled Lederman who thought of Mick solely as a guitarist and didn't realise he was also a proficient piano player. Mick travelled to join the band in Texas but on arriving drank heavily. Given the state he ended up in, Ian was about to pull him from the band, but Mick straightened out, started to play more than competently, and successfully completed the tour. This tour took place during a period when Mick was heartily sick of playing the guitar, complaining of the

The Long Road Home: 1977–1993

current adulation being heaped on guitarists who played a thousand notes a minute in a fast flashy style, which offended his own musical sensibility that 'less is often more'.

For the next couple of years Mick worked primarily in Canada, joining the band Payola$ on keyboards for their winter 82/83 tour. Although barely known outside their own country, Payolas had achieved two No. 1 singles in Canada. Mick also found time in 1982 to work with John Cougar Mellencamp. Tony Defries had approached Mellencamp while Mick was on the Rolling Thunder Revue tour and offered him a substantial advance to make demos of some of his new songs. The process of completing the subsequent album *American Fool*, produced by Mellencamp and Don Gehman, was somewhat drawn out and fraught. Mick was asked to come on board at a late stage and helped turn the album into what became a US No. 1. Mellencamp had almost given up on the now famous track 'Jack & Diane' until Mick suggested the use of baby rattles on percussion and a gospel choir ending. Mick's knowledge of studio techniques, incorporating the use of a gated reverb effect for the drum track, and his playing on the song, all led John Mellencamp to acknowledge that his hit single was primarily thanks to Mick. As with Lou Reed's 'Perfect Day', Mick was once again able to take the seed of an incomplete musical idea and improve it almost beyond recognition to produce a hit record.

In 1983 Mick was offered a well-paid gig with Bob Seger's touring band, but never one to chase the money, he opted instead to work with T Bone Burnett for a fraction of the pay, playing touring support for the Who. He also played on Burnett's album *Proof Through the Night*, on the tracks 'The Murder Weapon', 'The Sixties' and 'Pressure'. The year also saw Mick co-producing Toronto based singer-songwriter Lisa Dal Bello's album *Whomanfoursays*. Also known as Dalbello, she had been successful as a dance-pop singer, but the album marked her reinvention from mainstream pop into a much edgier alternative artist. They produced, played and mixed the whole album together, making extensive use of the new sampling technology offered by the Fairlight CMI digital synthesiser. The album opened up a whole new career for the artist in Europe and her home country Canada, the success of which she acknowledged was down to Mick. The music on the album is unlike anything he had helped create previously, and is certainly a long way from rock and roll. It demonstrates the sheer range of music that interested Mick, and his ability as a producer to help another musician find their unique voice and style.

In September '83 Bowie was performing in Toronto on his Serious Moonlight tour and suggested to Mick that he join them onstage to play 'Jean Genie', which he did on the second night. It was the first time in ten years that the two had shared a stage together. Mick borrowed Earl Slick's guitar for the track and much to the latter's horror proceeded to thrash it to hell, waving it above his head in a wild display of rock and roll showmanship. The audience loved it, but Earl was mortified at the risk and potential damage to his treasured guitar. It would be almost another decade again before Mick and Bowie would perform together at the Freddie Mercury Tribute at Wembley Stadium in 1992.

In 1984 Mick heard that his former Rats and Hunter-Ronson bandmate Geoff Appleby was seriously ill and flew back to Hull to visit. Geoff had suffered a stroke that May and was in Hull Royal Infirmary. He was showing no sign of recovery from his comatose state and his wife Moira and their family, including their 10-year-old daughter Sasha, were by his hospital bedside fearing the worst. Mick approached and spoke to Geoff, who woke, smiled and responded. It was the first indication of any cognitive functioning since his aneurysm. For the family it was as if Mick's presence had a miraculous effect and they were forever grateful. As friend Les Morfitt describes: 'That's the sort of guy he was. He came from one end of the world to see his best mate.' That autumn Mick had his own family issues to deal with: his father George became ill with cancer, and died on 9 November, and was buried in Hull's Eastern Cemetery. George's influence on his son probably gave Mick his need to be incessantly working. As Benny Marshall described, 'Mick had that fire burning inside of him. He wanted to get on all the time – "I've got to get on, I've got to get on" – he had a drive about him.'

Throughout the '80s that energy and drive meant he was constantly travelling for work across North America and Europe. In 1985 he was back in London with former Rich Kids singer Midge Ure, who had gone on to form Visage and then Ultravox. Midge wanted Mick to play guitar with his solo touring band. A film feature of their rehearsals was broadcast on 1 October on *The Old Grey Whistle Test*, with Mick playing guitar on the track 'Wastelands'. The liaison lasted only a couple of weeks. He was replaced by Glaswegian guitarist 'Zal' Cleminson who had played in the '70s with the Alex Harvey Band. Midge Ure had co-written with Bob Geldof and produced the massive Band Aid single 'Do They Know It's Christmas?' the previous year. With Geldof he'd set up the Band Aid Trust and then together they organised the global phenomenon that was Live Aid with its two benefit concerts in London

The Long Road Home: 1977–1993

and Philadelphia in July 1985. The late '80s saw Mick working on various projects with bands such as the Fatal Flowers, an Amsterdam-based blues rock band. Mick produced their second album in 1988 *Johnny D. is Back!* and their third *Pleasure Ground* in 1990, both of which sold well.

Towards the end of the decade Mick rediscovered his passion for playing the guitar and in 1988 phoned his long-time friend and collaborator Ian Hunter, saying he wanted to play with him again. It had been six years since they'd toured together, so they embarked on some low-key Hunter-Ronson Band dates in Canada that summer, followed by a series of dates that autumn in the States. 1989 saw them embark on a Scandinavian and European tour culminating in two sold out nights at the Dominion Theatre in London in February, the first time the pair had performed in the UK for around seven years. The show was recorded as part of the *BBC In Concert* series. That autumn they were on the road again in North America with a guest appearance by Joe Elliott at the gig on November 4, at Cleveland. Earlier in June and July that year Mick and Ian had recorded another album together in New York titled *Yui Orta*, which was released that October. Mick got substantially more Hunter-Ronson co-composer credits than on any previous album, as Ian realised that Mick rarely got well paid for his production or session work, and it was only through songwriting credits that he would earn some longer-term returns for his work.

One of the backing vocalists on that album was Swedish singer Carola Westerlund, whom Mick had met earlier that year when he played in Stockholm. Carola was part of the Swedish band EC2 with Estelle Millburne. Mick returned to Sweden to do some production work for the band and started a relationship with Carola. Mick's relationship with Suzi had broken down in the late '80s, partly as a result of being away from home for long periods of time. When their daughter was young, both Lisa and Suzi would go on tour with Mick, but as Lisa reached high school age that was no longer possible.

The new decade began with the Hunter-Ronson Band back on the road touring across Europe. Mick went to live in Sweden with Carola Westerlund, and their son Joakim, Mick's third child, was born on 15 April 1990. Mick was touring Sweden again with Ian in May and June 1991, by which time his relationship with Carola had also broken down. That year Mick produced the Swedish cult goth rock band Leather Nun's fourth album, *Nun Permanent*. It sounds remarkably fresh and accomplished 30 years on, no doubt partly due to Mick's production work, which delivers the raw energy of the band with echoes of Lou

Reed and Iggy Pop. The album never achieved the success it deserved, as distribution ground to a halt when the band's record company went bankrupt the year it was released.

Ronson fan and Bowie expert Kevin Cann had by this point built up a close relationship with Mick: 'He looked to me as being his manager for a while, but we never formalised it. He was struggling financially and I was trying to be a helping hand with general administration. At that time I was saying, *The way I can help you in the short term, is to help you set up a tour*. I wanted him to do his own music, 'cause he often used to play other people's material and rarely his own. I'd envisaged a "Mick Ronson Hits Tour" sort of thing. He said, "Yeah I'll do that." He hadn't got a record deal at that time and the tour was intended to help Mick get a new LP released and give him some cash he could take home to Sweden. We started to get a band together. He would go and listen to various bands. One particular one was suggested by a friend of mine – he had his own band who jokingly said, "Bring Mick Ronson along." I mentioned it to Mick, as we were in central London that evening, and he said: "Why not?", so we went to see this rehearsal. Mick picked up a guitar and played along with them. They were amazed he actually turned up. He had no airs and graces like that – he would happily sit in with a pub band given the chance."

Kevin's relationship with Mick often involved essential transport duties: 'He brought Joakim over with him in 1991 and I met him at the airport. I was a bit late that day and when I met him in the terminal he was there with baby Joakim and a baby buggy looking agitated. He said: "I thought you weren't coming, I was getting worried", but was relieved I was there. Another time, when I was dropping him off at Heathrow one evening, we were walking through the terminal and walked straight into Alice Cooper coming out of a shop. It was a lovely meeting, like they'd known each other forever, and Alice invited us to his show.'

That year Mick began to suffer from back pain. Kevin Cann could see that something had changed for the worse: 'Another time after that I picked him up at the airport and he was different. I was driving him and his conversation began to be a bit weird. He started by saying that he'd done some bad things in his life. I immediately felt he was telling me things I'm not sure I wanted to hear, so I blocked most of it out. But I believe it was generally a reference to his drinking and not settling down and that he wished he'd spent more time with his family. Eventually I asked him if something was wrong and he told me he wasn't well. As soon as we arrived at our destination, I called Maggi [Ronson] to tell

The Long Road Home: 1977–1993

her. I said, "There's definitely something wrong. I don't think he's very well." She was nursing at the time and said she would arrange to get him checked out, so I said, "I'll get him over to you." He had the hospital appointment the following day and that night Maggi called and said, "It isn't good – he's got terminal cancer."'

The diagnosis was sudden and shocking. Barely in his mid-forties, Mick had inoperable liver cancer. At one appointment he was told it was unlikely he would live to see Christmas. Kevin Cann again: 'Everything changed with his prognosis. I said to the tour promoters he was unwell – and he needs care – he can't do the tour. So we unpicked the tour we were setting up. He was still well enough to do things and still gigged from time to time, but a solo tour was out. He actually had two years of life from the point of knowing the diagnosis. But from then on it was more about organising what he needed.'

Friends rallied round as Kevin describes: 'People began sending him money to keep his head above water. Suzi had put out a distress call and collected some money. I was there when he needed me. His mum would phone me to tell me what flights he was arriving on. I said I would collect him from the airport whenever he needed. I would always be there to pick him up.' Mick needed to be in London for ongoing medical treatment. Former manager Tony Defries made sure he had a place to stay as Kevin recounts: 'Defries had a soft spot for Mick, always had a soft spot for him. Mick never had a bad word about him. Defries had been supportive as soon as he was told Mick was seriously ill. He had a lovely house in Hasker Street, but it had fallen into disrepair and needed a lot of work doing, so he paid for that to be done up, so Mick could stay there in his last months. It was very peaceful and comfortable, his family could visit, and it was close to where he was getting cancer treatment. It was also close to Hyde Park and he loved to walk there.' Other friends such as Ian Hunter and Joe Elliot helped where they could. Def Leppard covered 'Only After Dark' for the B-side of 'Let's Get Rocked' in early 1992, and Joe Elliot made sure they donated the royalties to help pay for Mick's soaring cancer treatment bills.

Mick refused to bow to any sense of the outcome being inevitable. In an interview with the *Hull Daily Mail* he insisted: 'I'm going to get rid of this. The doctors say it's incurable, but I don't believe anything is. People do go into remission and are still here ten years later. I feel really positive. I don't feel bad about it. I'm looking forward to fighting it and getting on with my life again.' He changed his eating habits and abandoned the full English breakfasts in favour of a vegetarian diet.

There were many more things he was determined to achieve with his music. In October '91 he toured Sweden with Graham Parker. He made sure that Tuesdays were free of commitments, and would fly home to London for chemotherapy and then return to Sweden the next day to continue touring.

Mick stayed positive throughout as Kevin Cann recalls: 'He was very buoyant about it, very upbeat, though we knew he wouldn't survive it. I felt his pain. And very soon he was starting to get major pain in his lower back. I remember we were driving along the Embankment one summer evening in '92 and he was clearly in pain, and it upset me greatly 'cause I felt it too. I wanted to tell the world – this amazing man, we are going to lose him. At Hasker St, the door would often go and a fan would be there on the doorstep. Mick would always go and chat with them. We had to rescue him a few times 'cause it was freezing cold. He always wore his shirt unbuttoned and his chest was always exposed. I was worried he'd catch a cold and I didn't want him to go down with anything else.'

In February and March 1992 Mick produced Morrisey's album *Your Arsenal*. During the sessions he confided with Morrissey some of the detail and extent of his creative partnership with Bowie, including the many guitar hooks he'd created, particularly those on 'Starman' and 'The Man Who Sold the World', for which of course Mick was never credited or paid. Morrissey was worried that the orchestration at the end of his album track 'I Know it's Gonna Happen Someday' was too similar to the end of Bowie's Ziggy classic 'Rock 'n' Roll Suicide'. Mick assured Morrissey that Bowie wouldn't sue him, as Bowie knew full well that Mick had written that arrangement for 'Rock 'n' Roll Suicide' in the first place. Kevin Cann recalls: 'He was in great pain when he was working with Morrissey. My then office in Gloucester Avenue, Primrose Hill, was close to the studio they were working in. I remember, I wandered down to the studio and we went outside for some air and he was holding his back, he was in a lot of pain. I said, "I wish you weren't working so hard." He said, "I can stop whenever I like. I'm enjoying it." It was always about the work with Mick. He loved being in the studio. So much so that he would often say yes to things before even thinking about it. He crammed in as much as he physically could in that last two years.'

Your Arsenal was released in July 1992 to highly favourable reviews and reached No. 4 in the UK charts. Mick's production work helped Morrissey make the transition from his previous indie-pop mode to a more muscular sound, thus rebooting his solo career. The album gave Morrissey a breakthrough in the States, where it reached No. 21 in the

The Long Road Home: 1977–1993

charts. At a point when Mick was in significant pain from his cancer treatment, he was still creating memorable work in the studio – a poignant indicator of what he could have gone to achieve had he lived longer.

On 20 April, Mick made what turned out to be his last onstage performance at the Freddie Mercury Tribute Concert at Wembley Stadium. It was broadcast worldwide and featured a star-studded cast of performers: Mick joined Bowie, Ian Hunter, Brian May, Roger Taylor and John Deacon onstage to perform 'All the Young Dudes' with Joe Elliott and Phil Collen from Def Leppard on backing vocals. Mick then went on to play Bowie's classic track 'Heroes'. Despite being in severe pain, it was a stunning finale performance from Mick. His Hull friend Les Morfitt was in the audience. 'When he came on you could see he was poorly and everybody knows he struggled. At the end of the concert we worked our way towards the side of the stage and went to this other area where Mick and a few others were round there signing autographs. He came across and was talking to us. He was asking how we were, and how did it go, and we just kept hold of his hand and we knew he was seriously ill and it was pretty sad.'

That summer Bowie asked Mick to play guitar on a funked-up version of the '60s Cream track 'I Feel Free' for his album *Black Tie White Noise*. In a knowing nod to Morrisey, Bowie also included the track 'I Know it's Gonna Happen Someday' off the *Your Arsenal* album. This was Bowie covering Morrissey sort of covering Bowie, with Mick as the lynchpin throughout. Mick also contributed on a version of Dylan's 'Like a Rolling Stone' which wasn't included on the album. On learning of Mick's illness Bowie offered the track for his *Heaven and Hull* album.

The idea of making what turned out to be his final album gave Mick the positivity and motivation to carry on working through the year and into 1993, and he was passionate about completing it. The roll call of friends and musicians that worked on *Heaven and Hull* is impressive, including Joe Elliott, Chrissie Hynde, John Mellencamp and Sham Morris, while the performance of 'All the Young Dudes' recorded at the Freddie Mercury Tribute Concert became the final track on the album.

Around this time John Cambridge in Hull had a phone call from David Bowie informing him that Mick was very ill. John had had no contact with Mick for over two decades following his unhappy departure from Hype in 1970, other than a brief and somewhat awkward chance encounter in Hull city centre some time after. Bowie gave John Mick's phone number and a few days later John called Mick and passed his own number on to the person who'd answered. Within minutes John got a phone call back: 'It was Mick. He was just as pleased to hear from me as I was from him. We was laughing and joking, and having a natter about the Rats and giggling, all this sort of thing. I didn't mention his cancer and he never really mentioned it, but I said to him, "You still come back to see your mum in Hull don't you?" "Oh yeh." So I said, "Listen, when you get back, Mick, give us a ring and I'll come round and see you and we'll have a right good chinwag. If not, I'll come down to London and we'll do the same there." He said, "Yeh. I'll really look forward to doing that John." But sadly that meeting never took place.'

On 29 April 1993 Mick Ronson succumbed to liver cancer and in the company of family and friends he passed away. Kevin Cann recalls: 'The last time I saw him he was very drawn. But I realised that I wasn't needed at that stage and I backed off a bit. I loved him to bits, but there were more important people for him to be with. He needed his family by his bedside. When he died, I hadn't been in the loop that week and didn't realise he had gone downhill so quick. Even though I'd had two years of knowing it was going to happen, it was still a great shock, and very upsetting for all of us close to him.'

A funeral service was held in London, on 6 May at the Church of Jesus Christ Latter Day Saints on Exhibition Road, attended by friends and family, including Stuey George and John and Angela Cambridge, who had travelled down from Hull. His eldest son Nicholas was also there. Nick had not seen his father in over 20 years and had never known him as an adult. For his mother Minnie, losing her son at such a young age was a heavy blow: 'In the end even his guitar was too heavy for him. He was always saying what he would do for everybody else if he became rich and won the lottery. He said he would buy the family a house and a car. We put a lottery ticket in his coffin with him when he died.' Mick's body was brought back to Hull and he was buried in Eastern Cemetery near the Ronson family home, in the same family plot his father George had been laid nine years before. Benny Marshall recalls: 'At the funeral as they lowered the coffin, some blossom blew from the trees, and Minnie said, "I'm sure that's a sign." I said, "Maybe you're right."'

Ian Hunter mourned the loss of his friend deeply and paid him a moving tribute by writing the song 'Michael Picasso', recorded three years after Mick's death. The song expresses that heart-rending grief felt after a loved one's passing, whilst at the same time honouring Mick's remarkable musical talent. It is an intimate, honest and heartfelt tribute to his close friend and collaborator.

The Long Road Home: 1977–1993

In Hull, Mick's death left many of those who knew him with a raw sense of loss. Steve Magee was deeply affected: 'I was absolutely heartbroken when he died. Although I hadn't seen him in a long time, he was such a genuine likeable person. Even when he was cutting the grass, I remember these pensioners coming out saying, "Michael, would you like a cup of tea?" And people waving at him shouting across the road, he was well known. Or at the music department, top floor at Hammonds and he'd be stood there just surrounded by people. He had hero worship even before he joined Bowie. I was devastated 'cause I always admired him. And I still think to this day, even though he'd played with all these famous people, I don't think it ever went to his head. I still think that if I bumped into him in the street after all these years, he'd still have the time and the courtesy to stand and have a chat with me as an old friend. He was a gentleman and a lot of people liked him and loved him.'

Mick's former Rats roadie and friend Ian Evans was distraught: 'It was just a sad, sad day when he died. I was really upset. I went home and got in the kitchen. I told my mother and I absolutely wept my eyes out. I couldn't stop for ages. She had a real job of consoling me, but it just came out, I couldn't control myself. It was just a thing that really affected me. We were very close and it didn't matter how far he was away, it was the fact that we'd gone through that period as a group and we just bonded. You'll always have that bond no matter. It took about an hour for my mother to console me, I was just so upset. I was absolutely devastated.'

Mick's friend Les Morfit still visits his grave. 'I've been back a few times. I've put the odd roll-up on top of the gravestone 'cause Mick smoked like a chimney and he used to like his rollies as he used to call them. I enjoyed my time, I enjoyed that era, but most of all I enjoyed his company and I loved him to bits.'

The inscription on Mick's gravestone reads:

Sweet Dreamer
To Know Him
Was To Love Him
To Live In The Hearts
Of Those Who Love You
Is Not To Die

12 The Legacy

The Legacy

Since his death, Mick has been remembered in countless articles, on social media and on film. His music has played a significant part in the personal soundtrack of many people's lives and has become more widely available through various posthumous releases. His home city of Hull has increasingly recognised his achievement, and alongside such icons as anti-slavery campaigner William Wilberforce, pioneer aviatrix Amy Johnson and the poet Philip Larkin, Mick is becoming part of the physical fabric of the city and held in the memory of its people.

A year after his death, to the very day, a memorial concert was held at London's Hammersmith Apollo, formerly Hammersmith Odeon, a venue closely associated with Mick. Organised by friend Kevin Cann and Mick's sister Maggi, the concert held on 29 April 1994 featured a stellar line-up of talent, gathered to celebrate the man and the music that was Mick Ronson. As Kevin Cann recalled: 'It was an incredibly difficult show to get on. Bands rehearsing in different parts of the country. Nobody giving us any timings. On the night I kept having to break it to the bands backstage to cut a number as we were going to run wildly over time and there was a serious penalty clause if we went on past an agreed local curfew hour. Gary Brooker thought he was going to be asked to drop "A Whiter Shade of Pale" – he was mightily relieved when I told him to definitely not drop that one!'

The concert, compered by Bob Harris, was a soundtrack to Mick's remarkable life and music career. John Cambridge, Ched Cheesman, Benny Marshall and John Bentley, along with Tony Visconti, recreated the Rats, playing 'It Ain't Easy' and 'I Feel Free'. Woody Woodmansey, Trevor Bolder, Joe Elliott and Phil Collen reconstituted the Spiders from Mars, along with Bill Nelson, Maggi Ronson and Phil Lanzen in the line-up. The Spiders performed a set with classic songs from the Ziggy years. Other artists included Dana Gillespie, Glen Matlock, Big Audio Dynamite, Gary Brooker, Bill Wyman, Andy Fairweather-Low, Henry Spinetti and Tex Taylor. The concert's headline set was from Ian Hunter with Roger Taylor and Roger Daltry, ending with the songs forever associated with Mick – 'Michael Picasso' and 'All the Young Dudes'. All performers gathered onstage for the 'Dudes' finale, including Geoff Appleby who, though unable to play after his life-changing stroke, could still attend in his wheelchair. A recording of the concert was later released as a CD on Citadel Music.

Ten days after the London Memorial Concert on 9 May, Epic Records released Mick's third solo album *Heaven and Hull*. Back in 1976 Mick was still under contract with RCA to produce a third album, but sales of his 1975 *Play Don't Worry* were less than anticipated and it was never produced or released. He had formed the Mick Ronson Band in 1976 and his intention was to release the band's studio work as his third album, but that too never came to fruition. *Heaven and Hull* thus became Mick's third solo album, completed after his death as a labour of love, with a lot of the work falling to Joe Elliott and Sham Morris, and many of Mick's friends rallying around to help finish the album. Tasked with the daunting responsibility of completing Mick's previous work on the tracks to a standard and style he would have wished, they overdubbed vocals, re-recorded parts and remixed tracks. Bowie contributed his version of Dylan's 'Like a Rolling Stone' from the *Black Tie White Noise* sessions. Chrissie Hynde added vocals to 'Trouble With Me' and John Mellencamp did the same for 'Life's a River', as did Ian Hunter on 'Take a Long Line'. Mick wanted his former Rats bandmates to play on the album, originally titled *To Hull and Back*, but his premature death made that impossible, which Benny Marshall still regrets: 'He wanted to do something with the Rats on the album. He "came back to Hull" with it, didn't he? He used the Humber Bridge as a focal point, it was *Heaven and Hull*, and it was like he always came back to Hull. I regret not doing that, I do really, that was my big regret because he was a mate."

In 1995, tracks from the recording of Mick and Ian Hunter's live shows as the Hunter-Ronson Band, at London's Dominion Theatre in February 1989, were released as a *BBC – In Concert*' CD. Ian Hunter's moving tribute 'Michael Picasso' was released on his album *The Artful Dodger*, initially only in Norway in 1996, but with a wider release in 2014. Ian continues to play the song regularly in his live set to this day. In June 1998 a CD of material by the Rats was released on the Angel Air (UK) label with the title *The Fall and Rise – a Rats Tale*. It contained all the band's singles, some further tracks featuring Mick on guitar and some previously unreleased recordings. This was followed by the 1999 releases of *Just Like This*' and *Showtime*, which made available the music recorded and played live by The Mick Ronson Band. In 2000 Mick's music from *Indian Summer*, the film that never got made, was finally released, offering a glimpse of a whole separate career Mick could easily have achieved as a successful film composer. In 2019 a 4-CD box set became available, titled *Mick Ronson Only After Dark – the Complete MainMan Recordings*, which was a reissue of his first two solo albums along with additional live tracks, demos and sessions recorded in 1976.

In 2007 Mick was posthumously awarded the Tommy Vance Award for Inspiration. At the ceremony in London in November that year, Suzi

The Legacy

and Lisa Ronson made acceptance speeches, with Lisa memorably saying of her father: 'He taught me that it's nice to be important, but it's more important to be nice.' In April 2013 the Institute for Contemporary Arts (ICA) in London hosted a Mick Ronson Fest to coincide with the Bowie Is exhibition at the Victoria and Albert Museum. It included film screenings and talks with guests Glen Matlock, Gary Kemp and Woody Woodmansey. Live music was performed by Maggi Ronson along with John 'Hutch' Hutchinson, who had played with Bowie in the late '60s. Maggi sang a selection of songs from her album *Sweet Dreamer*, which she had released as a tribute to her brother. That year also saw the passing of Mick's fellow Hull Spider Trevor Bolder who died in May from pancreatic cancer.

In 2016 the death of David Bowie occasioned worldwide mourning and a plethora of tributes, books and documentaries that continue to this day. The question is perennially raised as to whether David 'made' Mick, or whether it was Mick Ronson who 'made' David Bowie. There's no doubt that Mick with the Spiders from Mars gave Bowie the heavier rock sound and sensibility he was looking for at that stage in his career, turning him from the predominantly acoustic folk-rock balladeer to the full-on Ziggy rocker that ensured his worldwide success. In addition Mick brought his skill as a song arranger and an ability to orchestrate and conduct string arrangements. It's hard to envisage Bowie's success with so many of his classic tracks and albums from that period without Mick's stunning guitar hooks, his powerful scores and his skill in the recording studio. On the other hand, Mick at that time lacked Bowie's essential songwriting skills, and as the band Ronno had shown, it was unlikely Mick could achieve anything like national, let alone superstar status without the presence of a strong songwriter like Bowie. Even when leading a band, Mick always preferred being part of a team and collaborating in the creative process alongside a songwriter. After the Bowie partnership finished, he found his most successful collaboration with Ian Hunter. In the final analysis, the question is perhaps best answered by Ched Cheesman: 'Bowie needed Mick, and Mick needed Bowie in equal measure. They made each other'.

Mick's achievements have been celebrated in print and on film. In January 2003 *The Spider with the Platinum Hair* was published. Written by Americans Karen Laney and Eric Demattio, aka Weird & Gilly, this first biography of Mick is a well-researched account of Mick's career with a strong focus on his work in the States. In 2016 Woody Woodmansey published his autobiography *My Life with Bowie – Spider from Mars* followed by John Cambridge in 2021 with his memoir *Bowie, Cambo and all the Hype*.

On the film front, former Spandau Ballet's Gary Kemp presented the 2017 documentary *Passions: Mick Ronson*. Gary Kemp visited sites in Hull and London and managed to track down Mick's famous Les Paul guitar to Monaco, where it is owned by entrepreneur Simon Dolan. Back in 2007 a London-based film company Spontanuity started work on a documentary about Mick, but the film never saw release. Some of the footage was incorporated into Jon Brewer's documentary *Beside Bowie – the Mick Ronson Story*, which received a cinema and subsequent DVD release in 2017. The soundtrack of the film includes the Mick Ronson recording on Elton John's 'Madman Across the Water', Michael Chapman's 'Soulful Lady' on which Mick plays, and Joe Elliott's tribute to Mick with his version of 'This is for You'.

Beyond all the plaudits to Mick as a musician there is another legacy, that of his children: Nicholas, born in Hull in 1971, Lisa in America in 1977 and Joakim (Kim) in Sweden in 1990. All three have chosen to keep the Ronson surname. They have all been drawn at various times to perform music, but in contrast to their father chose not to follow it as a career. Nicholas Ronson had no contact with his father other than during a brief time as a toddler. He grew up in the shadow of his father's fame and legacy, yet never knew him as a child or adult. Nick spoke publicly about his father for the first time to the authors in 2021:

'I am very proud of my father's career achievements and the quality of the music he created both as a guitarist and as a producer. I'm aware that he garnered respect from the people he worked with throughout his career. I think it's fair to say he was regarded as a gentle and genuine talent from very early on in his career and these traits endured till his untimely death. In his role as a father, however, my experiences, regrettably, have been how shall I say...lacking.

Mum's relationship with Mick started when he was a gardener at the school she attended in Hull, so a good few years before I was born in October 1971. I've been told that at some point after this, mum and I went down to Haddon Hall, and I think I remember playing with Zowie, Bowie's son. I'm aware this period coincided with my father having a relationship with Suzi (Fussey) and mum and myself must have headed back up to Hull as a result, because we were at Nanna and Grandad's house in Bexhill Avenue for quite some time following this.

I have few memories of my early years, and certainly no definitive memories of being with dad, just a collection of vague images and

The Legacy

unsatisfied needs for a father's love. Perhaps I have subconsciously blocked out these thoughts and feelings, attempting to protect myself, or it could be due to a head injury I suffered just before my 16th birthday, who knows? At that time, whilst in hospital, I asked my Mum to send photos of me to Dad and explain the situation. I really needed him to be there for me. I think this was before he fell seriously ill. I know he received the photos, as they were found in a small black bag that he carried around with him when he died, but he never actually managed to make direct contact with me himself. The reasons for this are still unknown to me. I was, however, contacted when dad died in 1993. I went to my dad's funeral in London. It was unbelievably difficult going to the funeral. It felt surreal.

It has taken me a long time to resolve the whole situation in my mind, to attempt to understand other people's motivations and actions. I believe the clamour for fame and the subsequent efforts to maintain a certain image, led certain individuals, including my dad, to forget there was a child who simply needed his father. Having a family of my own only serves to further contrast these events. I married the love of my life, Emmaline in 2005, and since 2012, I have another love of my life, our daughter Lily! I'm sure I've passed on the Ronson musical gene to my daughter who plays piano beautifully. Who knows, maybe one day the musical legacy will continue.'

Nicholas, Lisa and Joakim all grew up with the legacy of a famous father known to millions of people worldwide, but only Lisa has the experience of a dad whom she knew in childhood and beyond. Kim Ronson has practically no memory of his father at all, being only three years of age when Mick died. Kim saw *Turn and Face the Strange* in August 2017 and said this of the show: 'It really enlightened me, seeing my own dad, with all the stories, all the people that's from Hull, since I didn't know much about my father's life in Hull. It was very touching, very moving. I cried at the end, quite a lot.'

In Hull there is still a strong living memory of Mick amongst many of the residents of his home city, although that age group are now in their senior years, so their numbers are inevitably diminishing. At the time of writing in 2022, many of Mick's former Hull-based fans, bandmates and musician friends are still alive, including Benny Marshall, Rick Kemp, Woody Woodmansey, John Cambridge, Ched Cheesman, John Bentley, Geoff Appleby, Eric Lee, Lou Duffy-Howard, Jeff Parsons and Rob Eunson, many of them still living in the city.

Hull held its own Mick Ronson Memorial Concert over the hot

weekend of 9–10 August 1997. The Saturday night gig was held at Hull's Ice Arena and included sets by Michael Chapman, Glen Matlock with his band Mustard, Mick Jones with Big Audio Dynamite, Colin Lloyd Tucker with Maggi Ronson, Steve Harley, and the Spiders line-up of Trevor Bolder, Woody Woodmansey, Joe Elliott on vocals and Phil Collen on guitar. Ian Hunter headlined once again. Also in the show were the Rats with Ched Cheesman, Benny Marshall, John Cambridge, Pete Allison and Brian Farr.

Another band that played that weekend was Yellow Monkey. The Tokyo band were influenced by Bowie and glam rock, and were big Mick Ronson fans. They were huge in Japan with three consecutive No. 1 albums along with 18 Top 10 singles. The band had organised a Mick Ronson Memorial Concert in Tokyo in May 1994, with successive events over the following years. That August weekend, hundreds of Japanese fans descended on Hull to see them play, and for a while the bemused residents of the city couldn't quite work out why Hull, even given Mick's reputation, had become such an international visitor destination. The Sunday concert was held in Queens Gardens with the dedication of the new Mick Ronson Stage. These weekend events were arranged by Kevin Cann and Maggie Ronson. In recent years the stage has fallen into disrepair, attracting criticism, but at the time it was a welcome addition to the city centre attractions.

Over the following years, friends and fellow musicians organised regular events at the Springhead pub in Hull, with Mick Ronson Legacy Concerts held there in 2010 and 2011. In April 2016 a Rock for Ronson concert was organised by Gary Marks to raise funds for the Mick Ronson Scholarship, offering financial support for young musicians wanting to pursue a career in music. Steve Harley and Cockney Rebel headlined the benefit gig at Hull City Hall with many local bands performing that night. In September the same year, an outdoor concert Ronson Rocks Greatfield was held on the grounds of a local community centre on Greatfield Estate. The event celebrating Mick's life in the area he grew up in, was unfortunately hit by the vagaries of the British climate, and there were massive downpours of rain.

Mick's achievement is also acknowledged and portrayed in the physical fabric of the city. In November 1994 Hull City Council named a new road Ronson Close in his memory. In 2016 a memorial plaque honouring Mick was unveiled at Hull City Hall by mother Minnie, sister Maggi, and Suzi and Lisa Ronson. A second blue plaque, in Hull's Paragon Station, was unveiled on 15 June 2017 by Woody Woodmansey.

The Legacy

Commemorating the three Hull Spiders from Mars, it celebrates Mick, Trevor and Woody: 'They were David Bowie's backing group in the first half of the 1970s and left for many of their musical adventures from this station.'

The most striking addition to the local landscape is the Michael Ronson Garden of Reflection in East Park. Located in the park where he worked as a gardener when playing with the Rats, it is an oasis of calm with a stunning central feature: a 2.4m (8ft) metal sculpture of Mick's Les Paul guitar designed by 18-year-old Hull student Janis Skodins, whose artwork was chosen by Mick's mother Minnie in a competition for local artists. At the opening ceremony, on 2 June 2017, Maggi Ronson spoke on behalf of Minnie who was too ill to attend: 'Mick absolutely loved his gardening job, so this couldn't be more perfect. We're very, very happy and I'm sure he'd be very proud.'

A recent addition to Hull's public artworks celebrating Mick is a large mural created in 2019 by Spray Creative artists with Lydia Caprani. Located on the wall above the Bilton Grange shops where Mick took deliveries on the Co-op van back in the early 1960s, the mural has a large portrait of Mick and references the flowers he tended in his day job as a gardener with the Council. In 2021 Hull artist Ed Ullyart created a new mural on Princes Avenue, close to where Mick would enjoy his take-away chips and curry sauce from Supabar. The mural portrays many iconic Hull musicians, writers and artists, with Mick Ronson sharing prominence with Roland Gift of the Fine Young Cannibals.

Minnie Ronson was unable to celebrate these recent civic acknowledgements of her famous son; she passed away peacefully on 11 June 2017 at the grand age of 93. She is buried in the same plot as Michael and husband George in Hull's Eastern Cemetery. In the years following Mick's death in 1993, singer Benny Marshall had regularly visited Minnie at her home on Milford Grove, where she lived for close on 60 years: 'I went there that many times I used to know exactly where Mick used to sit in the back kitchen. Whenever I came up to Hull I used to go down there and I used to spend many an afternoon with Minnie, chatting, putting the world to rights. The back kitchen was exactly the same. And she tells me: "That was Michael's chair. He used to sit sideways on to the table. He used to have his dinner on the table and his guitar on his knee. And he used to eat his dinner and play on his guitar." And I knew that, but I never used to say.'

In 2017 Hull was UK City of Culture. Mick Ronson was celebrated that year in various ways. In the opening event, Made in Hull, Mick featured prominently playing Bowie's song 'Jean Genie' in a film projected simultaneously on three building facades in Victoria Square to an audience of thousands each night during the opening week in January. Woody Woodmansey's band Holy Holy had previously performed in Hull in December 2014 at the Welly Club on Beverley Road, close to Mick's first family home. At that gig they showcased songs from *The Man Who Sold The World*. In March 2017 they were back in the city at Hull City Hall performing the entire *Ziggy Stardust* album live for the first time. The band featured Woody on drums, alongside Heaven 17's Glenn Gregory on vocals and Bowie collaborator and legendary producer Tony Visconti on bass.

2017 also saw the stage show *Turn and Face the Strange* premiere at the Freedom Centre in East Hull, close to where Mick grew up. Written and produced by us, the authors of this book, TAFTS is a multimedia stage show portraying Mick's life and career through live music, film and personal stories. We transcribed many hours of recorded interviews with friends, fellow musicians and fans of Mick Ronson. The range and richness of these stories formed a storyline for the stage show and are published here for the first time in this book.

In 2018 Wilberforce College in Hull refurbished its music department, theming the entire suite of studios and rehearsal rooms in honour of Mick Ronson, the Rats and the Spiders from Mars. The launch, attended by Maggi and David Ronson, saw the unveiling of a new mural portrait of Mick by Hull artist Mark Hebblewhite. The same year also saw a refurbishment of a different kind, albeit for young people too. Kexgill Property Group, who manage student accommodation, decided to redecorate one of their student houses in Hull and theme it as The Spiders from Mars House. With large-scale photographs and posters throughout, the house was launched live on BBC Radio Humberside to an enthusiastic throng of Ronson fans crammed into the lounge, while John Cambridge, Ched Cheesman, Bobby Joyce and Kristian Eastwood entertained with an unplugged set of songs from *Turn and Face the Strange*. The 2018 Humber Sesh Festival brought together onstage Mick's sister Maggi, Trevor Bolder's wife Shelly, and the sole surviving Spider Woody Woodmansey, who were all interviewed by BBC's David 'Burnsie' Burns.,

On one level, Mick's story is a simple universal one: that of a local boy made good. Whatever the circumstances of your start in life, whatever the context of the place, time and culture you are born into, with dedication, perseverance and sheer hard work, you will achieve

The Legacy

your ambition and fulfil your dream. Lynne Mitchell, the young girl who had a teenage crush on Mick back in the '60s when he worked the city's parks and playing fields, expresses it this way:

'I think for somebody like that who did it, and who worked hard to do it, it just goes to show what you can do with a bit of dedication. He was one of those people that everybody seemed to know. It was like having a member of the family making it – it's really lovely. He made a massive difference to a lot of people.'

Afterword

by Kevin Cann

As those who know me well know, I have many stories about Mick Ronson and many cherished memories of the great man.

Shortly after he died I mentioned to his sister Maggi that, as no one else seemed to be planning anything, I was determined not to let his passing go by without a public celebration. Michael's London funeral had been very poignant and all of his old colleagues, friends and family had filled the church in South Kensington with love and respect. I brought along my friend Sean Mayes, who had also known and toured with Mick back in those halcyon days and loved him too. Most of us shed more than a tear or two and then relived many happy memories with one another at the nearby wake. Michael's coffin was then transported home to Hull and buried next to his father's grave.

Maggi and I managed to spend the next months pulling together a rather large amount of exceptional musicians for a Memorial concert at the Hammersmith Apollo – the historic venue once known as the Odeon where David had famously broken his connection with the Spiders From Mars one warm summer evening in 1973. It was an amazing feeling to help the surviving Spiders put together a super group for that concert, particularly for that venue, and to work with so many fascinating and respected musicians for the event we staged in Mick's memory on 29 April 1994 – exactly a year to the day of his death.

Curiously, April 29 was also an important date in Michael's working chronology as it proved to be the last date of his first and only solo tour of the UK in 1974 (at Sheffield City Hall). I had seen him for the first time two days earlier at Hemel Hempstead Pavilion, and he was amazing. Forget all that waffle about Mick not being a good front man – he was a fabulous front man, and the memories of that night, of him thrilling the audience (with Trevor Bolder, Mike Garson, Ritchie Dharma, Mark-Carr Pritchett and Thunder Thighs among the legendary musicians and performers in his band) was something I've long cherished.

And at the Hammersmith Apollo in 1994, twenty years on from that first solo tour, there was a lot of love in the air too, and backstage was chock full of emotion. One of my fondest memories of that evening was after the finale, up in the small management office we had commandeered, being thanked by many involved in the show, but in particular by the wonderful Mick Jones from Big Audio (and The Clash of course). He put himself out to come and find me and shake my hand and give me a hug. It meant so much. But I was actually dead on my feet – I'd had barely two or three hours sleep in three days and nights leading up to show time and had another long night ahead of me. Every time I had a chance to eat I was called urgently to deal with another 'issue' during the build up so had barely eaten (we were in the building setting up and running sound checks for two days). It had been crazy, and so I was shell-shocked at the end and I'm sure hardly responded to Mick Jones as I would normally do. So I believe I never really had a chance to really thank him for all he did for us that night.

The whole build up for me was only made a little less stressful by my good friend Spizz – whose touring expertise and knowledge of musician's needs proved essential to the whole success of the evening, and Lana Topham – a noted and gifted film maker in her own right, who sat with me in the hours leading up to show time to help me sort through the evening's media running order (we had a lot of films and guests to be interviewed on stage between acts). I thank both Lana and Spizz again for all they did for Maggi and I that night.

But in the end, we did it in style, and we have a wonderful, good quality, multi-camera video recording of the whole evening, which I'm sure we'll make public at some point.

Which leads me to what followed. The plan always was to build a memorial stage in Hull's Queen's Garden Park – a place where Michael tended the flowerbeds and cut the grass back in the day, when he was a Hull municipal gardener. (It had previously been Queen's Dock, the walls of the gardens the original dock walls, the docks drained and filled with soil in 1930 to create attractive gardens.) It couldn't have been more perfect – or so we thought...

When it came to the launch in 1997, Maggi and I had arranged for a second Memorial concert in Hull, with another live-show the following afternoon at Mick Ronson's new – to be opened that day - covered stage (though many still refer to it still as the Mick Ronson bandstand). Large public gatherings also require a number of planning and safety

Afterword

meetings beforehand and I recall attending a number of those at the council's offices and town hall, and latterly at the police station, which fortuitously overlooked the band stand (I had naively believed that this ideal location would offer us the extra protection and support the new covered stage might need).

You can imagine my horror, then, when on the eve of that open air event, a senior policeman in police headquarters - half chuckling as he told me – recalled how the previous evening he and some colleagues had enjoyed watching some local youths sliding up and down the stage's brand new canopy, the one we had spent thousands putting in place for the community, before adding, "I knew it wouldn't last long." Still to this day I'm not sure he knew who he was talking to, but it was a crushing thing to hear on the eve of our celebratory launch party, and it was also sadly prophetic.

Looking back on it now, even given the ideal proximity of the stage with the Hull police HQ in full sight, it would have been nothing less than wishful thinking to expect the police to watch over it every night. Ultimately its location just outside their door offered it absolutely no protection at all, and those local youths quickly reduced our lovely stage to nothing. Within a week most of the heavy steel posts had significant graffiti damage (hundreds of names and silly comments scratched deep into the weather-proofed paintwork, which in turn then began to compromise the steel itself). It all just added to our woe.

The people that decided to use the canopy as a play slide started to rip the fabric and then, over the weeks and months, split the seams. From memory I think it only managed to survive a summer or two. But in that time it did fulfil some kind of purpose, including our glorious open air event - in Michael's name and memory - on a beautifully hot day too, and it left a lot of great memories for many people, even the great many who just turned up for a rare, free, open air event.

It was also the last time I ever saw David and The Spider's old roadie, Will Palin, who drove up from Cornwall in his trusty campervan with his wife just to see Mick's stage open. Will sadly died four years later in 2011.

I also recall that the gardens were full when the late South African Anglican Bishop, Desmond Tutu, spoke proudly from the Mick Ronson stage,

and I'm sure that, overall, we did at least start something tangible in Mick's name in Hull. The café behind the brick and concrete platform (the platform base still survives) is now known as The Mick Ronson

The Mick Ronson Story

Café. We had taken over that venue in 1997 as a green room/come changing room for the artists that day.

You can now also visit a beautiful guitar-shaped sculpture made in Mick's memory titled 'Sweet Dreamer', created by artist Janis Skodkins, in Hull's East Park (another attractive local park tended by Michael). Popular Mick Ronson Legacy concerts have regularly been staged at the Springhead pub in Hull and one cannot overlook and applaud the success of the ambitious Mick Ronson musical event, *Turn & Face the Strange*, by chance the brainchild of the authors of this excellent book.

And on an even more practical level, in more recent years Steve Harley once again came to the rescue.

After learning about what had happened to the original covered stage during a visit to Hull in 2015, Steve decided to do something about it and offered to put on a benefit concert. On hearing this, Hull council offered him the beautiful City Hall for free so that he could put on another wonderful fund-raising show for Mick. And this time, a far wiser Steve (who had, by-the-way, supported every Memorial event Maggi and I had staged) decided to make the money he raised work even harder by setting up a dedicated bursary fund for music students studying in East Riding. This has been successfully in place for nearly seven years now and is, in Mick Ronson's name, offering inspired students of music the assistance to make those extra important steps forward in their chosen careers. All of this was down to Steve and the musicians who supported him that evening.

The world would certainly be a much better place with more Steve Harley's, another very talented and humble man with a big heart.

So, that brings us to the summer of 2022 and beyond, because the Mick Ronson legend continues to grow and inspire and will never die.

This summer marked the 50th anniversary of Mick's enormous contribution to the legendary David Bowie LP, *The Rise and Fall of Ziggy Stardust and The Spiders From Mars* (the sound that was our future 50 years ago - timeless back then and remaining just as vital and fresh today). And in 2023 the Aladdin Sane 50th birthday will bring back massive memories for the many who joined the band wagon at that time and have remained loyal passengers ever since (witnessing the amazing Aladdin Sane front cover image for the first time sealed it all for me back in early 73 too). Incredibly, 2023 will also mark the 30th anniversary of Mick's passing.

From that moment in 1973, and up to the day he died, Mick Ronson was a big part of my life and somehow (and it's still something that

Afterword

makes me pinch myself), we became good friends too. And it wasn't hard to know the real Michael Ronson either. What you saw was what you got.

The wonder you felt if you were lucky enough to meet or encounter a musical genius like Mick Ronson, and the curiosity you couldn't help but contemplate at that intangible gift which enabled, someone like him, to create such beautiful music and melodies, was truly fascinating to experience. His humble gift and legacy has been appreciated by many millions of people around the world and looks likely to remain just as impactful for many, many more to come. What a legacy it is.

Hull and Yorkshire - be proud. Be *very* proud.

Kevin Cann, June 2022

Who's Who

Appleby, Geoff Rats and Hunter-Ronson bass player
Beck, Jeff Guitarist with the Yardbirds and the Jeff Beck Group. A big influence on Mick
Bentley, John Musician – Flesh, Squeeze
Bolan, Marc T. Rex glam rock star
Bolder, Trevor Bass player for Ronno and The Spiders from Mars
Bowie, David Singer, songwriter, actor, artist
Bradfield, Dave Drummer in three bands with Mick: the Mariners, the Crestas and the Voice
Cambridge, John 'Cambo' Drummer in the Rats, Junior's Eyes and Hype, who introduced Mick to Bowie
Chapman, Michael Hull-based folk singer-guitarist who gave Mick Ronson his first recording break
Cheesman, Keith 'Ched' Rats bass guitarist
Constable, John Chichester East Yorkshire stately home owner, promoter, manager of Hullabaloos
Cornell, Pat Owner of Cornell's Music Store, Hull, who sold Mick his famous Les Paul guitar
De Fries, Tony Bowie and Ronson's manager, head of MainMan
Dudgeon, Gus Producer of the single 'Space Oddity'
Evans, Ian 'Taffy' Rats roadie
George, Stuart 'Stuey' Roadie and security for the Rats, Bowie and others
Herd, Keith Owner of Fairview Studios, near Hull, where the Rats recorded early songs
Hunter, Ian Lead singer 'Mott the Hoople', Hunter-Ronson, the Ian Hunter Band and close friend of Mick
Irvin, Denise Mick's former fiancée, mother of his first son, Nicholas
Garson, Mike Pianist with David Bowie
Kemp, Rick Musician in the Mariners, with Michael Chapman and Steeleye Span
Lee, Eric Singer in the Aces and the Crestas
Marshall, Peter Benny Lead singer with the Rats
Mirfin, Pete Rats roadie, mechanic who serviced Bowie's car
Nelson, Sandra Mick's former girlfriend

Who's Who

Palmer, Alan Singer with the Mandrakes – later famous as Robert Palmer, singer of 'Addicted to Love'

Park, Ted Roadie with the Crestas

Renwick, Tim Guitarist with Junior's Eyes and other bands, including Pink Floyd

Ronson, David Mick's brother

Ronson, George Mick's father

Ronson, Joakim 'Kim' Mick's second son to Carola Westerlund

Ronson, Lisa Mick's daughter with Suzi Ronson

Ronson, Maggi Mick's sister

Ronson, Minnie Mother of Mick, Maggi and David Ronson

Ronson, Nicholas Mick's first son with Denise Irvin

Ronson, Suzi Mick's wife née Fussey, mother to Lisa

Simpson Jim Rats drummer when Mick first joined

Taylor, Clive 'Spud' Rats drummer between Jim Simpson and John Cambridge

Visconti, Tony Bass player in Hype, record producer for Bowie, Bolan and many others

Wayne, Mick Lead guitarist with the Hullabaloos, Junior's Eyes, Bowie

Westerlund, Carola Mother of Mick's second son, Joakim

Woodmansey, Mick 'Woody' Drummer with the Roadrunners, the Rats, Bowie and the Spiders from Mars

Mick Ronson Timeline

26 May 1946	Born in Hull. First child of George and Minnie Ronson.
7 January 1957	Sister Maggi born.
1958	Family move to 8 Milford Grove on Greathill Estate Hull, which remains his parents' home throughout their lives Mick learns the piano, recorder and violin.
1960	Leaves school at 14 and starts work at the Co-op, on a mobile grocery van serving the estates.
25 November 1962	Brother David born.
1963	Mick buys a guitar and hangs out on Saturdays at Gough & Davy's and Hammonds music departments, picking up guitar tips from local musicians.
22 November 1963	Joins the Mariners aged 17 at the instigation of Rick Kemp and plays his first public gig on the same day as the assassination of American president John F. Kennedy.
1964	Joins the Crestas and acquires the nickname Ronno. The Crestas gig regularly in the city and out of town.
1965	Suffers a severe electric shock during a Crestas gig at the Duke of Cumberland in North Ferriby. That autumn various band members leave the Crestas for 'proper' jobs and marriage.
January 1966	Aged 19, Mick moves to London to find work as a

Mick Ronson Timeline

	musician. Joins the Voice, a band that is part of a cult called the Process. In June the Voice disband. Mick struggles to make ends meet in London.
September 1966	Returns to Hull in debt. Gets job as a gardener with Hull City Council Parks Department. Joins the Rats with singer Benny Marshall, drummer Jim Simpson and bassist Geoff Appleby. Mick moves the band into the heavier rock sound of Jeff Beck, Jimi Hendrix and Cream.
April–May 1967	Clive 'Spud' Taylor replaces Jim Simpson on drums. Rats tour to France playing in Paris and Rouen. They return to Hull in debt.
October 1967	John Cambridge replaces Clive Taylor as Rats drummer.
Autumn 1967	Mick and John Cambridge write 'The Rise and Fall of Bernie Gripplestone', the Rats' only attempt at original material. They remain a covers band.
March 1968	The Rats support Jeff Beck at the Cat Balou Club in Grantham. Mick asks Beck to show him the riffs to 'Jeff's Boogie', which in turn becomes Mick's set piece 'Mick's Boogie'.
From June 1968	The Rats rename themselves 'Treacle' and under manager Don Lil are persuaded to develop a more melodic pop-rock sound.
September 1968	Geoff Appleby leaves the Rats and is replaced by Keith 'Ched' Cheesman on bass.
October 1968	Mick trades in his Fender Telecaster for a Les Paul guitar, emulating his hero Jeff Beck.
January 1969	The band drop the name Treacle and revert to the Rats.

The Mick Ronson Story

April 1969 — Mick sacks drummer John Cambridge, replacing him with Woody Woodmansey. John joins Mick Wayne's Junior's Eyes that summer and moves to London. Junior's Eyes becomes David Bowie's band.

August 1969 — Mick plays on Michael Chapman's album *Fully Qualified Survivor*. The Rats play the Burton Constable Hall all-nighter and then a Free Concert at East Park Hull supporting the Edgar Broughton Band.

28 September 1969 — Second East Park Free Festival gig in Hull with Michael Chapman, Mick with the Rats, John Cambridge and Mick Wayne with Junior's Eyes. David Bowie is on the bill, but doesn't perform.

November 1969 — Rats bassist Ched Cheesman is replaced by Geoff Appleby.

January 1970 — David Bowie and Tony Visconti search for a guitarist to join Bowie's new band Hype. John Cambridge suggests Mick Ronson, travelling up to Hull to recruit him. Mick is highly resistant to the idea of moving to London, but John persuades him to travel down to meet Bowie.

3 Feb 1970 — Junior's Eyes final gig and Hype's first at the Marquee. Bowie asks Mick to play on the session for the John Peel Radio Show, recorded on 5 February. Bowie asks Mick to join Hype. That month Mick gives up his job in Hull as a council gardener to move to London and announces his engagement to Denise Irvin in the *Hull Daily Mail*. Mick's leaving marks the end of the Rats. Bowie visits Hull, staying with John Cambridge's parents.

11 March 1970 — Hype perform at the Roundhouse, London as part of the Atomic Sunrise Festival. They wear

Mick Ronson Timeline

	stage costumes in what has been dubbed the first ever glam rock gig.
30 March	Hype play the Star Hotel Croydon. This turns out to be John Cambridge's last gig with the band.
6 April 1970	Bowie tells John Cambridge he is no longer needed, and he is replaced on drums for a second time by Woody Woodmansey. Recording starts for *The Man Who Sold the World* album and continues into May. Mick learns studio techniques and arranging skills from producer Tony Visconti.
August 1970	Mick and Woody split from Bowie, move back to Hull and recruit former Rats singer Benny Marshall. Hype tour with Trevor Bolder on bass because Visconti is busy producing in London. Hype renamed as Ronno and in November record in London.
January 1971	Ronno release the single '4th Hour of My Sleep' but lack of material means plans for an album are shelved.
10 April 1971	*The Man Who Sold the World* is released by Mercury in the UK, the first album on which Mick plays a pivotal creative role.
May 1971	With Ronno failing to make any impact, Mick rejoins Bowie and moves back to London, recruiting Woody Woodmansey on drums and Trevor Bolder on bass. The three Hull musicians become the line-up for Bowie's backing band the Spiders from Mars.
June 1971	Recording begins for *Hunky Dory*. Mick takes on Visconti's previous role as orchestral arranger. On trips back home to Hull he works on string

	arrangements and takes music theory lessons from his sister Maggi's piano tutor.
20 June 1971	Mick performs with Bowie at 5 a.m. at Glastonbury Festival.
August 1971	Tony Defries becomes Bowie's manager and lines up a new deal for RCA records.
September 1971	Mick flies to the States for the first time with Bowie and Defries. Mick, Woody and Trevor play their first gig together with Bowie on 25 September at Friars Club, Aylesbury.
14 October 1971	Mick's fiancée Denise Irvin gives birth at Hull Royal Infirmary to their son Nicholas. The relationship breaks down and Mick plays no further role in his son's upbringing.
November 1971	Recording for *Ziggy Stardust* begins at Trident Studios in London.
December 1971	*Hunky Dory* released in the US and UK.
January 1972	Bowie develops the Ziggy concept influenced by the film *A Clockwork Orange* and starts his and the band's makeover to glam rock, overcoming Mick, Trevor and Woody's initial resistance. Bowie declares he is gay. Try-out Ziggy gig at Friars Club, Aylesbury.
February 1972	UK tour of Ziggy Stardust starts in smaller pubs but builds to larger venues. Band performs on *The Old Grey Whistle Test* on BBC TV.
June 1972	Bowie, Ronson and Defries fly to New York for a promotional visit. Mick's second trip to the States within a year.
16 June 1972	*The Rise and Fall of Ziggy Stardust and the*

Mick Ronson Timeline

	Spiders from Mars released in USA and Europe. Mick is credited as co-arranger of songs with Bowie.
17 June 1972	Photographer Mick Rock captures the 'guitar fellatio' on tour at Oxford Town Hall and Defries ensures the photograph gets maximum exposure in music magazines.
6 July 1972	Bowie and the Spiders perform 'Starman' on *Top of the Pops* – a seminal moment bringing increased record and ticket sales for Ziggy. In Hull Mick's family receives homophobic taunts and their car is daubed with paint.
August 1972	Mick and Bowie co-produce Lou Reed's album *Transformer* with Mick writing the piano and string arrangement for 'Perfect Day'. Ziggy performs three sell-out shows at London's Rainbow Theatre incorporating mime and dance routines. Many fans adopt a glam rock look.
September–December 1972	First Ziggy tour of the States: 22 shows travelling by bus and train. Many of the songs for the subsequent album, *Aladdin Sane*, are written during the tour.
December 1972	Homecoming gigs at the Rainbow Theatre London. 'Starman' repeated on the BBC Christmas Day broadcast of *Top of the Pops*. Boxing Day broadcast of *The Old Grey Whistle Test* includes 'Queen Bitch'.
End of 1972	By now, Ziggy has sold over 95,000 copies in the UK and the same in the US. Mick has been on the road for 11 months with more than 90 performances. He has become a superstar guitarist, Bowie's essential song arranger, creative collaborator and co-producer of other

artists albums. Eighteen months ago, his career was at an all-time low. Now aged 26, he is an international star.

January 1973   *Ziggy Stardust* awarded a gold disc.

February–March 1973
                    Second Ziggy tour of the States; 17 shows in 6 cities with sell-out gigs and additional matinée shows.

April 1973   Tour of Japan with eight shows in five cities culminating in Tokyo. Conflict between Defries and Woody and Trevor over pay. Mick, forced to choose between loyalty to Bowie or loyalty to his Hull bandmates, is promised a future solo career managed by Defries. He agrees to keep the plan to retire Ziggy a secret.

13 April 1973   *Aladdin Sane* released in UK, Bowie's first No. 1 album. Mick credited as co-arranger with Bowie.

May–July 1973   UK tour of Ziggy with 41 dates and 15 matinée shows. Sold out gigs throughout with Ziggymania at its height.

28 June 1973   Ziggy at Bridlington Spa, the nearest gig to their home city of Hull for the three Spiders during their year and a half of touring. Hull teenager Gina Riley is the 100,000th person to see the show and gets VIP treatment.

2–3 July 1973   End of tour gig at London's Hammersmith Odeon. Bowie announces it is the last ever Ziggy performance. Trevor and Woody in shock and disbelief. Post-gig party at the Café Royal attended by many music and film celebrities.
                    Woody is sacked by phone a few days later, on the day of his wedding. Mick persuades Trevor to avoid any further conflict with Bowie and Defries.

Mick Ronson Timeline

July 1973 — Recording of *Pin Ups* album of cover tracks in France, retaining Trevor Bolder on bass. Woody is replaced by Aynsley Dunbar on drums. End of the road for the Spiders from Mars. Mick starts his solo career under Defries' MainMan management.

July 1973 — Mick holidays in Italy and starts a relationship with Suzi Fussey.

September 1973 — Recording for Mick's first solo album, *Slaughter on 10th Avenue*, in France, with Mike Garson on piano, Aynsley Dunbar on drums, and Trevor Bolder on bass, trumpet and trombone. For the first time Mick has total control over an album as producer, arranger, string conductor, musician and singer, and opts for an eclectic mix of music tracks rather than a rock-guitar dominated record.

October 1973 — RCA release *Pin Ups* in the UK and US. It goes straight to No. 1 in the UK and at this point Bowie has six albums in the UK charts, with Mick playing a key role on five. Mick performs in The 1980 Floor Show at the Marquee Club along with Trevor Bolder but without Woody Woodmansey. The 'recorded as live' event is broadcast on American TV in November and is the last outing for Bowie as Ziggy Stardust.

1974 — MainMan promote Mick as the new solo star with a massive billboard in Times Square, New York and exposure in the music press. Mick acts in a promo film for *Slaughter* with Suzi Fussey, shot on Tenth Avenue New York.

22–23 February 1974

Mick's debut solo concert at the Rainbow Theatre London with Mark Carr-Pritchard on second guitar, Trevor Bolder on bass, Mike

The Mick Ronson Story

	Garson on keyboards, and Ritchie Dharma on drums. The music press response is lukewarm with some suggesting that Mick appears nervous in the role of frontman.
March 1974	*Slaughter on 10th Avenue* album released by RCA reaching No. 9 in UK chart.
April 1974	UK 13-date tour of *Slaughter* receives mixed revues. By autumn poor US sales result in a proposed tour being cancelled.
July 1974	Mick starts recording for his second solo album *Play Don't Worry*, reverting to a stronger rock guitar vibe. As with *Slaughter*, Mick produces, arranges, conducts and plays a host of instruments on the album.
September 1974	Mick, increasingly uncomfortable in his role as a solo star and frontman, joins Mott the Hoople.
October 1974	Mick tours Europe with Mott the Hoople. The dream marriage soon turns sour with conflicts between Mick and the band, and Ian Hunter caught in the middle. By the end of December Mott the Hoople disband, but it marks the start of a life-long friendship and music collaboration between Mick and Ian Hunter.
January 1975	Mick records with Ian on his debut album *Ian Hunter*, bringing in his former Hull Rats bandmate Geoff Appleby on bass.
February 1975	Mick's second solo album *Play Don't Worry* is released by RCA to mixed reviews. Mick's solo career is effectively over by this point as he focuses on his work with Ian Hunter and freelance producing work.
March 1975	Two-week UK tour for Hunter-Ronson followed

Mick Ronson Timeline

                        by US tour.

From May 1975   Mick and Suzi move to the States and live in Manhattan, New York.

October–December 1975
Mick tours the States with Dylan and the Rolling Thunder Revue Band, playing variously alongside Joan Baez, Roger McGuinn, Joni Mitchell, Leonard Cohen, and Arlo Guthrie. The tour results in future collaborations with many of the musicians, including recording on Roger McGuinn's album *Cardiff Rose*.

April–May 1976   Second leg of the Rolling Thunder Revue Band with Dylan in the States.

26 May 1976   Mick's 30th birthday.

July 1976   Mick plays on Michael Chapman's album *The Man Who Hated Mornings*, but Chapman is not impressed by Mick being drunk. Only one track with Ronson appears on the album, ironically the song 'I'm Sober Now'.

Summer 1976   Mick parts company with MainMan and manager Tony Defries, taking on Barry Imhoff as his new manager. Moves to Woodstock in New York State with Suzi Fussey and buys a house there close to Bearsville Studios where he often records. Starts the Mick Ronson Band but fails to secure a record deal.

23 March 1977   Mick and Suzi marry in Woodstock and their daughter Lisa is born in August.

1978   Mick works in London producing *Ghosts of Princes in Towers* by the Rich Kids and *Storm the Reality Studios* by Dead Fingers Talk.

The Mick Ronson Story

October 1978 — Mick co-produces Ian Hunter's fourth solo album *You're Never Alone with a Schizophrenic*. The album's success leads to Mick touring with Ian for the next two years billed as the Ian Hunter Band with Mick Ronson.

1979 — Mick tours throughout the States with Ian Hunter, ending the decade with a gig at Hammersmith Odeon at the end of November.

1980 — European and US tour. *Welcome to the Club*, a double live album, is released in April. Mick and Ian perform around 120 gigs over 2 years of almost continuous touring

1981 — Mick forms a new band, the New York Yanquis, with Mick Barakan and tours the States that August. Works with Meatloaf on Dead Ringer. Works on a film project titled *Indian Summer* which is never completed.

October 1981 — Mick tours the States with Ian Hunter as his band's keyboard player, when Tommy Mandel is taken ill. It marks a period when Mick tires of playing the guitar.

1982 — Mick works mainly in Canada for the next two years. Plays keyboards with the Payolas. Also works with John Cougar Mellencamp on *American Fool*. Mick salvages the track 'Jack & Diane', turning it into a hit record for Mellencamp.

1983 — Works with Lisa Dal Bello in Toronto Canada, co-producing her experimental album *Whomanfoursays* released the following year.

September 1983 — Mick guests with Bowie on his Serious Moonlight Tour in Toronto, playing 'Jean Genie', marking a ten-year gap since the pair last performed

Mick Ronson Timeline

together in The 1980 Floor Show.

May 1984 — Mick's friend and former Rats bassist Geoff Appleby suffers a stroke. Mick flies back to Britain, visits him in hospital in Hull, and helps him gain a partial recovery.

9 November 1984 — Mick's father George Ronson dies of cancer aged 64 and is buried in Hull's Eastern Cemetery.

September 1985 — Mick rehearses in London with Live Aid co-organiser and former Rich Kids' singer Midge Ure, but the professional relationship founders and Mick is replaced for the tour.

26 May 1986 — Mick's 40th birthday.

1987 — Works with Dutch band Fatal Flowers, producing their second album *Johnny D. is Back!*, released in 1988 and their third *Pleasure Ground* in 1990.

1988 — After a six-year gap Mick tours again with Ian Hunter in June in Canada, and the States in the autumn, billed as the Hunter-Ronson Band. Incessant globe-trotting and touring result in the break-up of Mick's relationship with Suzi.

1989 — Hunter-Ronson Band tour Europe and Scandinavia.

2 February 1989 — Mick plays at the Melody Club Stockholm and meets Carola Westerlund. Flies back to Sweden to produce her band EC2 and starts relationship. Hunter and Ronson play their first UK show in around seven years with two gigs that February at London's Dominion Theatre, recorded and released as a BBC Live in Concert CD.

June–July 1989 — Ian Hunter's seventh solo studio album, *Yui Orta*, recorded in New York with five tracks

	credited to Hunter-Ronson, is released that October. Mick tours with Ian throughout the autumn in the States.
15 April 1990	Carola Westerlund gives birth in Stockholm to Mick's third child and second son, Joakim Ronson. Mick lives in Sweden with Carola but the relationship breaks down.
1991	Mick produces the Swedish cult goth rock band Leather Nun's fourth album, *Nun Permanent*.
April 1991	Mick suffers back pain, and in London sister Maggi insists he is checked out. Mick is diagnosed with terminal liver cancer and told he might not live till Christmas. Determined to fight the cancer, Mick changes his diet and continues working. In May and June he tours Sweden with Ian Hunter, and then in October with Graham Parker, returning to London each Tuesday for chemotherapy.
February–March 1992	Mick produces Morrissey's album *Your Arsenal*, released in July and reaching No. 4 in the UK charts.
20 April 1992	Mick plays guitar on 'All the Young Dudes' and 'Heroes' at the Freddie Mercury Tribute Concert at Wembley Stadium, which is broadcast worldwide and turns out to be Mick's final onstage public performance. That summer Mick records on Bowie's album *Black Tie White Noise*, released in April the following year. Mick works on his final album *Heaven and Hull* up to his death, with many friends contributing.
29 April 1993	Mick dies of liver cancer in London.
6 May 1993	Memorial Service for Mick is held in the Church

of the Latterday Saints in London. The following day Mick is buried in the same plot as his father in East Hull Cemetery.

1993

Joe Elliott oversees the finishing of Mick's posthumous album *Heaven and Hull,* released in May 1994.

Bands and Artists that Worked with Mick Ronson as Musician and/or Producer

The Mariners (1963–64)
The Buccaneers (1964)
The Crestas (1964–65)
The Voice (1966)
The Wanted (1966)
The Rats (1966–70)
Michael Chapman (1969 and 1976)
David Bowie & Hype (1970)
Hype / Ronno (1970–71)
David Bowie and the Spiders from Mars (1970–73)
David Bowie (1992)
Mott The Hoople (1972 and 1974)
Pure Prairie League (1972)
Milkwood (1972)
Lulu (1973)
Dana Gillespie (1973)
The Fallen Angels (1973)
Bob Sargeant (1974)
Ian Hunter (1975, 1978–82, 1988–91)
Mick Ronson Band (1975)
Bob Dylan (1975–76)
The Sundragon Sessions (1975)
Roger McGuinn (1975)
John Cougar (1976)
Kinky Friedman (1976)
New York Dolls (1976)
John Cale (1976)
The Rob Stoner Band (1976)
David Cassidy (1976)
Sparks (1976)
Hilly Michaels (1977)
Philip Rambow (1977)
Van Morrison (1977)
Roger Daltrey (1977)
Corky Laing (1977)
John Cale (1978)
Annette Peacock (1978)
The Rich Kids (1978)
Benny Mardones (1978)
Slaughter and the Dogs (1978)
Dead Fingers Talk (1978)
Roger C. Reale & Rue Morgue (1979)

Ellen Foley (1979)
Genya Ravan (1979)
David Johansen (1979)
The Johnny Average Band (1980)
Lennex (1981)
The Proof (1981)
Meatloaf (1981)
Payola$ (1981–1983)
Lisa Bade (1982)
Los Illegals (1982)
Les Fradkin (1982)
The Mamas and the Papas (1982)
The Mundanes (1982)
T Bone Burnett (1982–1983)
Perfect Affair (1983)
The Visible Targets (1983)
Lisa Dal Bello (1984)
X Davis (1984)
Ian Thomas (1984)
Urgent (1984)
Sandy Dillon (1985)
One The Juggler (1985)
Steve Harley (1985)

Midge Ure (1985)
Lisa Dominique (1986)
Andi Sexgang (1986)
Cody Meville (1986)
Rick Rose (1987)
Marie Laure et Lui (1987)
David Lynn Jones (1987)
Funhouse (1987)
The Phantoms (1987)
Fatal Flowers (1988 and 1989)
The Toll (1988)
Sham Morris (1988)
The Fentons (1988)
Marino (1990)
EC2 (1990)
Randy Vanwarmer (1991)
Leather Nun (1991)
Dag Finn (1991)
Casino Steel (1991)
Sonic Walthers (1992)
Morrissey (1992)
The Wildhearts (1992)
Graham Parker (1992)

Mick Ronson's Hull

1) The first Ronson family home at 1 Grosvenor Terrace, Grosvenor St, off Beverley Rd, where Mick spent his first childhood years. The original terrace has been demolished and replaced by modern housing.
Close to current 6 Grosvenor St, Hull HU3 1RU

2) Queen's Gardens. Location of the Mick Ronson Stage, opened in August 1997 during the weekend of the Mick Ronson Memorial Concert held in Hull.
Queens Gardens, Dock Street, Hull HU1 3DZ

3) Site of the former Gough & Davy Music Shop. where Mick mixed with local musicians on Saturday mornings in the early 1960s.
On Savile St, Hull HU1 3EF

4) Location of the former Hammonds Department Store and its Music Department run by Rick Kemp, where Mick would also spend time on Saturday mornings in the early 1960s.
1 Paragon St Hull HU1 3NA

5) Site of the former Gondola Coffee Club on Little Queen Street, where Mick and other musicians would often hang out.
Little Queen St, Hull HU1 3RA

6) Blue Plaque in Hull Paragon Station celebrating Mick and the Spiders from Mars, unveiled by Woody Woodmansey in June 2017.
Paragon Interchange Hull HU1 3QX

7) Site of the former venue Skyline Ballroom, where Mick played with the Rats supporting bands such as Pink Floyd in 1967 and the

Move in 1968.
9 Jameson St, Hull HU1 3EN

8) Site of the former Brickhouse Arts venue on Baker Street, where Mick played his last Hull gig in May 1971 with the band Ronno.
43 Baker St, Hull HU2 8HP

9) Brisbane Street (No. 9) where David Bowie stayed with John Cambridge's family in February 1970 when Mick first joined Bowie in Hype.
9 Brisbane St, Hull HU3 2HS

10) Site of the former Cornell's Music Shop on Spring Bank, where Mick bought his first Gibson Les Paul guitar.
29 Spring Bank, Hull HU3 1AF

11) Hull University Student Union. The only music gig David Bowie ever played in Hull in March 1970. The band was Hype, with Mick on guitar, John Cambridge on drums and Tony Visconti on bass.
Staff Refectory University of Hull, Cottingham Rd, Hull HU6 7RX

12) Hull Royal Infirmary, where Mick's first child, Nicholas, was born in October 1971.
Hull Royal Infirmary, Anlaby Rd, Hull HU3 2JZ

13) Site of The Phoenix Club – the only other place David Bowie played in Hull. He played bingo!
Site of A63 flyover where Hessle Rd meets Rawling Way HU3 2AF

14) Mural on Princes Avenue by Ed Ullyart of Hull musicians and

artists, with Mick featured prominently.
Clumber St Hull HU5 3QX

15) Halfway House Pub, a regular venue for local bands in the 1960s. Mick played there in the Mariners, the Crestas and the Rats.
595 Spring Bank West, Hull HU3 6LD

16) 99 St Georges Road, former home of Benny Marshall, lead singer with the Rats and where the band with Mick would often rehearse.
99 St Georges Rd, Hull HU3 3PU

17) Woodmansey Village Hall, where Mick rehearsed with the Rats, and later the band Ronno.
Woodmansey, Beverley HU17 0TR

18) Fairview Studios on Great Gutter Lane, established by Keith Herd, where Mick recorded his first studio tracks with the Rats from 1967 to 1969.
Great Gutter Lane W, Hull –HU10 6DP

19) Grave in Eastern Cemetery. Mick is buried in the same plot as his father George and mother Minnie.
Eastern Cemetery 1 Fremantle Ave, Hull HU9 4RH

20) East Park, Holderness Road, where Mick worked as a gardener with Hull City Council Parks Department. Hull Arts Centre hosted free concerts in the park in 1969, with Mick playing with the Rats. Location of the Mick Ronson Memorial Garden with guitar sculpture.
Holderness Rd, Hull HU8 8J

21) Andrew Marvell School playing fields, where John Cambridge recruited Mick for Hype in February 1970, setting him on the path to play with David Bowie.
Hull HU9 4ED

22) The Ronson family home from the late 1950s at 8 Milford Grove on Greatfield Estate.
8 Milford Grove, Hull HU9 5DJ

23) Mick Ronson Mural – Greenwich Avenue, Bilton Grange.
Greenwich Ave, Hull HU9 4UZ

24) Ronson Close, named in 1994 by Hull City Council in memory of Mick.
Hull HU9 4LL

Acknowledgements

A big thank you to all the following people who contributed their stories and memories of Mick Ronson, recorded by the authors and the *Turn and Face the Strange* project team in 2017 and 2020–21. Many of those stories appear in this book and you have all helped us tell Mick's story:

Alan Maskell, Alan Thurloe, Allan Abbey, Andy Richardson, Anne & Brian Gosling, Benny Marshall, Berit Westerlund, Carola Westerlund, Christine Park (formerly Kemp), Dave Bradfield, David East, David Harvey, David Wright, Dennis Wright, Eric Lee, Gary Marks, Gina Labrosse (formerly Riley), Graham Jenkinson, Ian 'Taffy' Evans, Janet Padwick, Jeff Parsons, Joanne Hill, Jim Simpson, Joakim Ronson, John Robinson, John Bentley, John Cambridge, John Close, Keith Cheesman, Kevin Cann, Kevin Hutchinson, Les Morfitt, Lou Duffy-Howard, Lynne Mitchell, Lyn Murfin, Maggi Ronson, Minnie Ronson, Malcolm Pearson, Mark Kay, Neal Owers, Nick Ronson, Pat Lee, Paul Denman, Paul Hudson, Paul Maxey, Peter Alton-Green, Pete Murfin, Phil Edwards, Ray Jordan, Richard Vickers, Rick Kemp, Rick Welton, Rita Carter, Rod Block, Robert Eunson, Sandra Goodare (formerly Nelson), Sasha Appleby, Sheila Gaynard (formerly Thornton), Shelly Bolder, Steve Magee, Steve Parry, Susan Baird, Susan Webb (formerly Fewless), Ted Park, Tony Ward.

The people who gave their time and energy to type up the many hours of audio story recordings:
Andy Medcalf, Darren Moore, Jane Birkinshaw, Jonathan Appleton, Rachel Kerr, Rachel Kerr, Tracey Frankish, Tracey Taylor,

The people who helped us with further research, gave permission for their material to be used, or supported the project in countless ways:
Charlotte Daly, Chris Dunnachie, David 'Burnsie' Burns, Derek McGill and the staff at BBC Radio Humberside, Hull College, the *Hull Daily Mail*, Jim Fletcher, John and Christine Bird, Les Morfitt, Lou Burnett, Madeline Bocaro, Mark Richardson, Martin Green and the team at Hull City of Culture, Mat Howlett, Michele Beadle and the staff at Hull History Centre, Phil Edwards, Richard Stott and the Kexgill Group,

Acknowledgements

Simon Forrester, Steve Ralphs, Tony Forrester and the staff at Freedom Centre, Tracey Taylor, Wilberforce College, Wyke College

The many brilliant artists, musicians and technicians who worked on and developed the stage show *Turn and Face the Strange*:
Anna Bean, Annabel Etheridge, Bethany Nicholson, Bobby Joyce, Carl Cooper, Catherine Ackroyd, Chris Heron, Ed Ullyart, Ellie Foody, Elliot Jarvis, Emily Hanover, Emily Tomlinson, Grace Burnett, Jason Addison, John Bentley, John Cambridge, John Warrener, Keith 'Ched' Cheesman, Kerrie Marsh, Kristian Eastwood, Lynsey Hester, Mark Richardson, Nathan Lynch, Pat Pretorius, Phil Keech, Rachael Jarvis, Rebecca Draper, Rob Cheung, Rob Mann, Tony Beasty,

And a special thank you to:
Kay Jarvis, whose work and attention to detail kept the TAFTS project on track, Cecile Piverotto for her Mick Ronson portrait illustrations, Karen 'Gilly' Laney and Eric 'Weird' Demattio aka Weird and Gilly for all their help, and publishers Andy Smith and Caroline Peden Smith, and editor Caroline Curtis at McNidder & Grace for all their encouragement and support.

Select Bibliography

Moonage Daydream – The Life and Times of Ziggy Stardust by David Bowie. Cassell Illustrated, 2005.
Bowie, Bolan and the Brooklyn Boy by Tony Visconti. Harper Collins, 2007.
Mick Ronson: The Spider with the Platinum Hair by Weird & Gilly. Independent Music Press, 2009.
Any Day Now: David Bowie The London Years 1947–74 by Kevin Cann. Adelita, 2010.
Starman: David Bowie – The Definitive Biography by Paul Trynka. Sphere, 2011.
Autobiography by Morrissey. Penguin, 2013.
Spider from Mars: My Life with Bowie by Woody Woodmansey. Sidgwick & Jackson, 2016.
The Age of Bowie by Paul Morley. Simon & Schuster UK, 2016.
Bowie Odyssey 70 by Simon Goddard. Omnibus Press, 2020.
Bowie, Cambo & All the Hype by John Cambridge. McNidder & Grace, 2021.

Magazines and Newspapers

Hull Daily Mail 13 February 1970, 5 January 1973, 18 April 1975, 1 June 2013
Disc and Music Echo 14 March 1970
Melody Maker 22 January 1972, 9 June 1973
New Musical Express 27 January 1973
Hit Parader March 1975
Rock Scene March 1975
Circus August 1975
Guitar Player December 1976
Nineteen January 1976
Beat Instrumental March 1980
Starzone 1984
Music Maker Holland September 1988
Classic Rock

Select Bibliography

Websites

For Mick Ronson:
https://www.facebook.com/mickronson/
http://www.maggironson.com/

For Ian Hunter and Mott the Hoople:
http://www.hunter-mott.com/
https://ianhunter.com/main/

For David Bowie:
https://www.bowiewonderworld.com/
www.5years.com
https://www.davidbowienews.com/

General:
www.loudersound.com
www.justabuzz.com
https://archive.bobharris.org/
https://www.lightscamerabackbeat.com/
recordcollectormag.com
https://bigsixties.blogspot.com
https://www.backseatmafia.com/
https://www.parisupdate.com/golf-drouot/
https://paristoric.com/
https://turnandfacethestrange.co.uk/

Image Section Photo Credits

1 *Mick playing at the Chestnut Cabaret*. Photo Madeline Bocaro.
2 *Photobooth pics of Mick and Keith 'Ched' Cheeseman*. Photo Keith Cheesman Collection.
3, 4 *Milford Grove on Greatfield Estate & Ronson Close*. Photo Garry Burnett.
5 *Mick in London in 1966*. Photo Les Morfitt Collection.
6 *Rats gig poster*. Photo Rupert Creed.
7 *Rats 1966 line up*. Photo Jim Simpson Collection.
8 *The Rats East Park Free Concert*. Photo Keith Cheesman Collection.
9 *Free Concert Flyer*. Photo Rick Welton.
10 *Former Hammonds Department Store*. Photo Garry Burnett.
11 *The original Fairview Studios*. Photo Garry Burnett.
12 *The later purpose-built Fairview Studios*. Photo Garry Burnett.
13 *Woodmansey Village Hall*. Photo Garry Burnett.
14 *John Cambridge*. Photo Anna Bean.
15 *Ched playing Mick's Les Paul guitar*. Photo Rupert Creed.
16 *Dave Bradfield*. Photo Rupert Creed.
17 *Keith 'Ched' Cheesman*. Photo Rupert Creed.
18 *Rats drummers John Cambridge and Jim Simpson*. Photo Rupert Creed.
19 & 20 *Hype promo*. Photo Jim Simpson Collection.
21 *Drummers John Cambridge and Woody Woodmansey*. Photo Rupert Creed.
22 *Montage of Hype in stage costumes*. Photo Ed Ullyart.
23 *Princes Avenue Music Legends Mural*. Photo Ed Ullyart.
24 *Mick Ronson mural on Greenwich Avenue shops*. Photo Garry Burnett.
25 *Mick with the Rats at Withernse*. Photo Keith Cheesman.
26 *Mick in tune and ready to play*. Photo Madeline Bocaro.
27 *Mick forever tuning*. Photo Madeline Bocaro.
28 *Gina Labrosse (Riley)*. Photo Rupert Creed.
29 *Trevor Bolder*. Photo Shelly Bolder.
30 *Ian Hunter and Mick*. Photo Madeline Bocaro.
31 *Kevin Cann, Mick and baby Joachim*. Photo Kevin Cann.
32 *The Spiders from Mars Plaque*. Photo Garry Burnett.
33 *East Park*. Photo Garry Burnett.
34 *Maggi Ronson with Guitar Sculpture artist Janis Skodins*. Photo Rupert Creed.
35 *Mick Ronson Memorial Garden*. Photo Garry Burnett.

Index

'4th Hour of My Sleep' 88, 181

Abbey, Allan 119
ABC 59
Aces 20, 34, 58, 176
Adamson, Chris 44
Advision 82, 88
'After All' 84
Aladdin Sane 53, 112–13, 115, 117, 174, 183–84
Alex Harvey Band 152
Alexander, George 91
'All the Young Dudes' 106, 113, 136, 157, 161, 190
Allison, Pete 166
Alton-Green, Peter 16, 20
American Fool 151, 188
Anderson, Miller 27
Angel Air 162
'Angel No. 9' 133, 140
Appleby, Geoff 23, 32–6, 39, 52–8, 67, 139–40, 152, 179–80
Appleby, Sasha 152
Arnesen, Pete 139
Artful Dodger 162
Atlantic Records 144

Bad Company 136
Baez, Joan 141–42, 187
Baker, Ginger 34
Baird, Susan 10, 11
Balanchine, George 129
Band Aid 152

Barakan, Mick 144, 150, 188
Barclay James Harvest 63
Barron, David 32
Battersea Power Station 60
Bearsville Picnic 144
Bearsville Studios 144, 187
Beatles 12, 13, 19, 21, 60, 104, 127
Beautiful South 45
Beck, Jeff 1, 19, 21, 27, 34, 40, 46, 54–7, 63, 67, 112, 122, 179
Bentley, John 23, 48, 53, 55, 66–70, 87, 94, 142
'Bernie Gripplestone' 45, 66, 179
Berry, Chuck 19–21, 100, 122
Beside Bowie: The Mick Ronson Story 164
Besnard, Jean 37, 40
Beverley Regal 19, 21, 24, 44
Big Audio Dynamite 161, 166
'Billy Porter' 133, 139, 149
Birdcage Club 42, 52, 123
Black Tie White Noise 157, 162, 190
Blakley, Ronnie 141
Block, Rod 9
'Blowin' in the Wind' 142
Blue Cheer 64
Blue Oyster Cult 150
Bolan, Marc 79, 85, 87, 89, 90, 127
Bolder, Shelly 10, 168
Bolder, Trevor 1, 10, 23, 53, 65–6, 87-8, 90, 97, 127, 130–36, 163, 181, 185
Bone 148
Bowie, Angela 43, 70, 76, 77, 80,

83, 85, 102, 110, 118
Bowie, Zowie 118, 124, 164
'Boy' 139
Boy George 108
Bradfield, David 18, 19, 25–8
Brewer, Jon 164
Brickhouse 90, 195
Bridlington Spa 2, 18, 118–20, 184
Bron, Gerry 88
Bronze 88
Brooker, Gary 161
Brown, Arthur 37, 45, 94, 101
Bruce, Jack 83, 127
Buckmaster, Paul 84
Buretti, Freddie 102, 131
Burnett, T Bone 141, 151
Burns, David ('Burnsie') 168
Burton Constable Hall 59, 62–3, 84, 180
Butterfield, Paul 144
Buttle, Brian 32, 33, 42

Café Royale 123
Cambridge, John ('Cambo') 3, 23, 36, 43–7, 54, 57–60, 64-8, 70–2, 76
Cann, Kevin 132, 138, 140, 154–58, 161, 166, 171
Caprani, Lydia 167
Cardiff Rose 143, 187
Carr-Pritchard, Mark 91, 132, 171, 185
Cat Balou Club 40, 46, 54, 57, 179
Cavern Club 89
CBS Records 137, 140
'Changes' 100
Chapman, Michael 17, 23, 61–2, 65-6, 70, 78, 84, 147, 166, 180, 187

Chateau d'Herouville 127
Cheesman, Keith ('Ched') 23, 42, 46, 48, 52, 57, 63, 73, 87, 147, 161, 165
Chen, Bobby 144
Chicken Shack 62
Childers, Leee Black 95–6, 111, 129
'Clorissa' 88
Chrysalis Records 150
Citadel Music 161
Clapton, Eric 34, 46, 56, 129, 147
Clash 150, 172
Cleminson, Zal 152
Clockwork Orange, A 102, 182
Close, John 48, 123
Cochran, Eddie 19
Cockney Rebel 166
Cohen, Leonard 141, 187
Collen, Phil 157, 161, 166
Collins, Phil 78
Connolly, Brian 122
Constable, John 59, 62
Co-op 13, 14, 16, 20, 50, 109, 167, 178
Cooper, Alice 101, 154
Cornells Music Shop 55, 195
Cornell, Pat 36
Cosey Fanni Tutti 90
COUM 90
Country Club 95
'Cracked Actor' 117
Cream 33–4, 83, 128, 157, 179
Crestas 4, 15, 20–7, 58, 133, 141, 178, 196

Dalbello, Lisa 151, 188
Daltrey, Roger 147
Dave Clark Five 33
David Bowie – see also Space Oddity
1–2, 23, 37, 43–6, 59, 60, 65, 67,

Index

71, 74–5, 79, 83, 96, 98, 112, 115, 120, 157, 163, 174, 180
Davis, Jay 144
Deacon, John 157
Dead Fingers Talk 49, 64, 148, 187
Dead Ringer 150, 188
Decca 78
Def Leppard 155, 157
Defries, Tony 1, 85, 91, 96, 100, 100–7, 110, 111, 116, 124, 128, 134–40, 143, 151, 155, 182–85, 187
Denman, Paul 74, 93, 108, 111
Dharma, Ritchie 132, 133, 171, 186
Diamond Dogs 130
Diddley, Bo 112
Do It Dog Style 148
Dominion Theatre 153, 162, 189
'Don't Be Cruel' 149
'Drive-In Saturday' 117, 130
Dudgeon, Gus 60, 61, 68, 84
Duffy-Howard, Lou 120, 165
Duke of Cumberland 21, 24, 52, 73, 178
Dunbar, Aynsley 127–28, 130, 133, 185

Eastwood, Kristian 168
EC2 153, 189
Eddy, Duane 13, 127
Egan, Rusty 148
Elliot, Dennis 139
Elliott, Jack 141
Elliot, Joe 139, 155, 157, 161–62, 164, 166, 191
'Empty Bed' 133
Entwhistle, John 147
Eunson, Rob 64, 148, 165
Evans, Ian ('Taffy') 11, 12, 36-7, 41, 43–4, 47–9, 159
Everly Brothers 19, 21

Fairview Studios 45-6, 57, 67, 196
Fairweather-Low, Andy 161
Faithful, Marianne 131
Fallen Angels 128
Fame, Georgie 33
Fantasia 70
Farr, Brian 166
Fatal Flowers 153, 189
'FBI' 150
Fender 36, 37, 55, 65, 83, 179
Ferris, Andy 80, 81
'Fill Your Heart' 97
Fine Young Cannibals 167
Fish, Michael 89
'Five Years' 100, 105
Flesh 53, 65, 87
Flowers, Herbie 91
Free 37, 54, 66, 84, 136
Freedom Centre 169
Friars Club 97, 103, 105, 182
Friedman, Kinky 141
Frost, Tony 112
Fry, Roger 70, 77
Fully Qualified Survivor 61, 65, 70, 78, 84, 147, 180
Fussey, Suzi – see also Ronson, Suzi 102, 103, 111, 124, 127, 164, 177, 185, 187

Gabriel, Peter 78
Garland, Judy 102, 108
Garson, Mike 112, 115–27, 121–22, 127–28, 130, 132–33, 171, 185
Gaynard, Sheila (formerly Thornton) 63

Gehman, Don 151
Geldof, Bob 152
Genesis 78, 90
Genesis P-Orridge 90
George, Stuey 24, 44, 45, 105, 112, 121, 158
Ghosts of Princes in Towers 148, 187
Gift, Roland 167
Gillespie, Dana 91–3, 161
Ginsberg, Allen 141
'Girl Can't Help It' 133
Glastonbury Festival 95, 182
Golfe Druot Club 37
Gondola Club 19, 45, 52, 194
Gonx 24
Gough and Davy 16, 36, 178, 194
Grappelli, Stéphane 38, 54
Gregory, Glenn 168
Griffiths, John 18
Grossman, Albert 144
Grosvenor, Luther (Ariel Bender) 136
'Growing up and I'm Fine' 129
Guam 141
Guthrie, Arlo 141, 187

Haddon Hall 71–2, 76–7, 79–82, 85, 89, 91–2, 102, 118, 124, 164
Halfway House 19-21, 23-5, 38, 196
Hammersmith Odeon (later Apollo) 1, 19, 66, 92, 120–22, 124, 132, 150, 161, 171, 184, 188
Hammonds 16, 17, 159, 178, 194
'Hang on to Yourself' 100, 121
Hard Rain 143
Harley, Steve 166, 174
Harris, Bob 96, 100, 105, 134, 138, 144, 161
Harrison, George 19, 21

Hartley, Liz 71, 76, 77
Harty, Russell 115
Harvey, David 10, 34, 35
Hawk, Johnny 20, 21, 25, 26, 34, 133
Heaven and Hull 157, 161, 162, 190, 191
Hebblewhite, Mark 168
Hendrix, Jimi 21, 33, 34, 42, 45, 46, 72, 142, 179
Herd, Keith 45, 196
Herman's Hermits 28, 91
'Heroes' 157, 190
'Hey Jude' 94
'Hey Ma Get Papa' 128
Hollies 19
Holly, Buddy 59
Holy Holy 168
Housemartins 45
Hudson, Paul 143
Hull, Kingston upon: 8
Hull Arts Centre 62, 196
Hull Brick Company 84
Hull City Council 30, 41, 49, 74, 166, 179, 196
Hull City of Culture 167
Hull Daily Mail 29, 42, 53, 74, 115, 155, 180
Hull Eastern Cemetery 5, 152, 158, 167, 189, 191, 196
Hull East Park 62, 64–6, 136, 167, 174, 180, 196
Hull Royal Infirmary 25, 97, 152, 182, 195
Hull Truck Theatre 90
Hull West Park 64
Hull University 77, 78, 195
Hullaballoos 43, 59
Hunky Dory 77, 84, 91–7, 100, 102, 107, 110, 118, 181–82
Hunt, Malcolm 27

Index

Hunter, Ian 1, 4, 106, 133, 136, 138–40, 149–50, 153, 155, 158, 162–63, 166, 186–190
Hunter-Ronson Band 139, 140, 150, 152–53, 156, 186, 189
Hutchinson, John ('Hutch') 163
Hutchinson, Kevin 73, 93, 94
Hynde, Chrissie 132, 157, 162

'I Feel Free' 157, 161
'I Know it's Gonna Happen Someday' 56
'I'm the One' 128
I'm the One 149
Imhoff, Barry 144, 187
Imperial Typewriters 10, 109
Ince, Frank 32, 33
Indian Summer 150, 162, 188
Institute of Contemporary Arts (ICA) 163
'I've Got You Babe' 131
Irvin, Denise 50, 67, 75, 90, 97, 124, 176, 180, 182
'It Ain't Easy' 16

'Jack & Diane' 151, 188
Jagger, Mick 1, 2, 16, 105, 121, 123
'Jean Genie' 112, 113, 117, 122, 130, 131, 152, 168, 188
Jelly Roll Blues Band 53, 87
Jenkinson, Graham 109, 118
John, Elton 84, 127, 164
Johnny D. is Back! 153, 189
Johnson, Amy 161
Johnstone, Davey 84
Jones, Mick 150, 166, 172
Joplin, Janis 144
Jordan, Ray 12

Joyce, Bobby 168
Junior's Eyes 43, 59, 60, 64–5, 67, 70–2, 80, 81, 83, 87, 180
Just Like This 144, 162

Kelly, Gene 129
Kemp, Gary 163, 164
Kemp, Lindsay 90, 110
Kemp, Rick 17, 18, 23, 61, 84, 89, 103, 124, 165, 178, 194
Kexgill Group 168
King, Peter – see also Marshall, Benny 32
Kinks 99, 127, 150
Kirke, Simon 136
Kitching, Mike 20, 25
Knopfler, Mark 129
Kontiki Club 19
'Kooks' 97
Kubrick, Stanley 102

Labrosse, Gina (formerly Riley) 119
'Lady Grinning Soul' 117
Laney, Karen ('Gilly') 163
Lanzen, Phil 161
Larkin, Philip 161
Leather Nun 153, 190
Lecore, Robin 32, 33
Led Zeppelin 34, 83
Lederman, Sam 150
Leeds Rollarena 120
Lee, Alvin 64
Lee, Eric 20, 23–4, 26
Lee, Pat 22
Les Paul guitar 1, 55–6, 164, 167
Let's Dance 106
'Let's Get Rocked' 155

207

'Let's Spend the Night Together' 117
'Life's a River' 162
'Life on Mars' 93, 94, 97, 118
'Like a Rolling Stone' 157, 162
'Lisa Likes Rock & Roll' 150
Lill, Don 53, 57
Live Aid 152
Locarno Ballroom 19, 79
'Lounge Lizard' 137, 139
'Love me Tender' 129, 149
Lulu 28

Mace, Ralf 80
'Madman Across the Water' 84, 164
Magee, Steve 105
'Maggie's Farm' 143
MainMan 96, 111–12, 116, 129–32, 136–37, 140, 162
Mandel, Tommy 150
Mandrakes 52, 62, 81
Mansfield, Dave 141
Man Who Hated Mornings, The 147
Man Who Sold the World, The 77, 82–5, 87, 89, 91, 97, 107, 112, 168
Mariners 4, 18–20, 25, 61, 141
Marks, Gary 166
Marquee Club 71, 72, 88, 130, 147
Marshall, Benny (or Peter) – see also King, Peter 23–4, 32–4, 37–9, 41, 46, 57, 60, 62, 64, 67, 74, 82, 84, 87–9, 91, 124, 152, 158, 162, 167
Marvin, Hank 19
Maskell, Alan 148
Matlock, Glen 148, 161, 163
Matthew, Brian 33
May, Brian 157

McCarey, Macs 129
McGuinn, Roger 141, 142
Meatloaf 150
Mellencamp, John Cougar 151, 162
Melody Maker 21, 103, 107, 130
Mercury, Freddie 94, 102, 152, 157, 190
Mercury Records 89, 91, 96, 112, 181
Mexborough Town Hall 22
Michael, George 108
'Michael Picasso' 1, 158, 161, 162
Mick Ronson Band 144, 162, 172, 187
Mick Ronson Only After Dark 128, 155, 162
Milford Grove 11, 75, 143, 167, 178, 196
Milkwood 93, 192
Millburne, Estelle 153
Mitchell, Joni 141, 187
Mitchell, Lynn 13, 50, 64, 109, 136, 169
Moog Synthesizer 79, 80, 149
Moon, Keith 2
'Moonage Daydream' 4, 66, 97, 100, 121, 132
Morfitt, Les 109, 120, 121, 123, 152, 157
Morris, Sham 157, 162
Morrison, Van 144, 192
Morrissey 156, 157, 190, 193
Most, Micky 28, 29
Mott the Hoople 10, 106, 134, 136–39, 186, 192
Move 45, 53
Murfin, Pete 44, 45, 75
Mustard 166
'My Mama Never Taught Me

Index

How To Cook' 149
Myers, Tim 20, 24

Needs, Kris 102
Needlers 47
Nelson, Bill 161
Nelson, Sandra (now Goodare) 18, 29, 38, 176
Nettleton, Barry 65, 84, 90
Neuwirth, Bob 140-42
New Musical Express (NME) 27, 115, 200
New, Steve 148
New York Dolls 148, 192
New York Yanquis 150, 188
Nice 62
Noone, Peter 91
Nun Permanent 153, 190

'Oh! You Pretty Things' 91, 105
Old Grey Whistle Test, The 105, 113, 134, 138, 140, 144, 152, 182, 183
'Once Bitten, Twice Shy' 139, 140
One of the Boys 147
'Only After Dark' 128, 155, 162
Orwell, George 130
Orwell, Sonia 130-31
L'Oubliettes Club 37
'Over the Rainbow' 108
Owers, Neal 45

Padwick, Janet 18
Paddingtons 46
Page, Jimmy 56, 73
Palmer, Robert (Alan) 52, 62, 81
'Panic in Detroit' 117
Paris 37-9, 72

Park, Christine (formerly Kemp) 17, 18, 124
Park, Ted 21, 24, 25
Parker, Graham 156
Parry, Steve 139
Parsons, Jeff 49, 56, 64, 90, 148–49
Paterson, Barry 32
Payolas 151
Peacock, Annette 128, 149
Peel, John 62, 72–3, 91, 95
Pennebaker, D.A. 121
'Perfect Day' 110, 11, 151
Phoenix Club 76
Phillips 81, 87–8
Pink Floyd 45
Pin Ups 53, 124, 127, 129–30
Pitt, Ken 85
Play Don't Worry 129, 133, 134, 139, 140, 162
'Play Don't Worry' 133, 140
'Pleasure Man' 128
Pleasure Ground 153
Pop, Iggy 96, 110, 154
Pork 95, 96, 101
'Power of Darkness' 88
Presley, Elvis 37, 129, 149
'Pressure' 151
'Prettiest Star' 78
Pretty Things 62, 127–28
Process 28
Proof Through the Night 151
Pure Prairie League 110
Pye Records 32, 137, 148

Queen 102
'Queen Bitch' 97, 105, 110, 113
'Questions' 149
'Quick Joey Small' 148
'Quicksand' 97

Rainbow Theatre 101, 110, 113, 132, 183, 185
Ralphs, Mick 136
Rats – see also Treacle 4, 23, 24, 32–9, 40–9, 52–9, 60–8, 71–5, 80–5, 112, 148, 158, 161, 162, 166, 168, 178–80, 194
RCA 96, 100, 106, 112, 116, 118, 121, 127, 128, 130–31, 134, 136–37, 140, 143, 161, 182, 185
'Rebel Rebel' 130
Red Guitars 45, 120
Reed, Lou 2, 4, 96, 102, 110, 111, 113, 123, 129, 133, 141, 151, 183
Reid, Terry 70
Renaldo and Clara 143
Renwick, Tim 64, 65, 70–2
Reverend Black and the Rocking Vicars 20
Revolver 46
Richards, Keith 21, 27
Richardson, Scott 128
Rich Kids 148, 152, 187, 189
'Ride a White Swan' (song) 87
Riley, Leon 122–3
Roadrunners 58
Robinson, John 20, 25
Rock, Mick 107, 111, 183
Rockpalast 150
'Rock and Roll Suicide' 100, 123, 156
Rodgers, Paul 136
Rodgers, Richard 129
Roger the Engineer 46
Rolling Stone 112
Rolling Stones 16, 18, 19, 59, 63, 117
Rolling Thunder Revue Band 141, 143, 151, 187
Rolling Thunder Revue: A Bob Dylan Story 143

Ronno (band) 46, 53, 65, 88–91, 163, 181
Ronson, family history 8, 9, 11, 12, 20, 124, 158
Ronson, David 14, 168
Ronson, George 5, 8–11, 16, 36, 40, 41, 152, 158, 167
Ronson, Joakim or 'Kim' 4, 153, 154, 164, 165, 190
Ronson, Lisa 5, 102, 144, 150, 153, 163–6, 187
Ronson, Minnie 5, 8–11, 30, 36, 40, 92, 109, 115, 119, 130, 158, 166, 167
Ronson, Margaret 10, 13
Ronson, Nick or Nicholas 4, 50, 75, 97, 124, 158, 164, 165
Ronson, Suzi – see also Fussey, Suzi 5, 102–4, 108, 111, 124, 127, 129, 134, 138, 140, 144, 153, 155, 162, 164, 166
Rouen 37–9, 179
Roundhouse 28, 65, 78–80, 95, 105, 180
Rossi, Mick 139, 148
Roxy Theatre 150
Rundgren, Todd 144
Rutherford, Mike 78

'Saturday Gigs' 137
Scott, Ken 127
'Sea Diver' 106
Sebastian, John 144
Seger, Bob 151
'Seven Days' 149
Sex Pistols 148
Shadows 12, 19, 129, 147
Shaar Murray, Charles 132
'She Shook Me Cold' 83

Index

Short Back 'n' Sides 150
Showtime 144, 162
Siffre, Labi 123
Simpson, Jim 32–5, 48, 76, 81
Skodins, Janis 167, 174
Skyline Ballroom 19, 34, 45, 63, 127
Slaughter and the Dogs 139, 148
Slaughter on 10th Avenue 127–30, 132–34
'Slaughter on Tenth Avenue' 129, 150
Slick, Earl 152
Soft Machine 84
'Soulful Lady' 164
Small Faces 64
Soles, Steven 141
Sombrero Club 92, 96, 102
'Sorrow' 130
'Space Oddity' 61, 65–7, 71, 77, 78, 107, 131
Space Oddity – see also David Bowie 60, 96, 112
Spandau Ballet 164
Spedding, Chris 84, 147
Spiders from Mars 1, 53, 66, 90, 95, 100, 117, 123, 124, 137, 163, 168
Spinetti, Henry 161
Spooky Tooth 136
'Spoonful' 32
Springsteen, Bruce 149
Squeeze 53
SRC 128
'Starman' 100, 103, 106–9, 113, 131, 156
Starr, Ringo 2, 121, 123
Stewart, Rod 1, 64, 121
Steeleye Span 17, 103, 176
Stereotones 32
Stoner, Rob 141

Storm the Reality Studios 148, 187
Stutt, Keith 65
'Suffragette City' 100, 106
Supabar 167
'Supermen' 80
'Sweet Dreamer' 159, 174
Sweet Dreamer 163

'Take a Long Line' 162
Taylor, Clive ('Spud') 36, 43, 56, 177
Taylor, Roger 102, 157, 161
Taylor, Tex 161
Temple Club 89
Temple, Henry 20, 25
Ten Years After 64
Thank Your Lucky Stars 33
The Man Who Hated Mornings 147, 187
'The Murder Weapon' 151
'The Sixties' 151
The Spider with the Platinum Hair 1, 82, 163
Third Ear Band 62
'This is For You' 133, 164
This is Spinal Tap 101
'Time' 117
Tommy Vance Award 162
'Too Much in the Skies' 149
Top of the Pops 21, 103, 107–9, 113, 131, 137, 182
Thunderclap Newman 62
Transformer 110, 111, 113, 183
Treacle– see also Rats 53, 54, 56, 179
Trident Studios 60, 61, 79–80, 82, 94, 97, 100, 129, 182
'Trouble With Me' 162
Truth 28, 46, 54

'Truth, The Whole Truth, Nuthin' But the Truth' 133, 139
Trynka, Paul 108
Tucker, Colin Lloyd 166
Tumbleweed Connection 84
Turn and Face the Strange 148, 165, 168, 213

Ullyart, Ed 167, 195, 196
Underwood, George 91
Ultravox 152
Ure, Midge 148, 152, 189
Uriah Heep 137

Vanilla, Cherry 95, 96, 111, 129, 134
Velvet Underground 110
Ventures 129
Vertigo Records 88
Voice 27–9, 179
Visage 152
Visconti, Tony 60, 67, 71–2, 76–80, 82–3, 85, 87–9, 92, 118, 161, 168, 180

'Waiting for the Man' 97, 110
Wakeman, Rick 94, 95
'Walk on the Wild Side' 111
Wanted 29
Ward, Tony 12, 49, 70
Warhol, Andy 95, 96, 101, 102
Washington, Geno 45
'Wastelands' 152
'Watch that Man' 117
Waters, Muddy 33
Watts, Michael 103, 104
Watts, Pete Overend 106, 138
Wayne, Mick 43, 58–61, 66, 70, 180

Weaver, Blue 139
Webb, Susan (formerly Fewless) 49
Welcome to the Club 150, 188
Welly Club 168
Welton, Rick 62–5, 84, 90
Wembley Stadium 152, 157, 190
Westerlund, Carola 153, 189, 190
White, Mrs 93
'White Light/White Heat' 110, 129, 132, 133
Who 37
'Who Are The Mystery Girls?' 148
Whomanfoursays 151, 188
'Woman' 133
Wilberforce, William 161
'Wild Eyed Boy from Freecloud' 94
Wonder, Stevie 85, 91
Woodmansey, Mick (Woody) 1, 23, 58, 74, 81, 127, 132, 136, 161, 163, 168
Woodmansey Village Hall 53, 57, 66, 87
Woodstock 64, 144, 187
World of David Bowie, The 78
Wright, David & Dennis 13
Wyeth, Howie 141
Wyman, Bill 161

X-Dreams 149

Yale, Martin 32
Yamamoto, Kansai 115
Yardbirds 27, 37, 46, 54, 59, 112, 127
Yellow Monkey 166
Your Arsenal 156, 157, 190
You're Never Alone with a Schizophrenic 149, 150, 188

Index

Yorkies 32, 36
Yui Orta 153

Zanetta, Tony 95, 111, 118
Ziggy –
    concept 100, 107, 182
    costumes 89, 102, 103, 106,
        108, 109, 112
    hairstyle 102, 104–6, 108, 109
    Hammersmith Odeon 121,
        122
    sexuality 101, 104, 108, 109
    tour of Japan 105, 118
    tour of US 111–3, 115–7
Ziggy Stardust and the Spiders from Mars, The Rise and Fall of 53, 106, 174
'Ziggy Stardust' 1, 97, 100, 101
Zimmerman, Robert – See Dylan, Bob 88, 140–43, 157
Zimmerman, Tucker 88

About the Authors

Rupert Creed, writer of *Made in Hull* – the opening event for Hull City of Culture. He co-wrote *Turn and Face the Strange* to celebrate the life and music of Mick Ronson. He was Producer for the BBC *Peoples War* project and has written and presented several documentary features for BBC Radio 4.

Garry Burnett, established author, co-wrote the critically-acclaimed stage show *Turn and Face the Strange*, the Story of Mick Ronson. He has most recently worked in collaboration with drummer John 'Cambo' Cambridge on his autobiography *Bowie, Cambo & All the Hype*.

Turn and Face the Strange: The Story of Mick Ronson The Stage Show

Turn and Face the Strange: The Story of Mick Ronson is a stunning multi-media show with a powerful rock band, string quartet, film interviews and live storytelling of the life and music of Mick Ronson. The legendary guitarist, album producer and arranger who was born on Greatfield Estate in Hull. From humble origins as a gardener and playing in local bands Mick Ronson went on to gain international success as the lead guitarist in the band The Spiders from Mars, and as a producer and arranger for David Bowie, Lou Reed, Ian Hunter and countless others.

This moving and joyous stage show premiered to a sell-out audience at Hull Truck Theatre. To find where the next show is touring and how to book tickets visit: www turnandfacethestrange.co.uk